Native America

INTERAMERICANA
INTER-AMERICAN LITERARY HISTORY AND CULTURE
HISTORIA LITERARIA INTERAMERICANA Y SUS CONTEXTOS CULTURALES
HISTOIRE LITTERAIRE ET CULTURE INTERAMERICAINES

VOLUME 9

Notes on the quality assurance and
peer review of this publication:

Prior to publication, the quality of
the works published in this series
is reviewed by external referees
appointed by the editorship.

Jeanette den Toonder / Kim van Dam /
Fjære van der Stok (eds.)

Native America

Indigenous Self-Representation in Canada, the U.S. and Mexico

PETER LANG
EDITION

Bibliographic Information published by the Deutsche Nationalbibliothek
The Deutsche Nationalbibliothek lists this publication in the Deutsche Nationalbibliografie; detailed bibliographic data is available in the internet at http://dnb.d-nb.de.

Library of Congress Cataloging-in-Publication Data
Names: Toonder, Jeanette M. L. den, editor of compilation. | Dam, Kim van, 1969- editor of compilation. | Stok, Fjære van der, 1987- editor of compilation.
Title: Native America : indigenous self-representation in Canada, the U.S. and Mexico / Jeanette den Toonder, Kim van Dam, Fjære van der Stok (eds.).
Other titles: Indigenous self-representation in Canada, the U.S. and Mexico
Description: New York : Peter Lang, [2016] | Series: Interamericana ; volume 9 | Includes index.
Identifiers: LCCN 2016038434 | ISBN 9783631640821
Subjects: LCSH: Indians of North America--Ethnic identity. | Indians of North America—Government relations. | Indians of North America—Intellectual life. | Indian literature—History and criticism. | Indigenous peoples—Mexico—Ethnic identity. | Indigenous peoples—Mexico—Government relations.
Classification: LCC E98.E85 N365 2016 | DDC 323.1197—dc23 LC record available at https://lccn.loc.gov/2016038434

ISSN 1618-419X
ISBN 978-3-631-64082-1 (Print)
E-ISBN 978-3-653-02620-7 (E-Book)
E-ISBN 978-3-631-69353-7 (EPUB)
E-ISBN 978-3-631-69354-4 (MOBI)
DOI 10.3726/978-3-653-02620-7

Peter Lang – Frankfurt am Main · Bern · Bruxelles · New York · Oxford · Warszawa · Wien

This publication has been peer reviewed.

www.peterlang.com

Table of Contents

Introduction

Jeanette den Toonder
Centre for Canadian Studies, University of Groningen

New Ways for the Future: Hemispheric Encounters

1. Definitions and self-determination

The different Indigenous peoples in the world constitute an important factor in redefining global cultural, national and political identities, as they share a common experience of colonization, deculturation and displacement and equally strive to achieve Indigenous rights and political autonomy. Their endeavor to create transnational networks of resistance has resulted in the formation of indigeneity, a notion that allows for Indigenous peoples to be considered as a global community.

In this volume, reflections on the key issues of sovereignty, self-government and self-determination are offered from a variety of perspectives, including political science, sociology, anthropology and literary theory. As Roger Maaka and Chris Andersen have stressed in their preface to the volume *The Indigenous Experience*, Indigenous experiences are extremely rich and heterogeneous and cannot be accounted for in one single book. This volume focuses on the experiences of several Indigenous groups in Canada, the U.S. and Mexico – in particular, the Inuit in Canada, the Choctaw in the U.S., and the Mixtecos and Tojolabal in Mexico – and strives to offer a more multifaceted understanding of North American Indigenous history, identity, community and forms of culture.

The United Nations Working Group for Indigenous Peoples which was installed in 1982 established a draft declaration on the rights of Indigenous peoples in which "common-to-all characteristics are identified, articulated, internalized, and [..] conceptualized" (Maaka and Andersen 11). The draft declaration completed in 1993 was based on the following working definition presented in the Martinez Cobo report of 1986:

> Indigenous communities, peoples and nations are those which, having a historical continuity with pre-invasion and pre-colonial societies that developed on their territories, consider themselves distinct from other sectors of the societies now prevailing on those territories, or parts of them. They form at present non-dominant sectors of society and are determined to preserve, develop and transmit to future generations their ancestral territories, and their ethnic identity, as the basis of their continued existence as peoples, in accordance with their own cultural patterns, social institutions and legal systems. (*U.N. Study of the Problem of Discrimination against Indigenous Populations*, U.N. Doc E/CN.4/Sub.2/1986/7/Add.4, at 29, para. 379)

This resulted in the Declaration for the Protection of Indigenous Peoples' Rights approved by the United Nations.[1] Even if the Declaration is non-binding for states, it serves as a powerful statement of universally accepted norms and provides a strong basis for arguing for greater legal protection for Indigenous rights.[2] However, as Manjusha Nair has argued, the concept of rights itself contains an inevitable paradox in the case of Indigenous peoples. Their legitimacy is based on collective property rights, but the recognition of these rights "originates in the idea of human rights that has the basis in Western liberalism and individualism" (Nair 5). As a result, the lawfulness of the concept of Indigenous peoples is "inherently linked to Western social and cultural changes since the 1970s" (Nair 5). From this Western perspective, Nair claims, a paternalistic and stereotypical image of the Indigenous' "pure and simplified form of life" (Nair 6) has emanated. This biased image is based on a romanticized idea of the traditional world of these communities and places them "outside the sphere of modernization" (Nair 6). Due to this image of "simple and undifferentiated society in the post-industrial discourse" (Nair 7), the United Nations' categorization of Indigenous peoples can be considered a-historical. In order for the Indigenous peoples to play a role of equal merit in society, this problem of historicity needs to be addressed.

It is therefore essential to shift the focus of legitimacy from the principle of property – where collective and individual rights clash – to that of historical self-determination. This particular form of self-determination takes into account "the fact that Indigenous peoples lived by their own laws, traditions and customs before they encountered colonizing powers as a crucial basis for a return to that status in the present" (Bennett 74). Mark Bennett, who considers self-determination a political or moral principle that can be applied to Indigenous peoples to justify their claims, also refers to the problems related to this application. Since the notion of self-determination is traditionally connected to nations and national groups, a frequently asked question involves the justification of self-determination. It has been argued that self-determination is indeed justified when considering Indigenous peoples' remedial right, based on "historical deprivation of territory (in terms of sovereignty or self-government), [..] the breach of autonomy agreements, and often [...] grievous breaches of human rights" (Bennett 96). In order to establish self-determination – which is a key element in orienting Indigenous-state relationships – different stages

1 http://www.un.org/esa/socdev/unpfii/documents/DRIPS_en.pdf.

2 Linda Tuhiwai Smith stresses that New Zealand, Australia, Canada and the United States refused to sign when the declaration was signed in 2009, "although subsequently, Australia, Canada and New Zealand have signed and the United States seems resolutely opposed" (119).

have to be completed: firstly, it is important to recognize prior sovereignty; secondly, to create an analogy with decolonization; and thirdly, to reorient the relationship between Indigenous peoples and the state. Furthermore, this relationship should be based on "mutual respect, consent and continuity" (Bennett 101). Recognizing prior sovereignty includes admitting that these peoples were deprived of their sovereignty by a colonizing power. Their current situation differs significantly from that of colonized peoples in Africa or Asia for example, who have been allowed to restore their different structures and rules through the decolonization process. In the case of Indigenous populations, there is a tendency to legitimize colonial power, as colonization has resulted in a democracy in which these populations are supposed to be "free and equal" (Bennett 107). Or, as Jeffrey Sissons has phrased it, post-settler states "claim to represent, fairly and legitimately, the descendants of both colonizers and colonized" (11). This argument however focuses on individual citizens instead of peoples, thus presupposing integration of Indigenous individuals within the colonizing populations and denying their decolonization. By recognizing prior nationhood and the analogy with decolonization, this situation of internal colonization can be transformed into a relation of equal and self-governing peoples, resulting in a renewed Indigenous-state relationship.

The principle of self-determination is also essential according to the UN Declaration on the Rights of Indigenous Peoples as it underlines "the right these communities" have to determine their own identity or membership in accordance with their customs and traditions. According to the chair of the Working Group, Professor Erica-Irene Daes, this foundational principle of self-determination entails a process "through which indigenous peoples are able to join with all the other peoples that make up the State on mutually-agreed upon and just terms, after many years of isolation and exclusion" (Daes 9). The comparison with "all the other peoples" refers to the existence of diverse cultures within a state. As James Anaya has argued, the increasing acceptance of cultural pluralism in Western societies enhances the possibilities for Indigenous peoples to develop autonomous governance and Indigenous institutions. Essential to Indigenous self-government is the development of these institutions on the one hand, and "their effective participation in the larger political order" (Anaya 111) on the other hand. By stressing this two-fold attachment, Anaya reflects on the way in which Indigenous peoples locate themselves within a global framework. Considering themselves distinct from, as well as part of, larger social and political units, they challenge "traditional Western conceptions that envisage mutually exclusive states as the primary factor for locating power and community, and the view promotes a political order that is less state-centered and more centered on people in a world of distinct yet increasingly integrated and overlapping spheres of community and authority" (Anaya 112). In order for constitutive self-determination to be achieved, the three conditions as formulated by Bennett – mutual respect, consent and continuity – seem to be vital. A fourth paradigm – constructive engagement – involves a constitutional covenant that may be decisive in changing Indigenous peoples and state relations. Roger Maaka and Augie Fleras have argued that constructive engagement "proposes a constitutional alternative to a colonial social contract" (345). This new constitutional order "secures and promotes indigenous rights, including the right to indigenous models of self-determining autonomy without, however, denying the equally legitimate claims to Crown rule and authority" (Maaka and Fleras 345). They nevertheless add that considerable controversy may be necessary in order to reach such a constructive engagement contract.

2. Transnationalism and Indigenous methodologies

Shared experiences and overlapping histories presuppose a productive comparison between Indigenous peoples across the world. Not surprisingly, therefore, the examination of connections between these global communities increasingly favors a hemispheric approach to Indigenous studies. As Antonio Barrenechea and Heidrun Moertl have stressed in their introduction to a recent special issue of *Comparative American Studies*, a growing number of scholars "argue for the planetary character of indigenous culture" (117) and explore the opportunities for considering indigeneity in a transnational context. Interdisciplinary approaches have also been promoted by associations and institutions, such as the Native American and Indigenous Studies Association (NAISA) and the International Association of Inter-American Studies/Asociación Internacional de Estudios Interamericanos (IAS/EIA). Such formal as well as informal affiliations between Indigenous peoples from different states in the Americas highlight "their common objectives in achieving greater cultural autonomy" (Sissons 14). Jeffrey Sissons has emphasized that, on the one hand, "the economic and political issues addressed by indigenous groups were and are depressingly similar" (13), but that, on the other hand, the cultural domain is characterized by its diversity. By opposing international policy favored by state politics and the form of modernity pursued by Indigenous peoples, Sissons contrasts the tendency towards homogenization in the first case and the need for cultural diversity in the second, a contrast necessarily including a duality between state and local interests. This perspective calls for a cautious application of the transnational approach, as each Indigenous group is (re)defining its cultural identity in its own way. This process of identification necessarily includes the re-appropriation of possessions taken from them by settler states. This re-appropriation of material culture, local customs or knowledge always involves a "renewed significance within alternative cultural frames" (Sissons 15), frames that should not be neglected. A number of critics have indeed stressed the existence of a certain tension between the nationalist orientation on the one hand and the transnational approach on the other, a strain that is primarily related to the global/local discussion. Furthermore, the transnational engagement should not exclude "internal transnationalism", a term referring to American native "national" spaces existing "inside the geography of the United States" (Huang et al. 8). Jessica Horton for example wonders if Native subjects "can simultaneously participate in transnational processes […], and continue to form and maintain deep local attachments" (3).

In her study *Mapping the Americas*, Shari Huhndorf focuses on the continuities and contradictions between these national and transnational orientations that have shaped Indigenous cultural production in North America. As discussed in the first part of this introduction, legal grounds for asserting self-determination and political sovereignty rest on the assumption that Indigenous communities are nations. This is particularly apparent when considering the term that Canadian Indigenous groups have proposed to identify themselves with the term "First Nations."[3] Even if "nationalism is an essential anti-colonial strategy in indigenous settings" (Huhndorf 3), it should be stressed that this nationalist approach is too restrictive from a scholarly perspective as many issues, such as gender, cannot be addressed by this method. The editors of the special issue "Charting Transnational Native American Studies" of the *Journal of Transnational American Studies* also consider the pragmatic importance of the nationalist approach as well as the risks of "oversimplifying complex tribal identities, erasing broad networks of interaction and community, and smoothing indigenous histories that have always included transnational elements" (Huang et al. 2). Their goal is to examine in what way transnationalism can be a useful analytical tool "for providing a deeper understanding of contemporary Native American Studies" (Huang et al. 1) by also considering in what way Indigenous conceptions of nationhood question Western understandings of the nation. Similarly, while scrutinizing the limits of nationalism, Huhndorf acknowledges the fact that the works of her corpus – Indigenous literature and culture of the 1980s and 1990s – "illustrate the enduring importance of indigenous nationalism" (Huhndorf 7). In her analyses of Indigenous cultural production, she insists on the interplay between tribal concerns

3 This notion does not include the two other Indigenous groups of Canada, the Inuit and the Métis.

and transnational dynamics, thus connecting the local and the global. If the tribal and the transnational are inseparable entities, Huhndorf's cross-border analysis does conclude that "transnationalism has come to occupy ever more expansive ground in Native cultural practices in recent decades and will likely continue to do so in the years ahead" (117). The editors of the special issue of the *Journal of Transnational American Studies* push this idea further by considering Indigenous experiences and realities as essential factors for restructuring the notion of transnationalism. Their focus on "Indigenous-to-Indigenous relationships and connections" (Huang et al. 3) establishes a comparative paradigm in which the traditional binary oppositions of center-margin, major-minor and center-periphery are replaced by a transnational turn. The transnational offers alternative geographies and histories in which national maps and histories are part of a large-scale global perspective.

Even if "persuasive arguments can be made" to embrace the transnational, Chadwick Allen doubts in his article "whether the 'nation' in 'transnational' can ever mean other than the settler nation-state" (2012.1: 17). By re-routing this thinking to center on Indigenous intellectual production, Allen proposes a trans-Indigenous methodology that he further develops in his study *Trans-Indigenous: Methodologies for Global Native Literary Studies*. Instead of focusing on the relationships between Indigenous nations and settler-states, Allen examines connections and crossings from Indigenous nation to Indigenous nation. By acknowledging the "mobility and multiple interactions of Indigenous peoples, cultures, histories, and texts" (Allen 2012.2: xiv), Allen distinguishes two related terms, "recovery" and "interpretation" (Allen 2012.2: xv), that have the potential to establish methodological approaches. The development of global Indigenous methodologies based on "juxtapositions of distinct Indigenous texts" (Allen 2012.2: xvii) should, however, not be at the expense of the diversity and complexity of Indigenous identities. Indeed, in Allen's study, distinct traditions and knowledge are respected by means of refined textual interpretations. As a result, multiple perspectives of divergent communities, languages and cultures meet within a trans-Indigenous framework. This constant dialogue between the local and the global does not prioritize the one over the other, as global Indigenous studies bring together "multiple distinct cultures and histories on a truly equal basis" (Allen 2012.2: xiii).

In her book *Decolonizing Methodologies*, Linda Tuhiwai Smith proposes a trans-disciplinary approach in order to develop an international comparative study of Indigenous communities. By focusing on social science research, she explores 25 projects examining themes such as cultural survival, healing, social justice and self-determination in order to establish an Indigenous research agenda.

Methodological approaches and Indigenous practices are combined within the projects, resulting in a stockpile of concepts for studying Indigenous issues from within. Testimonies, for example, can be studied as narratives of collective memory that enable a more nuanced understanding of these histories. The idea of collectivity is also present in the project of storytelling, which relates to oral traditions and stresses the function of stories to pass "down the beliefs and values of a culture in the hope that the new generations will treasure them" (Tuhiwai Smith 145). Concepts such as remembering and gendering are concerned with the destructive effects of colonization and historical trauma, but also present the challenge to heal and to restore through collective remembering and reinforcing traditional roles and responsibilities. The ability to create solutions and to imagine a future are examined by means of the projects of creating and envisioning. These are just some examples taken from the array of projects presented by Tuhiwai Smith covering issues resulting from colonization to the "transcendence" of what she calls the "basic survival mode" (Tuhiwai Smith 159) by means of establishing good relations and producing Indigenous knowledge. This research shows that methodologies can only be developed when Indigenous communities themselves are engaged in the projects. According to Tuhiwai Smith, these communities have to "draw on their cultural strengths and understandings to fundamentally transform themselves, determine their own futures, and contribute their unique knowledge frameworks to solving their own problems and those of a wider society" (Tuhiwai Smith 231). This ambitious agenda distinguishes itself by emphasizing active transformation and the role Indigenous cultural knowledge can play on a global scale.

Not only Indigenous cultural knowledge, but also environmental ethics can be considered an important issue that can have a significant impact on other cultures. As Allen shows with regard to the future of North American Indigenous peoples, changing attitudes toward the environment constitutes an "area of hope" (Allen 2012.2: 93) as there is a potential for "the settler nations to learn a more positive environmental ethic from American Indians" (Allen 2012.2: 93). Another essential element for a more positive future presented by Allen is the "strong belief in the persistence and resurgence of Indigenous peoples and cultures within the context of contemporary politics" (Allen 2012.2: 246). This focus on the continuity of Indigenous intellectual traditions in the twenty-first century does not, however, mitigate innovative transformations within the field of Indigenous practices. On the contrary, Allen's analyses of primarily artistic and literary works illustrate that artistic innovation is key to developing new systems of interpreting and appreciating Indigenous art. By asserting the cultural distinctiveness of Indigenous communities, Allen's goal is to demonstrate the literary and political power of the Indigenous by developing "new methodologies for literary interpretation" (Allen

2012.2: 141). His suggestion that it is possible to develop a "trans-Indigenous literary analysis based in multiple understandings of aesthetics" (106) is demonstrated by multiple readings of one single text and juxtapositions of multiple texts. Successive readings of the poem "Carnegie, Oklahoma, 1919" by N. Scott Momaday, for example, engage with cultural traditions and distinct artistic expressions while also demonstrating its political engagement. By juxtaposing Momaday's poem with "Sad Joke on a Marae" by Māori poet Apirana Taylor or "Blood Quantum" by the Hawaiian poet Naomi Losch, Allen offers various possibilities for "Indigenized methodologies of literary analysis and interpretation" (2012.2: 181). The focus on multiple Indigenous perspectives moves away from a pan-Indigenous approach and towards global Indigenous methodologies.

Allen's study partly seems to be a response to Margaret Kovach's investigation of how Indigenous knowledges can be integrated into research frameworks. In her book *Indigenous Methodologies: Characteristics, Conversations, and Contexts*, her main concern is to create space in academic institutions for Indigenous epistemologies. By presenting her personal experience as an Indigenous scholar at a Canadian university, by incorporating conversations she has had with other Indigenous academics and by focusing on story as an Indigenous research method, she traverses cultural paradigms and aims to transform methodological homogeneity in research. Through shared methods, Kovach argues, non-Indigenous researchers can also be informed by Indigenous knowledges.

The articles in this volume engage with the different investigations discussed in this paragraph and hope to connect Western and Indigenous methodologies by juxtaposing knowledges from various Indigenous communities. The contributors also hope to advance trans-Indigenous studies by examining intersecting themes within North American boundaries. The various perspectives explored in the different articles are expected to encourage productive dialogues across the US, Canada and Mexico-US borders.

3. Indigenous peoples in North America: intersecting themes

As the editors of *Comparative Indigeneities of the Américas* have argued, despite their "shared post- or neocolonial condition and [...] their geographical proximity, little dialogue has occurred between US and Canadian Indians and indigenous groups in the Américas" (Castellanos et al. 2). They offer a hemispheric approach through the examination of Indigenous experiences across the Americas, in particular by focusing on overlapping histories of native peoples on the one hand and mixed blood peoples on the other. Three concepts are fundamental to their approach: indigenism[4], mestizaje[5] and hybridity. The first two have been considered conflicting notions, as Chicana and Chicano scholars in the United States confiscated indigenismo in order to claim their Indigenous ancestry, a development viewed with great suspicion by Indian nations because they considered this an abusive application of indigeneity. Also, in Latin America and the Caribbean, the recognition of mestizaje was part of assimilation projects introduced by governments in order to eliminate indigeneity: "mestizaje has served as a liberal ideology that has tended to obscure social and racial inequalities under a guise of equality and multiculturalism" (Castellanos et al. 6). These tensions have been handled in various ways. By proposing "radical indigenism", scholars have defined a form of indigenism "relying on native cultural traditions and principles, rather than on hegemonic ideals" (Castellanos et al. 4), and in the case of mestizaje, the construction of mestiza cultural identity has shifted the focus from assimilation to anti-colonial practices and resistance. When compared to the United States, the phenomenon of mixed-raced peoples has a different connotation. Instead of being an instrument for assimilation, mestizaje rather referred to a situation of not belonging to society. Blood quanta being the major determining factor for membership of an Indigenous community, mixed blood people were considered products of miscegenation and subject to enslavement. The Métis in Canada form an exception as they are recognized in Canada "as a separate First Nation along with 'Indians' and the Inuit in Canada's written constitution, which was proclaimed in 1982" (McNab 67).

The third concept considered by Castellanos, Gutiérrez Nájera and Aldama, hybridity, is said to challenge essentialist frameworks and to offer Indigenous subaltern voices the possibility to destabilize colonial discourses. This notion is very much dominated by the context of postcolonialism. In one of the most influential studies on postcolonial culture, *The Location of Culture* (1994), Homi Bhabha defines hybridity as "the sign of the productivity of colonial power, its shifting forces and fixities; it is the name for the strategic reversal of the process of domination through disavowal [...] the revaluation of the assumption of colonial identity through the repetition of discriminatory identity effects" (Bhabha 159). With regard to Indigenous cultural discourses, it has however been argued that postcolonial theories fail to recognize the importance of essentialist elements

---

4 From Mexican *indigenismo*, which Castellanos et al. describe as a "problematic nationalist ideology that peaked in the mid-twentieth century" (2).

5 This notion does not only refer to "the cultural mixing of European, Indigenous, and/or African ideas and attitudes" but also to "elite ideologies, historical processes, and subaltern identities" (Castellanos et al. 5–6).

such as nationalism and sovereignty in order to gain self-determination. The Canadian novelist and essayist Thomas King, of Cherokee, Greek and German descent[6], notes that the postcolonial method neglects the fact that there were traditions, cultures and literatures in Canada and in other former colonies that existed before the arrival of the Europeans: "Pre-colonial literature, as we use the term in North America, has no relationship whatsoever to colonial literature" (King 2004: 184). King thus criticizes the fact that postcolonialism takes the advent of the Europeans in North America as a general starting point, cutting of Indigenous literatures from their traditions, "traditions that were in place before colonialism ever became a question" (King 2004: 185). Another problem according to King is the idea that postcolonial literatures are characterized by progress and improvement. He recognizes that the term postcolonial is appropriate for certain works[7], but vehemently opposes the implication that Indigenous writing is largely a construct of oppression. As an alternative, King proposes four new descriptors as "vantage points from which we can see a particular literary landscape" (King 186): tribal, interfusional, polemical and associational.

Tribal literature is literature shared among the members of a specific community and preserved in an Indigenous language. Polemical literature can either be written in an Indigenous language or English or French, but focuses always on the conflict between Indigenous and non-Indigenous cultures. Interfusional language, on the contrary, is a "blending of oral literature and written literature" (King 2004: 186). The language of communication is English or French, but the structure and rhythm of the text would derive from oral literature. The final descriptor, associational literature, concentrates on Indigenous daily life, focusing on the group rather than on the individual. The terminology proposed by King does not "depend on the arrival of the Europeans for its *raison d'être*" (King 2004: 189), but it cannot describe the full body of Indigenous literary work, as the essayist has himself admitted. King's discussion of the blending of oral and written literature in which different traditions meet, as well as the merging of the English or French language with Indigenous rhythm and style contribute to the transgression of boundaries and interactions between Indigenous storytellers. As King states in the introduction to his anthology *All My Relations*: "the advent of written Native literature has provided Native writers with common structures, themes and

6 King describes himself as a "contemporary Native writer" (185).

7 He mentions for example Métis authors Maria Campbell, *Halfbreed* (1973), and Beatrice Culleton, *In Search of April Raintree* (1983).

characters which can effectively express traditional and contemporary concerns about the world and the condition of living beings" (1992: Xx).

The combined expression of traditional and contemporary matters exceeds the postcolonial straitjacket and reaffirms the current significance of Indigenous epistemologies. This reaffirmation is also stressed by Angela Cavender Wilson in her essay "Reclaiming Our Humanity", in which a return to the ontological foundations is considered to be the essential way to strengthen Indigenous cultures in the globalized world. According to Wilson, recovery and reclamation of Indigenous knowledge and traditions are a necessary part of the scholarly agenda and a signifier of "cultural revitalization" (262). As discussed in the second part of this introduction, Chadwick Allen also foregrounds the importance of recovering Indigenous texts from history and from dominant discourses. This element of recovery, leading to cultural revitalization, is a first intersecting theme that connects Indigenous experiences in North America. Cross-cultural comparisons are increasing because of the growing mobility of Indigenous peoples and interactions between them. Migration strengthens cultural connections and identities across the hemisphere, but also challenges local practices. Migration can be seen as a threat as well as an opportunity. Thus, a second intersecting theme relates to the question of how migration incorporates specific local traditions on the one hand and "broader globally Indigenous fields of inquiry" (Allen 2012.2: xiv) on the other. Increasing Indigenous networks across the Americas is believed to have a favorable effect on the reinforcement of self-determination of Indigenous communities – the necessity of which has already been discussed in the first part of this introduction – and on local forms of governance. A third converging theme is that of sovereignty and autonomous governance.

These and related themes are examined in *Comparative Indigeneities of the Américas*, in which hemispheric Native or First Nations and Métis experiences are compared. Despite the fact that this book fosters a better understanding of connections between Indigenous communities in the United States, Canada and Latin America, it fails to include a third Indigenous group, the Inuit. This omission is justifiable when considering that the focus of this study is put on the U.S.-Mexico and Latin American-Caribbean experience. It is, however, remarkable that the situation of the Inuit is generally examined separately, instead of being incorporated in comparative studies.[8] We therefore propose to broaden the scope of the

8 Several studies such as Marie Wadden's book *Where the Pavement Ends: Canada's Aboriginal Recovery Movement and the Urgent Need for Reconciliation*. Toronto, Douglas & McIntyre, 2009 discuss and compare the First Nations, Métis and Inuit experiences,

hemispheric discussion by including the Inuit experience in it. By also examining the developments in the Arctic, this volume proposes to expand the study and comparison of Indigenous encounters in North America.

In the case of the Inuit, the most striking of the intersecting themes is that of sovereignty and governance. As scholars have argued, the "Nunavut Land Claims Agreement between the Inuit of Nunavut and Canada, signed in 1993, is considered to be one of the most extensive and successful examples of such agreements"(Van Dam 14).[9] The creation of a territory for the Inuit, Nunavut ("Our Land"), makes this land claim particularly unique. The Agreement focused on ownership of the land, but it also included the commitment to create a Nunavut Government. On April 1, 1999 territory and government were created and established. As a result, "many of the ambitions of the Inuit were realized: land ownership [...]; resource use and management [...]; self-government and self-determination, and compensation" (Van Dam 20). Apart from Nunavut, three other Inuit regions exist in Canada: Nunavik (James Bay, Northern Quebec), Inuvialuit Settlement Region and Nunatsiavut (Labrador). All Canadian Inuit are represented at the federal level by Inuit Tapiriit Kanatami ("Inuit are united in Canada"), created in 1971 and based in Ottawa. Outside of the four Inuit regions, approximately 25% or 15.000 Inuit live in the south or urban centres. All the Inuit of the circumpolar Arctic, including the Inuit of Alaska, Russia, and Greenland, are represented by the Inuit Circumpolar Council.[10]

Despite the assertion of rights to sovereignty and governance, the realization of self-determination in Nunavut and the creation of Inuit organizations, the question has been raised if Inuit Arctic sovereignty really exists. In her newspaper article "Fund Inuit, not Canadian, Arctic Sovereignty" (2009), Marie Wadden criticizes the stationing of Canadian troops in order to guard the Arctic borders. She argues that "Inuit are once again on the sidelines, forced to watch a parade of southern military types who will bring with them a negative social impact

---

but these books generally focus on the national situation and not on transnational or hemispheric issues.

9 See for example K. Cameron and G. White. *Northern governments in transition, political and constitutional development in the Yukon, Nunavut and the Northwest Territories.* Montreal, Institute for Research of Public Policy, 1995 and J. Hicks. "The Nunavut Land Claim and the Nunavut Government: political structures of self-government in Canada's Eastern Arctic." Ed. H.K. Petersen and B. Poppel. *Dependency, Autonomy Sustainability in the Arctic.* Ashgate, Aldershot Brookfield, 1999. 21–53.

10 See the website of the Inuit Knowledge Centre: http://www.inuitknowledge.ca/content/inuit-government.

that no one has bothered to measure or mitigate".[11] According to Wadden, this is exemplary of the Canadian government policy that disregards the sovereignty of Canada's Indigenous nations rather than supporting it. The negative social impact of federal government measures shows that there is a need for Inuit-run development projects as well as for programs of transmitting Inuit culture and knowledge.

Restoring lost traditions and giving access to heritage by committing oral traditions to text[12] or by broadcasting information on traditional Inuit lifestyle and practices in English as well as Inuktitut[13], are examples of the intersecting theme of recovery. This theme covers a broad range of issues, from cultural aspects to matters of health. An important aspect of recovery is for example raising awareness of the legacy of residential schools by giving attention to the impacts of mental and physical abuse that still affect survivors and their families. Healing initiatives focusing on the family and community and on combining the mind and body are taking place that also help people reconnect with their cultural roots. This is also strongly related to another essential matter that is widely examined with regard to recovery, namely health conditions and social determinants of health. The examination of health risks related to factors such as climate change, the economic situation, and environmental dispossession are not specifically related to Inuit communities, as many Indigenous nations face similar problems. When focusing for example on the land "as a fundamental component of Indigenous culture, and central to [their] health and wellness" (Richmond & Ross 404), physical displacement from their lands and territories "has negatively affected the collective well-being of Indigenous populations" (Richmond & Ross 404).[14] Displacement in this sense is understood as relocation. In their book *Tammarniit (Mistakes)* (1994), Frank James Tester and Peter Kylchyski present an overview of Inuit relocations in the Eastern Arctic and discuss the considerable hardships the Inuit faced.[15] Relocation schemes were put in place by the Canadian government

---

11 See: http://www.theglobeandmail.com/globe-debate/fund-inuit-not-canadian-arctic-sovereignty/article4214072/.

12 An example is Beverley O'Brien's book *Birth on the Land – Memories of Inuit Elders and Traditional Midwives*, Iqaluit, NU, Nunavut Arctic College, 2013.

13 See the Aboriginal Peoples Television Network (APTN): http://aptn.ca/.

14 Richmond and Ross note that Community Health Representatives of First Nation and Inuit communities across Canada have identified six health determinants: balance, life control, education, material resources, social resources, and environmental /cultural connections.

15 A striking example is the 1953 High Arctic relocation, when Inuit families were forcibly relocated to the uninhabited and inhospitable High Arctic, 1500 kilometres north of

for many different Indigenous communities. These relocations and other effects of government policy are criticized in the final report of the Royal Commission on Aboriginal Peoples issued in 1996, which hopes to repair the damage to the relationship between non-Indigenous and Indigenous peoples.[16]

Inuit history is strongly characterized by nomadic ways of living and migration. For nearly a half-century now, the Inuit have been migrating to southern urban centers. Urban migration is present in all of Canada's Indigenous populations, but is has been argued that the differences many Inuit face are unique, because they usually come from small communities of only a few hundred. Research shows that "communities are not fixed or unified entities and that issues such as housing, language and discrimination both unite and create barriers for Inuit in the city" (Patrick & Tomiak 55). According to Donna Patrick and Julie-Ann Tomiak, community building and increased access to services in the city are essential elements for social and cultural well-being. As a result of migration, Inuit linguistic and cultural practices are jeopardized. As Patrick and Tomiak argue, language programs and strategic use of resources are important ways for maintaining cultural practices.

The various examples taken from the Inuit situation support the application of the three intersecting themes as a foundation for comparative research on North American Indigenous experience. These intersecting themes therefore shape the structure of this volume: the first part focuses on the theme of recovery in relation to the literary field, the theme of governance will be examined in the second part through examples of conflict, public government and citizenship and the theme of increased global movements in relation to the preservation of local traditions will be developed in the final part of this volume.

4. Recovering sovereignty through self-governance and cultural expression

In the first part of this volume, Daniel Chartier and Grit Alter discuss the role of written literature in Inuit culture by focussing on the significant role that the Inuktitut language and storytelling play in maintaining a strong and distinct Inuit identity. Chartier offers a first historical interpretation of the evolution in Nunavik, the Inuit region of Québec. He presents this, on the one hand, by comparing it to written literary forms practiced by First Nations, and, on the other hand, by examining the specificities of the blend forms of Inuit oral heritage and Western written tradition.

their traditional homeland of Nunavik, in northern Québec. In 2010, the government of Canada presented its apologies for this relocation.

16 See http://www.aadnc-aandc.gc.ca/eng/1100100014597/1100100014637.

He argues that Inuit literary history, by creating a space of its own, can both give access to heritage through the study of oral persistence in writing and raise awareness of the originality of certain literary forms. Thus, recovery in literature is a matter of space, as Grit Alter also shows in her analysis of Inuit children's literature. She underlines the importance of the institutional space of the publishing industry, in which Inuit authors increasingly claim ownership of their stories, as Inuit culture has too often been represented by cultural outsiders. By countering the existing stereotypes from within, new spaces of cultural identity can be created in literature. The theme of recovery takes on the form of a re-imagination of Inuit stories from an Inuit perspective. Alter, like Chartier, underscores the importance of two elements in particular, the preservation of the oral tradition on the printed page and the usage of Indigenous language in which agency is expressed. In contemporary children's books, the inclusion of phrases in Inuktitut is closely associated with the image of North as a home and a strong connection to the land. At the same time, new spaces of self are created when the child protagonists explore different geographical and temporal spaces. As a result, Alter argues, contemporary Inuit life is based on knowledge of the past through storytelling. The power of Indigenous storytelling is furthermore stressed in Hans Bak's article on the American Indigenous author LeAnne Howe. Bak discusses the theme of recovery as a re-examination of American history in which Indigenous and mainstream (his)stories are interconnected and interact mutually. His analysis of LeAnne Howe's literary work concentrates on the recovery of an erased history and on the search for an Indigenous epistemology in which empirically verifiable truth and knowledge through story are merged. By exploring the theme of recovery, the articles in this section of the anthology demonstrate that re-connections to and re-imaginations of Indigenous past and identity create new spaces and developments in Indigenous literary history that enrich transnational literary studies.

The three articles of the second section discuss the reconfiguration of Indigenous peoples' relationship with the state and state institutions as an essential condition for Indigenous social development as well as for establishing Indigenous citizenship models and new types of government. Andreas Huck's article on the conflict situation in British Columbia with regard to the proposed Northern Gateway pipeline shows that First Nation's poorly integrated involvement in assessment processes in BC can be followed back to Canada's colonial past. A first step to improve First Nations' involvement in the review process of the Northern Gateway project is therefore to critically reflect First Nation-government-relations against the background of Canada's colonial past. By approaching the problem from Social Impact Assessment theory, Huck argues that external conflict mediation can help to solve different levels of the conflict. However, in his conclusion he also emphasizes the active role the Canadian federal government should play in fostering a real negotiation by acknowledging community needs and community self-determination. Conflict and negotiation are also at the baseline of Merel de Buck's analysis of the alternative education project of the civil society organization *Centro de Apoyo Comunitario Trabajando Unidos* (CACTUS) in the Mixtec Baja region of Mexico. The project's goals are to offer quality education to the Mixtec community and to emancipate students in terms of citizenship. De Buck considers the school of CACTUS as a place where dispute and mediation takes place between the local community and the state. Traditional relationships between these actors have been based on cultural difference as a criterion for exclusion. De Buck argues that the school of CACTUS functions as a tool to overcome exclusion and to contest dominant citizenship regimes in Mexico. As a result, the experience of citizenship is changing and increasingly being produced in permanent negotiations in which local actors and states collaborate. In the case of Nunavut, as Kim van Dam argues, the Inuit have successfully established a form of aboriginal self-government and as such it is one of the most far-reaching examples of how aboriginal people have regained power within their nation states. The Inuit have chosen to fulfil their ambitions with a conventional public government with a mandate common for these types of government. They have successfully introduced important Inuit values into the governance system, most notably the concept of Inuit Qaujimajatuqangit – Inuit traditional knowledge. Nevertheless, the Nunavut government has very limited financial power as the federal government is still in control of taxes, land and resource development. As a result, the territorial ambition of Nunavut to encourage self-reliance and self-sufficiency may therefore be jeopardized.

The three very different examples analyzed in this part demonstrate that, by means of conflict and negotiation, a fundamental change of the Indigenous peoples' relationship with the state can be achieved. Such an improved relationship, in which Indigenous traditional values are recognized, fosters self-determination and self-governance.

In the third and final section of this volume, Wil Pansters mentions the Zapatista uprising in Mexico as an example of the changing relationship with the state and an affirmation of a renegotiation of this relationship on their terms. When discussing resistance against oppressive power relations in Mexico and the increasing political awareness of Indigenous communities, Pansters also focuses on the international context, as the formation of global human Indigenous rights and the creation of transnational networks has considerably contributed to a re-articulation of Indigenous identities. He further presents the debate about the relationship between collective and individual rights as a key element in changing Indigenous identity politics in Mexico. In this debate, women's interpretations of gender rights were essential for developing alternative ways of thinking that go beyond binaries. In their article on the practices of berry picking and sharing by Inuit women in the community of Inukjak, Simard-Gagon and Desbiens also challenge the binary structures that drive traditional Western theories of gender based on the divide between public and private spheres. Their focus on the example of berry picking illustrates the need for flexible gendered skills within the complexity of contemporary context. They not only examine berry picking as a contribution of Inuit women to territoriality, but they also insist on the agency of women in connecting two systems in contemporary economy, that of market economy and territorial systems of subsistence. Their analysis is therefore an important contribution to a better understanding of Inuit women's experiences and role in society. Traveling further south, to the state of Oaxaca in southern Mexico, Martin Berger examines the cultural tradition of the game of *pelota mixteca* and compares the views of players of the game on the one hand and of the Mexican government on the other. Berger argues that the conception of the game as an ancestral tradition by the Mexican state led to the promotion of the game as a tourist attraction, whereas the players themselves believe that the game can only be saved from extinction by promoting it as a more widely played sport. If the government underscores the tradition of the game, the players argue for a detraditionalization of the game: only taking the game out of the sphere of the cultural particular will guarantee its survival. This example underscores the significance of situating Indigenous cultural traditions in a wider framework: the promotion of these traditions and values worldwide not only ensures their survival but also enriches global culture.

Works cited

Allen, Chadwick. "A trans*national* Native American Studies? Why not studies that are trans-*Indigenous*?" *Journal of Transnational American Studies* 4.1 (2012.1). https://escholarship.org/uc/item/82m5j3f5.

–. *Trans-Indigenous. Methodologies for Global Native Literary Studies.* London (Minneapolis), The University of Minnesota Press, 2012.2.

Anaya, James S.. *Indigenous Peoples in International Law.* Oxford/New York, Oxford University Press, 1996.

Barrenechea, Antonio and Heidrun Moertl. "Hemispheric Indigenous Studies: Introduction." *Comparative American Studies* 11.2 (June 2013): 109–23.

Bennett, Mark. ""Indigeneity" as Self-Determination." *Indigenous Law Journal.* 4 (Fall 2005): 71–115.

Bhabha, Homi K.. *The Location of Culture.* London and New York, Routledge, 1994.

Castellanos, M. Bianet, Lourdes Gutiérrez Nájera, and Arturo J. Aldama (ed.). *Comparative Indigeneities of the Américas. Toward a Hemispheric Approach.* Tucson, The University of Arizona Press, 2013.

Daes, Erica-Irene A.. "Some Considerations on the Right of Indigenous Peoples to Self-Determination." *3 Transnational Law & Contemporary Problems* 1 (1993): 1–12.

Dam, Kim van. *A Place Called Nunavut. Multiple Identities for a New Region.* Groningen, Barkhuis Press (Circumpolar Studies 5), 2008.

Horton, Jessica. "Alone on the snow, alone on the beach: "A global sense of place" in *Atanarjuat* and *Fountain*." *Journal of Transnational American Studies* 4.1 (2012). https://escholarship.org/uc/item/54p2f9pq

Huang, Hsinya, Philip Deloria, Laura Furlan, and John Gamber. "Charting Transnational Native American Studies." *Journal of Transnational American Studies* 4.1 (2012). http://www.escholarship.org/uc/item/3w4347p6

Huhndorf, Shari M.. *Mapping the Americas: The Transnational Politics of Contemporary Native Culture.* Ithaca, NY, Cornell University Press, 2009.

King, Thomas. *All My Relations. An Anthology of Contemporary Canadian Native Fiction.* Norman and London, University of Oklahoma Press, 1992 [1990].

–. "Godzilla vs. Post-Colonial." Ed. Cynthia Sugars. *Unhomely States: Theorizing English-Canadian Postcolonialism.* Mississauga, Broadview Press, 2004. 183–190.

Kovach, Margaret. *Indigenous Methodologies: Characteristics, Conversations, and Contexts.* Toronto, U of Toronto P, 2009. Print.

Maaka, Roger C.A. and Chris Andersen. *The Indigenous Experience. Global Perspectives.* Toronto, Canadian Scholars' Press Inc, 2006.

Maaka, Roger C.A. and Augie Fleras. "Indigeneity at the Edge: Towards a Constructive Engagement." Ed. Roger C.A. Maaka and Chris Andersen. *The Indigenous Experience. Global Perspectives.* Toronto, Canadian Scholars' Press Inc, 2006. 337–357.

McNab, David T.. "Métis Voices and Sovereignty. Reflections on Métis Resistance to Imperial Layers of Colonialism in Canada." Ed. M. Bianet Castellanos et al.. *Comparative Indigeneities of the Américas. Toward a Hemispheric Approach.* Tucson, The University of Arizona Press, 2013. 67–80.

Nair, Manjusha S.. "Defining Indigeneity. Situating transnational knowledge." *World Society Focus Paper Series*, 2006.

Patrick, Donna and Julie-Ann Tomiak. "Language, culture and community among urban Inuit in Ottawa." *Études/Inuit/Studies* 32.1 (2008): 55–72.

Richmond, Chantelle A.M. and Nancy A. Ross. "The Determinants of First Nation and Inuit Health: A Critical Population Health Approach." *Health & Place* 15(2009): 403–411.

Sissons, Jeffrey. *First Peoples. Indigenous Cultures and Their Futures*. London, Reaktion Books Ltd, 2005.

Tester, Frank J. and Peter Kulchyski. *Tammarniit (Mistakes): Inuit Relocation in the Eastern Arctic 1939–63*. Vancouver, UBC Press, 1994.

Tuhiwai Smith, Linda. *Decolonizing Methodologies. Research and Indigenous Peoples*. London & New York, Zed Books, 2012 [1999].

U.N. Study of the Problem of Discrimination against Indigenous Populations, U.N. Doc E/CN.4/Sub.2/1986/7/Add.4, at 29, para. 379.

Wadden, Marie. "Fund Inuit, not Canadian, Arctic Sovereignty". *The Globe and Mail*, August 18, 2009. http://www.theglobeandmail.com/globe-debate/fund-inuit-not-canadian-arctic-sovereignty/article4214072/.

Wilson, Angela Cavender. "Reclaiming Our Humanity: Decolonization and the Recovery of Indigenous Knowledge." Ed. Peter A. French and Jason A. Short. *War and Border Crossings: Ethics When Cultures Clash*. Lanham, Rowman & Littlefield Publishers Inc., 2005. 253–263.

Part I: Literature, Recovery and Space

Daniel Chartier
Research Chair on Images of the North, Winter and the Arctic, Université du Québec à Montréal

The Social and Cultural Context of Inuit Literary History

Inuit literature already has a specific place in world heritage, since it is seen as a testimony of the possibility for man to live in the toughest conditions[1]. *Written* Inuit literature is more particular: it develops at the end of the twentieth and the beginning of the twenty-first century, at a time when books and magazines are challenged by new media and new publication forms. It shares with other native artistic expressions a strong political meaning, considered either postcolonial or, as some suggest, not yet postcolonial. It also conveys rich oral and sculptural traditions, in its inventive new ways of making literature. However, as the few researchers on this literature point out, Inuit works received no or little critical attention, and they are almost never part of university curriculum (Kennedy). All these facts combine to form a fascinating case for research, which poses considerable methodological challenges.

Nunavik Inuit literature, which appears to be both part of a greater Inuit whole (including Nunavut, Greenland, Northwest Territories) and exclusive in its situation – at the crossroads between Inuktitut, English and French languages – poses specific challenges to the literary historian.

The objective of this article is to examine some of the parameters within which we can think of a first historical interpretation of the evolution of written literature in Nunavik, the Inuit region of Québec, which, as of 1959, signals the beginning of a written self-representation of the Inuit.

1. Inuit literary and cultural contexts

Inuktitut, which is considered by linguists as one of the most complex languages, has been in written form for just over one hundred and fifty years[2], which explains its

1 For example, critics of the first translations of Inuit literature in Indian languages, *The Harpoon of the Hunter* in Marathi and Hindi, demonstrate the universality of Inuit culture, beyond the difficulties of translation and the gap between social situations. See for example Apoorva Puranik, 2016.

2 For an account of the development of written Inuktitut, see Ken Harper, 1983.

short linguistic[3] and literary history. Although not endangered, compared to most native minority languages in North America, Inuktitut survives in part thanks to the work of dynamic organizations, like the Avataq Cultural Institute in Québec[4]. Inuktitut plays a significant role in maintaining a strong, distinct identity and culture among the Inuit[5]. According to Noel McDermott, literature in Inuktitut has a future, but "encouragement and support" will be needed to ensure that Inuktitut writers "get their work published and distributed" (Langgård and Thisted 237).

As early as in the 1930s, a traveler to Nunavik recorded that most Inuit could read and write, despite the lack of a formal educational system. Written Inuktitut was then mainly used for religious ceremonies. Since pen and paper were difficult to obtain, like any other manufactured material, Inuit writing was limited as a result. The scarce presence of trees, the fragility of caribou and seal skins left little to write on: carvings made of bones or stones sometimes allowed oral traditions to be kept in a material, symbolic form.

Even if Inuit from all territories share a common linguistic base, the large number of dialects and the lack of a standardized language among the Inuit of Nunavut, Nunatsiavut, Nunavik and Greenland makes it difficult to exchange written texts in Inuktitut among Inuit men and women. Furthermore, the use of two writing systems, syllabic form in Nunavik and in parts of Nunavut, and Roman orthography for others, poses a considerable challenge to cultural and literary exchanges.

The retention rate of Inuit language is among the highest of Indigenous peoples of the Americas: 80% of Inuit in Nunavut and 90% in Nunavik speak Inuktitut (McDermott 225). That being said, and partly because of the difficulty of linguistic exchanges between Inuit, most writers in Canada choose English as the language of literary writing. A number of texts are written and published in Inuktitut, and to a lesser extent, in Nunavik, in French. Greenland has a longer literary tradition, and it publishes a larger number of texts and books. A substantial proportion of it is in Greenlandic (the rest being in Danish).

---

3 The first complete Nunavik Inuktitut dictionary was completed by Taamusi Qumaq and published in 1990 as "The Real Inuit Words".

4 Founded in 1980, Avataq received its mandate from the "elders" of Nunavik. Today, the Institute has a complete range of programs and services, including: an Inuktitut promotion and preservation program, a genealogy program, a Nunavik museums program, a Nunavik Inuit art collection, an archaeology department, an artist support program, a documentation and archives center, local cultural committees, traditional skills courses, as well as a research and publications service. [http://www.avataq.qc.ca/en/Institute/About-us/Background-Information, July 2012].

5 See for example Jean-Philippe Chartrand, 1986.

Traditionally, Inuit value narratives to convey their lifestyle, legends and even historical facts, sometimes dating back hundreds of years. According to Nunavik writer and filmmaker Zebedee Nungak, "amazingly, the human memory served as an archive for these [stories]." Nungak considers that "one of the strongest traditions of Inuit has been the preservation of culture and identity through *unikkaat* (stories) and *unikkaatuat* (legends)" (62).

Some oral literary forms are specific to Inuit; this is the case for what Nungak calls "daily narrative". He writes:

> Another feature of Inuit daily life was the "daily narrative". The family would re-group at the end of the day, and recount the events and happenings of the day. A natural extension of this forum was the reciting of legends and stories by the more elderly members of the family (62).

The integration in daily life of "fiction", as Western culture would call it, is the convergence of talking about daily life and storytelling.

The reader will also note that Inuit stories (both from Nunavik and from Greenland) demonstrate a specific conception of time compared to Western narratives. In Taamusi Qumaq's book (2010), for example, a chapter begins with a return to the events described in the previous chapter, a clear sign of a trace of orality. A different time conception also appears in the fragmented narratives and the multiplication of literary forms (eg, Kelly Berthelsen), in which the book is the focal center of a multiplicity of time scales and perspectives, which can confuse the reader but demonstrate the characteristic use of literature by Inuit writers.

Most practiced written literary forms resemble those of aboriginal people, comprised mainly of tales and legends, but also of journalistic essays, dictionaries and life stories, some novels, children's literature and poetry, and – more rarely – theatrical plays.

Regardless, Inuit culture today seems in danger of survival: according to Markoosie, author of the first Inuit novel in Canada, *Harpoon of the Hunter*, "much of our oral history has been lost or no longer told by those who possess such knowledge of our past" (37).

However, much remains to be done to integrate written literature in Inuit cultural habits, and to adapt the forms to their ways. In addition to the usual difficulties of young writers, an Inuit writer faces a series of additional pitfalls. According to Nungak,

> Since Inuit traditions are oral and not literary, Inuit have had to process through a transition to find a suitable "zone of comfort" in the field of written literature. In past times, writing seemed to be something for "others" to do, and was not at all a pre-occupation of Inuit. For a long time, it seemed that Inuit were neither meant, nor expected to be, writers.

> That is, in the way that *Qallunaat* [white men] have been authors, poets, and producers of written works for centuries (64).

Today, writers such as Zebedee Nungak have developed a satirical style that is part of an assertion of a political identity and a post-colonial position. Others such as Taqralik Partridge have developed an art midway between performance, poetry and spoken word, thus keeping the oral tradition alive into a renewed and urban art form. It is interesting to note that Taqralik Partridge's works are mainly published via short videos on YouTube, the best way to reach Inuit people according to the artist, who nevertheless also writes and publishes stories. She won a prize for the best short story written in English in 2010 (Rogers 3).

The absence of a publisher or literary magazine in Nunavik and Nunavut, and the fact that there is still no geographic center for Inuit cultural and literary consecration, keep the development of a literary life fragile.The challenges and the failings of the education system exacerbate this fragility. Even today, only a minority of Inuit complete their basic schooling, while a tiny fraction of them succeed in obtaining a graduate degree. The significant demand for skilled labour allows Inuit graduates to easily obtain a professional job, leaving few of educated people to develop a cultural and literary life.

Yet Inuit authors have been writing for half a century. In doing so, they have been facing steep obstacles. They have long been unrecognized and overlooked. In 1985, Margaret Harry asked: "Where are the Indian and Inuit writers? Many white Canadians, including those who consider themselves well read, cannot name a single Indian or Inuit writer" (Harry 146). Today, twenty-five years later, Harry's remarks still apply, despite a few exceptions.

2. Nunavik cultural situation

Inuit are one of the few aboriginal people who live in many territories, covering all the Arctic and including Siberia, Alaska, Northwest Territories, Nunavut, Yukon, Nunavik, Nunatsiavut and Greenland. In Greenland, Canada and Alaska, they are about 150,000. In Nunavik, Québec's northern region, they are 14,000. The population of Nunavik is among the youngest in Québec: one person in two is less than 20 years old.

The Inuit of North America are not, strictly speaking, Native Americans, although they are an Indigenous people; their ancestors are generally believed to have come to America several thousand years after the arrival of Native Americans. For the Cree and Innu (historically called Montagnais) peoples, Nunavik's Inuit represent the first wave of immigrants to America, followed by the Vikings, French, and English a few decades later. However, the same political questions arise concerning the Inuit and Indians. The largest land claim process in Canada's history led, in 1999, to the creation of Nunavut, a territory designed as the new home for much of Canada's Inuit. In addition, to honour the claims of the Inuit of Nunavik, in Arctic Quebec, the Quebec government created the Kativik Regional Government under the Convention of James Bay and Northern Quebec Agreement, creating the region of Nunavik. This agreement, signed in 1975[6], was followed by the official recognition by the Quebec government as early as 1983 (one of the only governments to have ever done so) that "the aboriginal people of Quebec are distinct nations that are entitled to their culture, their language, their customs and traditions and to the right to orient themselves the development of their own identity"[7].

European influence on the Inuit is considerable: first by the imposition of a social and economic system that was foreign to their society, then by the appearance of new diseases and by an abandonment of traditional culture, which resulted in social and family problems, but also in an increase in living standards and education. These improvements also show serious inequality and cultural loss and lead to an adaptation to new modes of dissemination of culture and knowledge: sculpture, drawing and lithography, and finally written literature and cinema.

The political, military and cultural presence of non-natives among the Inuit has clearly had an impact; however, today, the Inuit are fighting to keep and adapt their ways in order to preserve their distinct culture: they are encouraging the teaching and speaking of Inuktitut, the preservation of values and stories about the past, the use of various forms of modern communication (radio, television and the Internet) as well as the development of oral practices (song, spoken word, etc.) and, of course, written literature.

If it manages to keep its language, an Inuit community continues to share a strong common heritage with other Inuit populations, even if its inhabitants speak it with great variations, often due to loans from various European languages: English, French, Danish and German. They therefore have a shared language base, but they practice it with differences according to their geographical location. On the other hand, communities that lose the ability to communicate in Inuktitut (mostly towards English) also diminish their ability to exchange with other Inuit around the Arctic.

---

6 For more information on the Convention, see Alain-G. Gagnon and Guy Rocher, 2002.

7 This statement was followed in 1985 by the "Motion portant sur la reconnaissance des droits des Autochtones", voted at the Assemblée nationale du Québec on March 15th, 1985. See: *Amérindiens et Inuits. Portraits des nations autochtones du Québec*, Secrétariat aux affaires autochtones, Gouvernement du Québec, 2009, p. 10.

Due to the extension of southern political and cultural powers and influence on the Arctic and the establishment of separate regional administrative structures, most Inuit created a double identity for themselves: Pan-Inuit and regional, in parallel to a commitment (which varies depending on their situation) towards the states to which they are linked.

From the outside, the Inuit represent, for European culture and philosophy, the image of man in front of the essential, a living witness of asceticism which would be natural, and not cultural, as Michel Onfray demonstrates in his essay *Esthétique du pôle Nord* (2002). This leads to the universal recognition of Inuit human and cultural experience, but also to a folklorisation of Inuit culture and values, weighted by the concept of "authenticity". For example, if anthropologists have been very interested in Inuit communities, their special attention has left behind contemporary forms of expressions, often a product of a mixed heritage. The work of Nunavik writer Markoosie clearly illustrates this effect: his traditional novel *Harpoon of the Hunter*[8] received great reviews and was published in book format in several languages, while his other novel, *Wings of Mercy*[9], which describes the life of a plane pilot in the Arctic, was never published as a book. If they want to survive, the Inuit need to strongly defend their right to modernity (Chartier 2005), which necessarily implies the right to create new, hybrid and cross-cultural cultural forms.

Regarding the Inuit territory in Quebec, Nunavik is particularized by a striking demographic and economic growth (which does not eliminate serious social problems, including a high suicide rate, violence and unemployment), by a very high level of use of the Inuktitut language and a singular trilingual context, with French, English and Inuktitut.

3. The concept of "written text" in Nunavik Inuit culture

Among the Nunavik Inuit, the concept of "written text" arises from the introduction of writing by Edmund James Peck in 1877 (Evans), and it was not until a few decades ago, at the end of the twentieth century, that the first signs of written Inuit literature became visible.

The establishment of a Western education system (1932: 1st mission school; 1949: 1st federal school; 1963: School Board of New-Quebec) has increased the

8 The Inuktitut (French/Inuktitut) edition of this text, *Le harpon du chasseur*, was published by Les Presses de l'Université du Québec, coll. "Imaginaire | Nord Jardin de givre", 2011 [1969].

9 Published in 5 parts in *Inuktitut Magazine*, from Summer 1972 to Autumn 1973.

knowledge of writing, but primarily for the benefit of a foreign language: English. It was only after 1978 that Inuktitut was offered in schools.

During this transition period, "written text" had a symbolic place, linked to an external power (often religious), in a world that was previously based on orality. However, the appropriation of writing by the Inuit gradually led to the appearance of the first texts, scattered in newspapers and periodicals, and – for some – in the form of books.

These precious early texts mark the beginning of self-representation of the Inuit and a way to preserve their heritage. *Inuktitut Magazine*, first published in 1959, signaled the beginning of an Inuit written literature in Nunavik. The first literary works written by Inuit – including *The Harpoon of the Hunter*, which has just been republished and which was the first Inuit novel in Canada in 1969 – are a blend of forms that draw on both Inuit oral heritage and Western written literary tradition. According to some critics, such a blend diminishes the "authenticity" of the narrative: what the novel gains in formal innovation and literariness, it loses in representativeness of authentic culture. To avoid this problem, Inuit writers have no choice but to assert their right to create works in the same way as writers from all other modern cultures: through a meshing of self and other.

4. Inuit literary history methodology

Inuit literature grounds its interest and relevance not so much by the quantity of its productions than by the fact that it constitutes a symbol that has universal value for human experience. For the Inuit, including Markoosie, this commitment takes the form of a duty of memory, which shows how it is now necessary to communicate through writing in order to transmit their vision of the world.

As Clara Mongeon-Bourbonnais demonstrated in her literary study of Zebedee Nungak (from Nunavik), Inuit literature – like many other colonial literatures – is overwhelmed by the figure of the "Other", which can be understood by the figure of the "*Qallunaat*". This figure appears in the first Inuit texts as a surprise (Qumaq), fear, threat, and then in a continual challenge that must be discarded (Nungak) and overcome (Berthelsen).

From a methodological standpoint, it is tempting to apply the excellent work done on Canadian and American First Nations literature to Inuit literature, partly because these studies are particularly fertile and abundant. However, if it is possible to consider these studies in an understanding of Inuit literature, one must also remember to apply them with caution because of fundamental differences between Inuit and First Nations (or Native Americans). It is true that Inuit culture shares with First Nations cultures an oral origin, certain identity themes and a postcolonial perspective. However, Inuit culture differentiates itself on many fronts, including legal, historical, cultural, geographic and linguistic ones:

- First, the Inuit of Canada, unlike the First Nations, were never subject to the *Indian Act;*
- Because of their remoteness and isolation, the notion of hybridity, which correctly applies to varying degrees to the First Nations, had a different and lesser impact among the Inuit;
- Canada's Inuit are part of a larger whole: they belong to a people living in territories of different jurisdictions in five countries: mainly in Nunavik, Nunavut and Greenland, but also in Nunatsiavut (Labrador), in the Northwest Territories, Alaska and Siberia;
- This situation contributes to the existence of a pan-Inuit identity, intellectually defended by Greenlandic Aqqaluk Lynge[10], but also to regional differences, accentuated by the establishment of institutions specific to areas administered by the Inuit;
- Finally, the Inuit share a common linguistic background, beyond their differences. Also, unlike most of the First Nations who have difficulty maintaining their languages, Inuktitut remains strong among communities and is used in contemporary culture.

From a literary point of view, the literature of Nunavik displays some characteristics of a so-called minor literature (a concept developed by Gilles Deleuze and Félix Guattari[11], and redeveloped by Jean Bessière), which is a literature written in the same language as that of a literature of greater importance: for Nunavik, this is the case of Greenland, literarily well-endowed, with over 100 publications a year.

As Nelly Duvicq demonstrated in her PhD thesis, the concept of "postcolonialism" is not generally accepted by Inuit authors and critics: first, they reject the fact that they live in a *post*-colonial society, since they do not control their own political and social destiny; second, they believe that Inuit literature must be understood from its own sources, without reference to external concepts (such as postcolonialism), which are often applied without consideration of the particular situation of the Inuit.

Within Canada, each Inuit region eventually developed institutions that account for its own peculiarities, which has implications from a cultural, linguistic

10 His poetry clearly speaks about this desire to perceive Inuit identity as a whole: *Taqqat uummammut aqqutaannut takorluukkat apuuffiannut / The Veins of the Heart to the Pinnacle of the Mind*, 2008; *Des veines du cœur au sommet de la pensée*, 2012 [2008].

11 *Kafka. Pour une littérature mineure,* Paris: Éditions de Minuit, 1975.

and literary perspective. For example, Keavy Martin chose to study only the literary productions of Nunavut in his PhD thesis (2009). In the case of Nunavik, this difference is accentuated, as previously mentioned, by the fact that it is the only Inuit territory at the confluence of three languages in which texts are produced and published: Inuktitut, English and French.

In conclusion, and from a methodological point of view, the Nunavik corpus has characteristics that differ from other Inuit territories, but also others that make it part of a larger body. Moreover, one can find useful concepts for understanding Inuit literature in the numerous studies on Native American literature, but these must be carefully adjusted because of the unique characteristics of this culture.

5. Conclusion

Since the work of Margaret Harry and, more recently, that of Keavy Martin, we can see how the Indigenous literatures and especially Inuit literature pose a reception problem that questions the rules found elsewhere in the process of establishing literary aesthetic judgments (Chartier, 2000). Harry found that, in many cases, Indigenous and Inuit literatures are evaluated through a critical process of ignorance or praise which does not consider the aesthetic value of the works. However, a unique literary aesthetic exists: it can be found in the origin (both oral and visual), the context (both pan-Inuit and regional), and in the preferred forms (both short stories and autobiography) of Inuit literature. This Inuit literary aesthetic is characterized, as Karen Langgård and Kirsten Thisted have recently shown in the circumpolar context, by a postmodern voice (which includes forms that combine the written and the oral, like spoken word, songs, web videos, and multimedia blogs). An Inuit literary history might also require its own literary theory, as Langgård suggests in the context of her own research on Greenlandic literature. I believe this situation calls for considerations relating to the social and cultural context of Nunavik, the transition from oral to written and oral persistence in writing, literary reception issues which blur the reading and the appreciation of texts, and finally, an analysis of the recurrence and the originality of certain literary forms, including the presence of autobiography and postmodern feminist and gender perspectives. All these issues justify the necessity of a broad questioning of literary history methodology in order to take into account the specificity of Inuit literature.

Works cited

Amérindiens et Inuits. Portraits des nations autochtones du Québec. Secrétariat aux affaires autochtones, Gouvernement du Québec, 2009. Print.

Berthelsen, Kelly. *Je ferme les yeux pour couvrir l'obscurité.* Québec: Presses de l'Université du Québec, 2015. Print.

Bessière, Jean. "Penser les littératures émergentes. Émergence et institution symbolique." *Littératures d'émergence et mondialisation.* Ed. S. Faessel and Michel Pérez. Paris: In Press éditions, 2004. 47–65. Print.

Chartier, Daniel. *L'émergence des classiques.* Montréal: Fides ("Nouvelles études québécoises"), 2000. Print.

–. "Introduction. Définir des modernités hybrides. Entre société, patrimoine, savoir, pouvoirs contemporains et culture autochtones." *Globe. Revue internationale d'études québécoises* 8.1 (2005): 11–16. Print.

–."The First Inuit Novel Written: A Significant Literary and Social Achievement. Markoosie, *Harpoon of the Hunter.*" *Le harpon du* chasseur. Markoosie Patsauq. Québec: Presses de l'Université du Québec, 2011. 169–180. Print.

Chartrand, Jean-Philippe. *Internal Colonialism and Inuit Ethnic Identity Maintenance. The Relevance of Inuktitut Language Retention for the Ethnic Survival and the Adaptation of Inuit to Development and Modernisation in the Canadian North.* Diss. Ottawa, Carleton University, 1986. Print.

Duvicq, Nelly. *Les écrits du Nunavik depuis 1959: problématiques et conditions d'émergence d'une littérature inuit.* Diss. Université du Québec à Montréal, 2015. Print.

Evans, K. "Edmund James Peck. His Contribution to Eskimo Literacy and Publishing." *Journal of the Canadian Church Historical Society* 26.2 (1984): 56–68. Print.

Gagnon, Alain-G. and Guy Rocher (eds.). *Regard sur la Convention de la Baie-James et du Nord québécois.* Montréal: Québec/Amérique, 2002. Print.

Harper, Ken. *Writing in Inuktitut. An historical perspective.* Ottawa: National Museums of Canada, 1983. Print.

Harry, Margaret. "Literature in English by Native Canadians (Indians and Inuit)." *Studies in Canadian Literature* 10.1–2 (1985): 146–153. Print.

Jacobsen, Birgitte (eds). *Cultural and Social Research in Greenland 95/96. Essays in Honor of Robert Petersen.* Nuuk: Ilisimatusarfik, and Atuakkiorfik, 1996: 158–170. Print.

Kennedy, Michael P.J. "Canadian Inuit Literature in English. A Critical Bibliography." *From Oral Tradition to Rap. Literatures of the Polar North.* Ed. Karen Langgård and Kristen Thisted. Nuuk: Ilisimatusarfik/Forlaget Atuagkat, 2011. 189–222. Print.

Langgård, Karen and Kirsten Thisted eds.. *From Oral Tradition to Rap. Literatures of the Polar North*. Nuuk: Ilisimatusarfik/Forlaget Atuagkat, 2011. Print.

Lynge, Aqqaluk. *Taqqat uummammut aqqutaannut takorluukkat apuuffiannut / The Veins of the Heart to the Pinnacle of the Mind*. Montreal and Hanover: International Polar Institute, 2008; *Des veines du cœur au sommet de la pensée*. Québec: Les Presses de l'Université du Québec, "Imaginaire | Nord Jardin de givre", 2012 [2008]. Print.

Markoosie. *Harpoon of the Hunter*. Montreal: McGill-Queen's University Press, 1970. Print.

Martin, Keavy. *Stories in a New Skin. Approaches to Inuit Literature in Nunavut*. Diss. University of Toronto, 2009. Print.

–. "Is an Inuit Literary History Possible?" *American Indian Culture and Research Journal* 34.2 (2010): 67–80. Print.

McDermott, Noel. "Canadian literature in Inuktitut." *From Oral Tradition to Rap. Literatures of the Polar North*. Ed. Karen Langgård and Kristen Thisted. Nuuk: Ilisimatusarfik/Forlaget Atuagkat, 2011. 223–244. Print.

Mongeon-Bourbonnais, Clara. *La figure du Qallunaat: Zebedee Nungak et la prise de parole inuite*. Diss. Université du Québec à Montréal, 2014. Print.

Nungak, Zeebedee. "Contemplating Inuit presence in literature." *Inuktitut Magazine* 104 (Winter 2008): 62–67. Print.

Onfray, Michel. *Esthétique du Pôle Nord*. Paris: Grasset, 2002. Print.

Puranik, Apoorva. "Marathi take on Arctic life". *Mid-day* (Mumbai), January 15th, 2016, 10. Print.

Qumaq, Taamusi. *Inuit uqausillaringit / Les véritables mots inuit. Un dictionnaire des définitions en inuktitut du Nunavik (Québec arctique)*. Montréal and Inukjuak: Institut culturel Avataq and Québec, Association Inuksiutiit Katimajiit, 1990. Print.

–. *Je veux que les Inuit soient libres de nouveau, 1914–1993*. Québec: Presses de l'Université du Québec. 2010. Print.

Rogers, Sarah. "Taqralik Partridge wins top writing prize for short story." *Nunatsiaq News*, December 10th, 2010, 3. Print.

Hans Bak
American Studies, Radboud University Nijmegen

Erasure and Recovery: History, Identity and Indigenous Epistemology in LeAnne Howe's *Miko Kings* (2007)

> "We are American history, we are American literature.
> Every track and trace of the American experience
> runs through our communities. We have been the transformers
> so much more than we are ever credited to have been."
> Susan Power, *The Grass Dancer* (1993)

Prelude: "The Story of America"

Both novels written by Choctaw author LeAnne Howe – the award-winning *Shell Shaker* (2001) and, more recently, *Miko Kings* (2007) – are grounded in a firm belief in the power of Native story, not just as a means of sustaining and empowering Native people to create identity, history and community in mutual interaction, but also as a means of affecting and transforming American culture and history at large. "Native stories are power", Howe has argued in an essay entitled "The Story of America: A Tribalography": "They create people. They author tribes. America is a tribal creation story, a tribalography" (29). In the essay, Howe advances a revisionary view of history as a symbiosis of Native and mainstream (his)stories, emphasizing how the interconnectedness and mutual interaction has in effect transformed American history. Her argument is sophisticated and multi-leveled. It focuses in part on the familiar contention that without the assistance of Native tribes the early white settlers would not have stood a chance of survival, but underlines the significance of *story*: "creation stories gave birth to our people", she says, but goes on to emphasize that "our stories also created the immigrants who landed on our shores", in effect making the immigrants into Americans. "When the foreigners arrived and attempted to settle in the upper Northeast, they had nothing to eat, nothing to sustain them but their faith in biblical stories. Indigenous people told them new stories of how to live in our world" (29–30).

Her most compelling argument, however, is that it was the power and persistence of a tribal story over centuries that effected the creation of America: "when the European Founding Fathers heard the stories of how the Haudenosaunee unified six individual tribes into an Indian confederacy, they created a document, the U.S. Constitution, that united immigrant Europeans into a symbiotic union called America" (37). Howe offers powerful historical evidence for her argument that a Native story served as "a kind of cultural template for the New World", the Founding Fathers in effect using and respecting Indian ideas as the building of the new US government unfolded. American Indians, she claims, are in effect the "ghost writers" (42) for "the story of America" and deserve recognition as such.

Howe's argument is partly rooted in a scientific theory of symbiogenesis, which holds in essence that evolution is the result less of competition among life forms (a popular distortion of Darwin's survival of the fittest) than of "continual cooperation, strong interaction, and mutual dependence" (34). Howe transposes this insight into the cultural realm and applies it to the process of "contact" as not so much a form of conflict as of dialogic "networking", in which both sides permanently transformed and interacted with each other. She also exposes "the prejudice inherent in the belief" that tribal stories are forms of myth, folklore, or fiction (36), demonstrating that in effect many tribal insights and forms of orally transmitted knowledge have recently been "proven" to be rooted in historical "fact" by scientific research: thus, birds (which figure prominently in the Choctaw world view as creators, tricksters, and healers) have been demonstrated to possess forms of memory not unlike humans. In *Miko Kings*, as I hope to show, Howe's belief in the equal validity of mythical knowledge and verifiable scientific truth assumes central place.

Stories, Howe advances in her essay, not only have the power to bridge "sacred" knowledge and scientific truth, they also have the power to make connections across human cultures and cultural divides. It was Howe's grandmother who, by passing on tribal stories, taught her the power of story to "create": it "brings forth knowledge and inspires us to make the eventful leap that one thing leads to another" (32). Howe also underscores the function and nature of storytelling as a communal, not an individual act; in the words of Louis Owens, "For the traditional storyteller, each story originates and serves to define the people as a whole, the community" (43). Storytelling, then, in Howe's view is "a cultural bias" of tribal people: "tribalography comes from the native propensity for bringing things together, for making consensus, and for symbiotically connecting one thing to another" (42) over time; "our stories are unending connections to past, present, and future" (47). Storytelling thus locates identity at the junction of history and the future: "textual space" becomes "a contemplative reflection of identity"(44). It may even become a way of "expanding our identity" as it holds the possibility of working a symbiosis, a cross-cultural connection between Indians and non-Indians: thus "tribalography creates a literary and literal past" (46) for both Natives and non-Natives.

Howe's two novels effectively enact the ideas on story and history embedded in her essay.[1] In what follows I intend to demonstrate how *Miko Kings* is centrally informed by three interwoven thematic motifs, the origins of which can be traced back to Howe's essay.[2] First, by imaginatively reconstructing how native ritual and ceremony lay at the root of American baseball, *Miko Kings* aims to write Indians back into U.S. history through the metaphor and analogy of sports, Indian baseball becoming a "template" for Indigenous – and, by extension, American – history. By recovering a lost segment of the native past, effectively erased through colonialist practice, Howe ingeniously recreates an episode in turn-of-the-century Oklahoma history (1897–1907) as a prism for issues and dilemmas that remained pivotal to Indigenous life, culture and politics through the twentieth and into the twenty-first century. Secondly, Howe underscores this motif – the recovery of an erased history – by interweaving it with the personal quest of the principal narrator, Lena, for re-connection to her tribal and ancestral past as the prerequisite for re-constituting personal and tribal identity. In exploring both motifs, *Miko Kings* effectively draws on a register of postmodern devices to dramatize native time as a continuum of past, present and future, in which – as Howe has argued in her essay "The Story of America: A Tribalography" – "story" can function as a launching pad for making the "eventful leap" across time and space, and in which the distinction between imaginary truth and historical accuracy, between science and sacred knowledge, dissolves. Thirdly, then, Howe infuses both thematic strands with what one might call the search for an Indigenous epistemology: advancing the equal claims to truth of empirically verifiable scientific truth and tribal knowledge through story, myth and ritual, she posits the possibility of (necessity for?) a symbiosis which, as Lena suggests at novel's end, may bring a mode of higher, transcendent knowing which has the power to heal.

---

1 For an analysis of *Shell Shaker* in relation to Howe's essay, see my "Seeking Balance Through History and Community: The Presence of the Past in LeAnne Howe's *Shell Shaker*" (2001) in *The Challenges of Native American Studies: Essays in Celebration of the Twenty-Fifth American Indian Workshop*, Barbara Saunders & Lea Zuijderhoudt (eds.) (Leuven: University Press, 2004), 303–321.

2 The analysis of *Miko Kings* which follows appeared in adapted form as part of a longer essay entitled "Games Indians Play – Reflections on Sports as Cultural Practice and Historical Template in Contemporary Native American Literature and Film" in *Twenty-First Century Perspectives on Indigenous Studies: Native North America in (Trans)Motion,* edited by Birgit Däwes, Karsten Fitz, and Sabine N. Meyer (Routledge Research in Transnational Indigenous Perspectives No. 1), published by Routledge New York and London, 2015 101–123.

1. Baseball: template for Indian and American history

Just as, in her essay, LeAnne Howe offers a convincingly imagined argument that Native peoples are in effect the ghostwriters of the "story of America," so in *Miko Kings* she freely interweaves historical fact and imaginative reconstruction to posit Native peoples as the ghostwriters of one of America's most cherished and mythological sports, baseball. She challenges the commonly held belief – a now discredited historical fabrication – that baseball was invented in 1939 in Cooperstown (site of the baseball Hall of Fame) by Abner Doubleday, a Union Army general in the Civil War who reputedly fired the first shot at Fort Sumter. Instead, Howe claims, or has one of her fictional characters claim, "base-and-ball" was "a sacred game" (43)[3] deeply rooted in Indigenous ceremony and ritual. Games that were precursors of modern-day baseball (toli, stickball, lacrosse) were played among tribes as early as 400 years ago, even before white settlers came. The games performed a central function in tribal life and culture, stickball providing martial training for warriors, and base-and-ball fostering diplomacy between tribes. Indian baseball, claims Ezol Day (a young Choctaw woman) in the novel, unlike the modern-day "assimilated" version that became America's national pastime, was "a sacred game" that reflected "mathematical codes that harness cosmic forces" (43). It showed that, contrary to widespread belief, tribal culture was rooted not in the sort of myths that settler culture so easily dismissed as mere folklore or superstition, but in an Indigenous mode of *science* that reflected a native cosmology and a different understanding of time: "From the mound, a pitcher was the embodiment of the center pole that could access the Middle, Upper and Lower Worlds," Ezol explains (39), so that a star pitcher like Hope Little Leader came close to being a shaman, a "healer" in touch with the spirit of nature, whose pitches worked "in collaboration with the earth's mathematical system" (44). Ezol continues to affirm that in the Choctaw language there is no distinction between "science" and "the sacred" as modes of knowing or sources of cognition: "Indians in North and South America built cosmic observatories in the form of mounds and pyramids, very complicated structures that require geometry. A stomp dance and a baseball game mimic natural phenomena, such as tornado winds, that are counter-clockwise" (43). Ezol is convinced (and writes a scientific article to prove her point – she even tries but fails to get it patented by the U.S. Patent Office) that Europeans and Choctaws steer by a different sense of time, and that this makes it highly unlikely that baseball could be a white invention: "How plausible is it that white people,

3 All subsequent page references, given parenthetically in the text, will be to the 2007 edition.

who live by the clock and sword, would invent a game without time, one that must be played counter-clockwise?" (42). Baseball is a game with "no time limit" – it is "*past time*" and "for a reason".

Indian baseball, then, is (or was) a wholly different affair from the secularized and watered down version that was "assimilated into America's consciousness." As Ezol reminds us, mainstream American baseball was founded on the exclusion of blacks and Jews, to reflect "all-American" values. By contrast, "base-and-ball, *our game*, was created so that we could include everyone. We played the game to collaborate with other tribes, the stars, and with the great mystery" (43–44).

As Howe's novel shows, this original form of Indian baseball was completely erased from America's collective memory, its history lost, as from the early decades of the twentieth century on, Indian teams playing white teams were recurrently exposed to new rules and regulations imposed – seemingly gratuitously, and often in mid-game – by the director of national leagues. Thus the appropriation of baseball by the Anglo colonizer reduced a "sacred game" to a mere sport, eradicating the ritual element that sustained the individual warrior-player and destroying the dimension of spirituality and community-building.

Howe's novel seeks to restore the fictional history of a mythical all-Indian baseball team, the Miko Kings, which legendarily won the 1907 Twin Territories championship in a blood-curdling final against an Anglo team made up of veterans from Fort Sill, the U.S. Seventh Cavalry. Spicing her account with Indian humor referencing a tragic history of genocide, Howe's reclamation imagines the games between Indian and white teams as self-conscious re-enactments of the Indian battles that were still within human memory in 1907: for the Miko Kings, a team composed of Choctaw, Cherokee, Chickasaw and mixed-blood players, battling the U.S. Seventh Cavalry on the diamond field is infused with the traumatic memory of genocide and a sense of historical retribution – with the memory of Little Big Horn still vividly alive, it becomes "Custer's Last Stand" all over again, a historical echo exploited tragic-comically in the tauntings by coaches back and forth. Sports media present the games in rhetoric that pitches "the red man against the white man" or references "Custer's Last Stand, Strike Two," conveniently blurring the distinction between the Southeast Choctaws playing ball and the Plains' Indians (Sioux) who fought Custer.

Howe pitches the novel at a fulcrum moment in Indigenous history: the early 1900s, when Indian baseball is about to be subjected to mainstream rules and regulations; when Indian Territory is about to become the state of Oklahoma; when federal Allotment policy is at its height; and when a booming capitalist expansionism hits the native inhabitants of the town of Ada, Oklahoma, hardest and most mercilessly. The historical analogy is highlighted with painful alacrity: just as the sacred game of baseball is subjected to colonizers' regulations (such as the division of playing time into innings), so the federal policy of assimilation reaches its traumatic height in the division of Indian land into parcels of private property, a policy which systematically destroyed the land-base of many tribal cultures and disrupted the kinship structure and community foundation of Indigenous life. On Christmas day of 1906 a young Choctaw woman believes her grandmother "died of a broken heart because we are losing the battle against allotment. Hordes of white people are moving into Indian Territory and stealing our lands" (162). With the deprivation of land, also Indian identity is up for grabs as a result of the colonizers' enforced practice of registration on the Dawes Rolls. Ezol, our native storyteller from the past, insists that "documents lie" – she contests the truth of "identity" on the tribal rolls and exposes the corruption involved in Dawes allotment policy, with 75,000 whites applying for a place on the tribal rolls in order to claim land: "No one will ever know who they really are if they rely on paper identities issued by the federal government. Documents cannot be trusted" (29). Allotment thus exposes Indigenous peoples to the immorality and corruption that comes with the invasion of a booming capitalist expansionism. A Choctaw woman rails against "the epidemic of forgers, fraudsters, grafters, and thieves" flooding Ada, and a newspaper editorial proclaims: "Nothing will stop the Indians from being swindled out of their land, or disappearing from the face of the earth. Except a war" (29). As part of her effort at recovering lost episodes of Indian history, Howe resuscitates the forgotten history of the Four Mothers Society, an association which fought against allotment and sought to restore "the old ways", even to the point of sending a delegation to Washington DC.

It is against this backdrop of exploitation and corruption that Choctaw Henri Day seeks to run for mayor of Ada on a ticket of legalized gambling and game-playing on Sundays. As he struggles hard against his own vulnerability to gambling and corruption, he seeks to turn historical developments to Indigenous advantage by launching an all-Indian baseball team, building a ballpark in Ada, and founding an independent Indian baseball league. In 1904 he is convinced that "[f]or Indians playing ball is in the blood" (104) and that "[w]ith allotment and statehood coming, Choctaws need to stick together more than ever" (113). As a result, he wants to capitalize on economic opportunity and place native peoples at the center of it: "A league of all Indian baseball teams will demonstrate that the people from different tribes can own something together. It will be the country's first inter-tribal business, an alliance that will spread across the whole U.S." (112).

Howe thus shows Indigenous peoples in the U.S. balancing on the edge of extinction and erasure: on November 16, 1907, "[w]ith the creation of Oklahoma, with the privatization of tribal lands, everything changes. Indians will be written out of Oklahoma's picture. And history." (23) Using baseball as metaphor and analogy, *Miko Kings* aims to write Indians back into Oklahoma (and U.S). history. The attempt to recover the lost history of a baseball team is effectively used by Howe as a fictional wedge into the past, a means of touching upon a widening gyre of themes, dimensions of Indian history, issues of cultural loss and identity (and even representation, of natives in early film as well as in literature, from *Arabian Nights* to Longfellow's *Evangeline*). Howe thus convincingly shows how the early years of 1897–1907 were a prism for issues and dilemmas that would remain pivotal to Indigenous life, culture and politics through the twentieth and into the twenty-first century.

2. Identity and Indigenous epistemology

But *Miko Kings* is far from being your ordinary historical novel. Formally, it plays upon a familiar register of postmodernist devices: in collage-fashion, it freely interweaves multiple narrative strands across different moments in historical time, it presents multiple narrative voices and focalizers, and offers a fragmented and non-linear structure. Omniscient narration alternates with personalized storytelling voices. Prose gives way to the visual presentations of newspaper clippings, film stills, photographs, and even the visual reproduction of 50-plus pages from an entire journal-cum-scrapbook of handwritten and manually typed pages. Throughout, the status of truth/ "reality" (fiction or fact, history or fancy?) remains indeterminate, as we readers are catapulted between the present and various moments in the past, with the freedom of imaginary time-travel, Howe spinning past, present and future into a harmonious continuum of time. As one of the storytelling voices in the novel has it: "Time is like a majestic dance. … Observe how I can step forward or backwards or sideways and form multiple patterns that intersect" (44). Howe invites us readers to join in the Indigenous dance of time. It takes a leap of the imagination.

Such fictional strategies also govern the novel's second theme – the quest for personal and tribal identity through re-connection with an erased ancestral past. Our principal narrator in the present is Lena Coulter, a thinly disguised autobiographical version of LeAnne Howe. In 2006, Lena, who is half Choctaw, half Sac and Fox, finds herself in a symbolic position: having turned her back on her native past and identity, she worked as a journalist in NYC before, driven by restlessness and hunger "to see the world," she relocated to Amman in Jordan where she became involved with a Palestinian journalist who dies in a terrorist attack on the Days Inn. In the wake of 9/11 she feels as uprooted and shiftless as ever, "a nomad, searching the world for something I couldn't quite name" (20). At this moment she is summoned home by a voice ("The time has come to return home") – "the land of my ancestors had tracked me down and was speaking. At age 47 I clung to it like a lamp against the darkness" (20). The theme is a familiar one in Indigenous fiction: salvation lies in a return to native roots and the land of one's ancestors. In the summer of 2006 Lena finds herself in Ada, Oklahoma, working to restore and renovate the house she inherited from her grandmother, who built it on allotment land in 1906. Her mother having died a week after giving birth to her, Lena has always felt orphaned, un-grounded, un-centered: "I felt she'd abandoned me, that somehow my umbilical cord to the center of her had been severed, completely detached before I was born, setting me adrift to fend for myself, with only an absent father" (17). The frame narrative to the novel, then, gives us the story of Lena's personal quest for surcease from orphanage, for re-connection to her lost past and identity.

That personal quest becomes inextricably tied to the larger history of Southeastern tribal culture, as – in knocking down a wall in her grandmother's house – Lena discovers a leather U.S. mail pouch hidden in the wall, which contains a diary by one "Ezol" as well as documents, newspaper clippings and one photograph relating to an Indian baseball team, the 1907 Miko Kings Champions. Hooked, and haunted by the faces of the individual players on the photograph, Lena sets out to reconstruct their lost history, but her explorations in historical archives bring her to a dead end. Though she finds traces that an actual Indian baseball team existed, the history of the Miko Kings appears to have been effectively erased from record. "It was then that Ezol appeared. Perhaps my need to know brought her across time and space. Her spirit entered the house and placed the team's history on my shoulders, heavy as foreign epaulets" (22).

With Ezol as her guide, Lena imaginatively reconstructs the history of the Miko Kings during regular nightly visitations of Ezol, who, seated in her grandmother's chair, speaks to (and through) her as a spirit voice from the past, helping her to undo the erasure and recover the past. "That night, she unwrapped the team's stories as one might open birthday gifts. Out of order, but with a gift for celebration" (22). In Ezol's reconstruction, the distinction between history and fiction dissolves: imaginary truth is on a par with strict historical accuracy, Ezol's stories offering an Indigenous mode of knowing that is outside or beyond (yet on a level with) scientific proof. Ezol's voice speaks through Lena's narrative voice: the two become indistinguishable, as the native storytelling-spirit from the past (Ezol) merges with the verifiable fact-hunting researcher (Lena). The novel thus exemplifies what I have termed an Indigenous epistemology: Lena listens and takes dictation, "caught up in a virtual world of her making". "She is the narrator; I the medium, intermediary, stenographer, and servant to the story." As Ezol's stories spin connections across time and space, Lena makes herself "invisible by breathing life onto the page, and then exist there, side by side with the words and images" (24). The story of the Miko Kings, then, is a collaboration; this is "our book" (29), with Ezol and Lena becoming "mirror images of each other" (44).

The lost and erased past is thus recovered largely through the imaginative reconstructions based on Ezol's nightly stories, in which "time opens like a coffin" (33) as Ezol unfolds in vivid detail the early twentieth-century history of Ada, Oklahoma. But Ezol is not entirely fictional: born in 1879, she is the niece of Henri Day, owner of the Miko Kings. She attends Good Land Indian Orphanage (one of the oldest boarding schools, founded in 1848) until age 21, after which she becomes a postal clerk in Ada, where she becomes involved with the Miko Kings and dies in a fire at age 28. Much of Ezol's story is told through her (fictionalized) diary, 50-plus pages of which are represented visually and verbatim in the novel. Evoking echoes of Zitkala-Ša's *Schooldays of an Indian Girl* (1900), the diary offers a moving glimpse into the boarding school life of a young orphaned girl (she loses her mother and twin sister at an early age, while her father simply disappears), as she is subjected to a ruthless process of acculturation, the forced abandonment of "the old ways" and adaptation to the white man's ways through schooling, linguistic dispossession and Christianization. Ezol, whose name derives from the French Isole (for "isolation" or "insulation" – against death, after the demise of her twin sister), keeps merciless track of the number of her days at Good Land and ends her every entry with "Si apela. Help me." She reveals herself as a shrewd, fast learner, with a knack for languages and science, and early develops a theory about differences between time for whites and Indians, which she seeks in vain to have patented. She sees patterns in the universe, with the help of an "eye tree" inside of her, a metaphor some critics have read as indicating symptoms of autism (Russell). Her tutors at the orphanage believe she suffers from "genius symptoms" as well as attacks of nervous agitation. Through her diary we witness the rise of the Miko Kings to championship glory, concomitant with the rise of corruption, nightly raids by the Ku Klux Klan, the tragic consequences of allotment, and her infatuation with the Miko Kings' star-batter, Blip Bleen.

Among the rich cast of characters fully and vividly brought to life in the novel, two briefly deserve illumination here: the intersecting stories of Hope Little Leader and Justine Maurepas. Hope Little Leader is one of the Indigenous voices whose story is given full play in the novel. In 1907, Hope was the Miko Kings star-pitcher who could throw "a lightning ball that blisters the imagination of the spectators at the game" (192) and marshal cosmic power in the act. In 1969, at the time of the Vietnam War and the release of the Beatles' *Abbey Road* album, Hope finds himself in an elderly home in Ada, attended to by a male nurse named "John Lennon" and a cross-dressing, war-protesting nurse named Kerwin. Close to death, nearly blind from diabetes, he is badly mutilated – the hands which used to throw the magical pitches are now amputated to resemble "two giant sea horses with curled fleshy ends for tails" (58). Nicknamed "No Hands", he suffers from morphine-induced visions in which he revisits his days of glory on the baseball mound, his years at boarding school, and his amorous involvement with a mixed blood (black-red) female activist, Justine Maurepas, with whom he fathered a daughter, Evangeline, in 1908.

Justine's story is likewise fully "recovered" in the novel, as she tells her life to an African-American historian who is researching her legendary contribution as "Black Juice" to the history of Black Nationalism. Hers is a searing story of terrorist violence, abusive oppression, and the discriminatory pain suffered by a woman of mixed French, Indian and black ancestry, at the hands of whites (the Klan) as much as Indians, who in their superiority to "colored" people show themselves uncannily imitative of whites in upholding the color line. The complex history of relations between natives and peoples of mixed Indigenous-colored descent is another dimension brought back to life and light by Howe's novel. Now, in 1969, Justine regrets having turned her back on her greatest love, Hope, in the mistaken conviction that he was "weak" and could not protect her against racist violence. Hope, likewise, in 1969 mourns her departure at the time: "She is pleasure clasped to memory like a fastball to a glove" (191).

In Hope's account, as in Ezol's, we slide fluidly back and forth in time, between the early 1900s and 1969. We learn how he came to attend the historical bi-racial boarding school Hampton Normal School for Blacks and Indians, which first admitted native children in 1877, not permitting the two races to mingle (later it evolved into a famous college for African-Americans; it stopped admitting Native children in 1917 for lack of federal subsidies). Howe evokes the brutal regime of enforced acculturation with searing sharpness. At Hampton Hope was a most recalcitrant and rebellious kid, an inveterate runaway who after every attempt was imprisoned in solitary dark confinement, where he fantasized about a teaching aide he was passionately in love with, Dusky Long-Gone Girl. He is finally released and placed with a baseball team, hoping this will bring him the discipline and self-control he sorely lacked at Hampton. To become a baseball hero is his dream, and he makes good, leading the Miko Kings to win the Twin Territories championship against the Seventh Cavalry. Or did he? Though supposedly Hope starred in the very first film ever made about Indian baseball, a 1909 film ominously entitled *His Last Game* (a 14-minute reel which Howe actually discovered in the Library of Congress), Howe keeps her readers in tantalizing uncertainty about what happened at the crucial moment in the final game: did Hope throw the cinching ball and lead his team to glory? Or do we give credence to the speculative possibility that, discouraged by the sudden departure out of his life of his great love Justine, Hope capitulated to the temptation offered him by a gambling syndicate to take the money and run? Two competing versions are held out to the reader: in one he throws the game, the Miko Kings lose, and Hope is pursued on his flight by several of his former teammates, who retaliate for his act of betrayal by chopping off his hands at the wrists. In another version, he throws the miraculous pitch, tapping into "the Choctaw's source of power" (218), and makes the decisive heroic catch that wins the championship for the Miko Kings. This is the vision he sees just before he dies, the memory of a last grand gesture: "He raises up the sea horses to make one last heroic catch" (215). Reality? As Ezol has told Lena many times, "reality is manifest from what we see and how we speak of it" (219). Howe thus reasserts the issue of epistemological truth, and keeps us hovering in a limbo of ambivalence between two versions of historical reality, haunted by our own craving for verifiable certainty over against visionary revelation, for scientific truth over storytelling truth. Touché.

3. Finale: towards celestial knowledge as a mode of healing

In the end, the frame narrative of Lena's personal quest is also brought to resolution, a moment of healing. Through Ezol she discovers that her grandmother Cora may have been involved in the corruption that led to the demise of the Miko Kings and even in the death-by-fire of Ezol at 28. If her grandmother was a biological ancestor, in Ezol – in effect her grandmother's cousin – she now discovers a spiritual ancestor. As Lena had intuited early in the novel: "We must be [related]. She reads me like a book" (41). Working in tandem with her newly found ancestor Ezol, Lena has reconstructed a shared history and legacy into the future: "we have recreated the past – telling the story of not just her relatives, but mine too." Like a true storyteller, Lena has thus brought past-present-future in harmonious relation, and in the process found her "center" of identity. In unearthing and "recovering" the story of the Miko Kings, rescuing it from erasure, Lena has at the same time recovered the story of her own family and discovered a new ancestor in Ezol: she has "truly turned back time" in a "collaboration" with Ezol (220), she has found surcease from the feeling of loss and abandonment she had suffered, as Ezol now reaffirms herself as the ancestor Lena should have had: "Lena, I may not be your blood grandmother – but I should have been. And I have always been with you in spirit. That is the true story I came to tell" (221). Ultimately, recovering the lost history of the Miko Kings, Lena has also recovered her personal lost history and re-established roots with her ancestors. And such, as Lena realizes at novel's end, is "celestial knowledge," a mode of sustaining and transcendent awareness in which science and story come together: a symbiosis of verifiable and recordable truth and "sacred" spiritual knowledge which has the power to heal – "Such is the sacred made manifest in the flesh of the page" (221).

Works cited

Howe, LeAnne. "The Story of America: A Tribalography." *Clearing a Path: Theorizing the Past in Native American Studies*. Ed. Nancy Shoemaker. New York and London: Routledge, 2002. 29–48. Print.

–. *Miko Kings: An Indian Baseball Story*. San Francisco: Aunt Lute Books, 2007. Print.

Russel, Bryan. [Untitled review of *Miko Kings: An Indian Baseball Story*]. E3W [Ethnic and Third World] Literature. University of Texas. Web 22 Feb. 2012. http://www.cwrl.utexas.edu/orgs/e3w/Howe.

Grit Alter
English Department Westfälische Wilhelms-University Münster

"Ready to Shout of Joyous Things": Claiming Space for/in Inuit Children's Literature

> "Everywhere Ukaliq looked, she saw gifts. Even the hardest ground would grudgingly provide stones and wherever Ukaliq's family lived, the little girl would stack the stones into friends.
> Some of Ukaliq's stone friends looked ready to shout of joyous things. Some seemed filled with sorrow. Some pointed past the horizon or towards a lake. Through the long nights of winter or through the endless days of summer, Ukaliq's stone people rose, like sentinels, from the earth that cradled them." (Ulmer n.p.)

This quote from Ontario-based Mike Ulmer's *The Gift of the Inuksuk* (2004) introduces a young Inuk girl who may have first created an Inuksuk. In his children's book, Ulmer offers one version of the origin of the stone people who have provided guidance and protection for the Inuit for hundreds of years. Ulmer, who himself is not part of the Inuit community, does not want to tell an Inuit legend; rather, it is his hope that "a little girl I have called Ukaliq can represent the wisdom that made the Inuit rich partners in the bounty that is the natural world" (Ulmer n.p.). Whereas this attempt could be criticized in terms of authenticity and appropriation[1], Ulmer has been successful in providing space for the Inuit in bookstores and moved Inuit culture into the focus of a publisher (Sleeping Bear Press, based in Chelsea, Michigan), and thus allows children to read books in which Inuit children are not only represented, but are represented in a positive light. Inuit and non-Inuit children alike have the opportunity to learn about the Inuksuk, a symbol that is essential to Inuit culture.

---

1 As Edwards and Saltman explain, "the issue of appropriation of culture and voice has continued to polarize members of the writing and publishing community [...]. Some writers and publishers believe that only members of a specific ethnic or cultural group have the aesthetic and moral right to give voice to that group's experiences and beliefs. Others adamantly declare that with appropriate research, sensitivity, and imagination, it is possible to create authentic stories and characters, even if they are not part of the writer's personal life experience" (206).

The following essay offers insights into Inuit children's literature, be it written by members of the Inuit[2] community themselves or books in which Inuit culture is represented. Besides the First Nations and the Métis, the Inuit form one of the three constitutionally recognized groups of Indigenous peoples in Canada, but they are often pushed to the margins, not only due to North America's geography, but also within First Nation's children's literature. This essay aims at introducing to the reader current Inuit children's books and at discussing how they negotiate cultural and linguistic identities. The analysis will focus on an intersectionality of geographic, temporal, social and cultural spaces.

In this essay, "space" is to be understood on different levels. It refers to the actual space of Inuit children's books in bookstores and libraries, but it also refers to the "space" Inuit protagonists occupy within the books and how this representation establishes cultural and identity spaces. As will be seen from references to elaborations on Inuit children's literature, recent Inuit children's books show that spaces of Inuit protagonists have shifted to a more authentic and holistic representation, which counters existing stereotypes and enables Inuit to be seen in a different light. In order to elaborate on space for and in Inuit children's literature, aspects such as gender, language, story-telling, home and family as well as lifestyle support the argument that Inuit protagonists deserve and need place, space, and shelves to enable Inuit and non-Inuit children alike to negotiate spaces of cultural identity – and that Inuit characters are indeed *ready to shout of joyous things*.

1. Gender representation in Inuit children's books

In 2011, Robert David investigated the representation of Inuit in contemporary British and Canadian non-fiction books and, among other aspects, recognizes that a strict ascription of gender-roles entails sexist notions, also in the representation of Inuit. Despite the traditional division of activities in Inuit families, the focus is most often put on the "visually more interesting male role as the hunter or the choice of a narrative that follows a boy learning hunting skills from his elders" (David 145), and not on the "equally important role of women in taking the product of the hunt and making sure that maximum use is made of it for food and clothing" (Davis 145). In a similar sense and with reference to Sherrill Grace's elaborations of adventure novels from the north, Björn Sundmark indicates that "girls and

2 This essay focuses on the representation of North American Inuit in English literature for young readers. In accordance with the frame of this edition, other circumpolar Inuit peoples (in Greenland, Alaska, Northern Europe, or Russia) and their literary achievements shall not be considered.

women are absent or play an insignificant role" (Sundmark 155) in fictional texts. However, in four of the six books that are included in this essay the protagonist is female; in two of these texts, the girl is the one who saves her father and brothers[3]. In *Missuk's Snow Geese* (Renaud 2008), Missuk's father sets out for his hunt and leaves wife and daughter behind. Missuk dreams of becoming as skilled a snow geese carver as her father but for her it is difficult to "find the graceful bird in the stone" (Renaud n.p.). She is also not good at sewing. She rather goes outside to enjoy the beginning of spring that brings the frozen tundra back to life. She lies down in the snow watching snow geese flying across, and moves her arms and legs to leave bird-shaped imprints in the snow. When she returns home, a heavy snowstorm sets in which prevents her father from coming home. Being afraid of what might happen, she falls asleep and when he is back the next morning learns that it were her snow geese in the snow that led her father home. Knowing that her imprints of snow geese have saved him, she gains confidence in her carving. Thus, Missuk is not only the main protagonist of the narration, but she also becomes the heroine of the story as she saves her father and guides him home. Interestingly, in order to do so, she does not need an ulu, the traditional knife of the Inuit, but she uses her whole body and the pleasure of watching the migrating flocks return home and feeling the snow underneath her warm clothes to reconnect her father with the family, to reconnect her confidence in carving geese with herself and, in finding the gift of traditional Inuit art through feeling the land, she also reconnects herself with Inuit tradition and lifestyle[4]. Missuk additionally establishes her position as a loving daughter, and her space in Inuit future, as she will be able to perform traditional chores. Even if those may remain within a certain gender divide, Missuk is not marginalized or made insignificant as a girl, but presented as an essential member of the family who secures the survival of the father as well as Inuit traditions of carving and sewing, and thus, occupies essential social space within her family and community of the Inuit.

Also in Mike Ulmer's book *The Gift of the Inukshuk* (2004), the female character functions as a savior of her male family members. Mike Ulmer's story revolves around the young girl Ukaliq who uses stone figures to help lost caribou hunters find their way home. In the beginning of the story, the girl "just" builds stones

---

3 As David and Sundmark refer to silenced female voices in Inuit children's literature, the books under investigation in this essay which presented male voices will not be discussed in this section in order to counter David's and Sundmark's position.

4 For a detailed and non-fictional account of Inuit lifestyle the book *Uqalurait: An Oral History of Nunvaut*, edited by John Bennett and Susan Rowley, is highly recommended.

on top of each other, making "friends" being her only intention. It is only when her father and brother embark on an annual hunt of the migrating caribou, that those friends of stone gain meaning of survival as they allow for the hunt to be successful and guide the men home. When a threatening snowstorm covers the land, Ukaliq asks her younger siblings to help her create more "stone friends" as "they will help return our brothers and father" (Ulmer n.p.). Within the "empty landscape", as it is often perceived by outsiders, the children's plan turns out to be successful and those Inuksuit gain significance as landmarks that distinguish open space from places which are home to the people and offer secure guiding through the vastness of the land.

In some of Michael Arvaarluk Kusugak's tellings of Inuit stories and legends, female protagonists carry the plot and are active agents in telling the stories (*Northern Lights, Arctic Stories, Promise*). *Arctic Stories*, to refer to one example, collects three short stories which tell different incidents of fictional Agatha in Repulse Bay. One of these is her community's encounter with an airship that flew over Repulse Bay in 1958. Never having seen such a thing in the air before, the people in Repulse Bay are scared and try to run away from it. Despite having to run as fast as she could, Agatha keeps yelling at the airship to turn around and go away. While she is increasing her yells, the airship finally turns around and the people of Repulse Bay praise "Agatha for saving the day!" (Kusugak *Arctic Stories* 14). In the other two stories of this collection, Agatha befriends a raven, goes to school and rescues Father Fafard from drowning in the ice-cold sea.

All of these stories present the female protagonist as an active agent on the land and within strong community ties. One may object that in the stories mentioned above, the female protagonists serve the male, as is the case with Missuk and Ukaliq in securing the survival of their fathers and brothers, or serve the community, as Agatha yells away the intruder from the outside. However, those Inuit children's books offer strong and confident female role models, which, according to Sundmark and David, would be mostly absent from Inuit literature for young readers. Kusugak, Renaud and Ulmer inscribe the female into spaces of power and action and offer current examples that make the female in Inuit children's literature visible beyond traditional chores.

2. Landscape and community in Inuit children's literature

Despite its generalizing notion, one can say that Canada perceives itself as an Arctic country, a pride that is, for example, reflected in foundational texts such as the national anthem ("The true North strong and free!"). However, as such it is addressed in "two competing visions [...] as homeland or frontier" (Kassam 433).

As Kassam explains, the conception of the North as a frontier has Southern roots and is "motivated by a desire to exploit natural resources [...], is myoptic and simplicistic" (433). The vision of the North as homeland "originates from those who live, work, and play there", it is "informed by thousands of years of indigenous use of the land and sea", it is a reality "characterized by diversity and complexity in the population demographic, culture, and economy" (433). This differentiation allows stating that by the majority of Canadians the North is perceived as a harsh environment, too threatening to live in, and too far away to be included in general considerations of Canadian identity. In literary spaces this could be ascribed to the wilderness, dangers and loneliness protagonists usually encounter, e.g. in *Juggling Fire* (Bell) and *The Middle of Everywhere* (Polak) (Sundmark 156). When describing the Canadian North as a "difficult land to live in" and as "inhospitable land" (David 142), one needs to be aware of the perspective from which such judgments are made. As also David maintains, despite its harshness that I identify from my middle European point of view, the North has been a region which has been able to sustain its people for millennia (142). In current children's books, therefore, the North is also presented as home to people, who live there as residents, not as visitors, researchers or explorers. Although the snow storm in *Missuk's Snow Geese* threatens her father, it is also the snow in which Missuk leaves marks which guide her father home. Although she is frustrated for not being able to carve and sew, that is using the resources of the land to perform life-saving and life-improving tasks, the beginning spring, the returning snow geese and the comforting snow contribute to Missuk's happiness and ease. Also in *The Gift of the Inuksuk* it is a snow storm that threatens Ukaliq's father and brothers, while it is the stones piled up to stone people which guide the hunters home and secure their survival. When the stone people are built, the book shifts to a pedagogical tone and explains that those stone people are now called Inuksuk – in the image of man –, which can nowadays be found not only in the North but around the world to indicate dangerous passages and to point travelers toward home. Thus, the notion of guidance and security that surround Inuksuk still remains. These examples show that people need to adapt to their environment and natural surroundings if they have to and want to survive in the harshness of the North. Underestimating the weather and individual action make the North dangerous, not being and living there.

A similar notion can be recognized in Edwardson's *Whale Snow*, a story about Amiqqaq who wanted to join the whale hunt but was not allowed to for his young age. From his father he learns that the last time the whalers hunted a whale was the day when he was born. As a sign of respect and gratefulness for the whale, the boy was named after the Amiqqaq crew. The reader follows Amiqqaq's experiences and feelings on the day when the group of whale hunters returns to the village after a successful hunt. *Whale Snow* mirrors the importance of community relations and their interdependency when a whale is caught and the families come together to celebrate. As the community members have divided the whale among themselves and gather in Amiqqaq's home to celebrate, he learns about the importance of community, mutual support and reliance and the necessity to honor the "spirit-of-the-whale" (Edwardson n.p.).

3. Space of time – existence and modernity

"It is only within the last two decades that stories about and by Canada's Aboriginal peoples have begun to move beyond the past to show contemporary Aboriginal families living in the modern world" (Edwards and Saltman 201). This is not only visible in the emergence of aboriginal-owned and -operated publishing houses since the 1980s (Cf. Edwards and Saltman 201), but also in the plots and illustrations of recent Inuit children's books. Edwardson, for instance, has Amiqqaq's father arrive in a skidoo when he returns from the hunt and has Amiqqaq's grandmother use a fully equipped kitchen to prepare food, both of which exemplify current Inuit lifestyles. When the whalers, nevertheless, live in tents and use dogsleds, the continuing adaptation to the land also becomes visible. This is also mirrored in the illustrations that supplement the written story, in which modern housing as well as igloos are presented. In children's books, the illustrations carry an essential part of the narration. Perry Nodelman's estimation that "whether we are conscious of it or not, illustrations always convey information, not just about what things look like, but how we should understand and what we should feel about the things depicted" (Nodelman 6) gains essential importance. This is especially the case when realizing that Ulmer's story and Melanie Rose's illustration in *The Gift of the Inuksuk* create spaces of temporal, spatial and therefore also cultural distance – a critical remark that needs to be focussed despite the positive comments that were made regarding landscape and the representation of gender. While the double-page illustrations throughout the book show a snow-covered landscape, a tee-pee and igloo here and there, and the occasional rocks, the final page is rather different. The colors are warm; there is a lake, a family (that rather looks Caucasian) in a canoe, and a huge Inuksuk in the foreground. The snow is gone, the ice has melted, and no Inuit is in sight. "To this day Inuksuk wait for paddlers and canoeists" and "greet travelers along highways" (Ulmer n.p.) – from the illustrations one gathers that the Inuksuk obviously no longer guide hunters home, not to speak of the caribou, which according to the picture have vanished as well. But at least, the Inuit's message is still around for everyone to romantically perceive and enjoy: "you are not alone" (Ulmer n.p.). For the tourists, this is good to know. But where have the Inuit gone? What has happened to all the snow and ice – and where is Ukaliq? With the final page, Ulmer's story parallels what Wiegand already observed in 1992: "Inuit [...] are a people who have been defined in children's books almost exclusively in terms of their past" (123) – despite his book being published in 2004. As they are no longer represented in the final page, the Inuit do not have any connection to the present; Inuit culture is placed in an imaginary space in the past. All that remains is an idea, a legend, a memory represented by a stone figure which used to be a "friend" (Ulmer n.p.), surrounded by a romanticized version of cultural identity. As "images [in terms of representation of minorities] usually replicate the popular social values and moral attitudes of the time and of the culture, often without the realization that the child is unconsciously absorbing these values and attitudes from the images presented" (McKenzie 201–202), it is especially important that children read literature that refrains from re-establishing and implementing false ideas of the Inuit, such as that of a vanishing people. However, Ulmer's book re-constructs the temporal and spatial gap which his book may actually have attempted to fill. Carmen Luke maintains that educators need to understand "how the public texts of everyday life construct our understanding of the world, and position persons to take up various social, political and cultural identities" (Luke 20). Therefore, it is important that readers use the absence of the Inuit in the final pages of Ulmer's book to reflect upon it critically and use other books for intertextual references so that they can de-construct the spaces Inuit occupy in children's literature. Through this critical reading, Inuit and non-Inuit children alike have the option to not only find *themselves*, but also *find* themselves in the stories they read (Cf. West and Harris 77).

This quest of finding representations has certainly been supported by political changes as well. As Schwartz observes, the "creation of Nunavut as an official territory has had a huge impact [...]. Its concrete existence catapults the non-Inuit audience into the present, creating along with it an ability for cultural outsiders to leave behind old stereotypes and conceptualize a contemporary Inuit story" (Schwartz n.p.). However, Ulmer's publication counteracts this very notion. From the back cover of the book the reader learns that Ulmer lives in Hamilton, Ontario. One could harshly say that, obviously, a book about the Inuit is needed in order to remember the Inuit and offer them space in bookstores. Rather than encouraging more Inuit writers to find voices in the publishing industry, the story of the Inuksuk also *needs* to be written by an author, who "keeps an Inuksuk at home but does not need it to find good fishing" but to remind him "of the way the Inuit [...] live a simple life and only consume what they need". While Mike himself is able to enjoy "modern" means of fishing and "riding the wave of progress", the Inuit do not need to worry about those things and just "go with the snow". Although he attempts to offer spaces of cultural contact, Ulmer's children's book supports the romanticized imagined space of the Inuit and ignores the many aspects in which they exist in a place that other people may consider to be harsh and life-threatening. That geographic, social and cultural spaces seem to be clearly differentiated is even supported and the gap increased when the tourists in the canoe and the Inuit do not even meet. Additionally, this raises questions of authorship, ownership and appropriation. If Ulmer occupies the space of telling this story, Inuit writers will find it more difficult to speak for themselves.

It may until recently have been "virtually impossible for a native writer to find a publisher; and, despite the recent proliferation of periodicals produced by the [...] Inuit themselves [...]" (Harry n.p.) and although "there are still proportionately very few books" (Harry n.p.), the publishing landscape has changed, not least with the establishment of the first Inuit-owned publishing company Inhabit Media in Iqaluit[5]. Within the past few years, Inhabit Media has published a number of highly recommendable retellings of Inuit stories and legends. For instance, two children's books can be mentioned as examples of the successful path this publishing house is taking[6]:

- *The Giant Bear* by Jose Angutingunrik (2012), which tells the story of a brave hunter who encounters nanurluk and, based on his cleverness and elaborate hunting skills, manages to outsmart the bear, or;
- *The Legend of the Fog* by Qaunaq Mikkigak and Joanne Schwartz (2011) about a man who meets a giant on the tundra and is able to save himself and his family by releasing the first fog into the world.

Special emphasis needs to be put on Inhabit Media's publication of *The Qalupalik* of Elisha Kilabuk in 2011, which was awarded the Book of the Year Award ("Quill & Quire's" n.p.) by the renowned Canadian literature magazine *Quill and Quire* in 2011. In their justification for this choice it can be read that "[m]ainstream attention to Inuit culture is still relatively rare. The introduction of Inhabit Media's Unikkakuluit series, featuring traditional stories presented by contemporary Nunavummiut storytellers and artists, should be a big step toward resolving this issue, especially if the quality of the first picture book is any indication of what's to come" ("Quill &

---

5 Although Inhabit Media is focused in this essay as the first publishing house in Iqaluit, it should not be ignored that other publishers exist in the North, for example Alaska Northwest Books.

6 Further examples are Sakiasi Qaunaq's *The Orphan and the Polar Bear* (2011), Ibi Kaslik's *Tales from the Tundra* (2010), Donald Uluadluak's *Kamik: An Inuit Puppy Story* (2013), Marion Lewis' *Kaugjagjuk* (2011), Rachel Qitsualik's *Under the Ice* (2012), or her collection of frightening Inuit folklores *Shadows That Rush Past* (2011).

Quire's"). A further critical incident can be seen in the process of the publication of Kusugak's first story *A Promise is a Promise* in 1988. Annik Press was first unwilling to accept the manuscript and it was only after a collaboration of Robert Munsch and Michael Kususgak was arranged that the book was eventually published. When *A Promise is a Promise* turned out to be a bestseller, Annick Press was "more willing to issue subsequent stories without the intervention of a non-Aboriginal author with mainstream name recognition" (Edwards and Saltman 203).

Authors such as Michael Kusugak contributed to the perception of authorship and ownership of Indigenous stories and legends within multicultural literature. As Schwartz notes, "stories of the Inuit have been imagined by cultural outsiders. It is time for the stories to be de-imagined and re-imagined from within. A people must tell its stories to itself, and in this globalized world, to everyone else. They must tell them in their own way, with their own voice and with an openness to sharing their stories with other cultures" (Schwartz n.p.). Inhabit Media serves as an example that Inuit voices are not only heard but also printed. From another perspective it could also be said that Inuit writers not necessarily depend on "mainstream" publishers but can turn to local sources to be included in literary spaces. Still, this critical issue leads to two further aspects of space which need to be considered: the near substitution of storytelling as performance by books and the space that is offered to Inuit languages within the Canadian publishing industry.

4. Story-telling, the printed page and languages of Inuit children's literature

Among the writers discussed in this short essay, it is especially Michael Kusugak who manages to keep oral tradition alive on the printed page and to inscribe Inuit discourses into Canada's literary canon. In his books he talks about his own experiences of "grow[ing] up in a place like Repulse Bay", but he also uses the "wonderful stories that had been passed down from generation to generation, for hundreds, thousands of years" (CBC "interview") his grandmother told him as a child as a foundation for his books. Writing those in English, he is "able to reach a wide audience and one that until recently had not heard an authentic voice from the North" (Schwartz n.p.). Although the book is a static object in which voice, body movements and gestures can hardly be represented as vividly as "a sensual experience of oral storytelling" (Schwartz n.p.), ironically the book would be the vehicle which preserves and passes on the traditional stories to future generations of Inuit children as well as opening windows to a non-Inuit audience (Schwartz n.p.).

In order to create vibrant voices on the pages, Inuit authors often use storytelling features in their texts and thus adapt the printed space to oral storytelling. In this sense, Kusugak, for example, incorporates traits of a storytelling voice using repetitions when introducing the main protagonist in *Baseball Bats for Christmas* (1990/2006) as "a very asthmatic boy. Arvaarluk was seven years old, and Arvaaluk was very asthmatic" (n.p.). The author also directly addresses the reader and offers "l]et me tell you a thing or two about Repulse Bay" (*Baseball Bats* n.p.), thus turning the reader into listener. Additionally, the oral tone is retained in rather short sentences, especially at the beginning of new paragraphs ("In 1955, though, trees arrived in Repulse Bay. There were six of them. They came by aeroplane."), and onomatopoeia such as "flop, flop, flop" for "skis bouncing over the snow drifts" or "Rooaaarrrr!!!!" for the plane flying above the people's heads. Moreover, Kusugak's stories often end with the terms "Taima" or "Taimakalauq" which in Inuktitut indicate the end of a story, meaning "that's all" or "that's all for now". This would in printed text not be necessary as the book as such is simply finished, but it remains an important feature in oral storytelling.

Furthermore, authors of Inuit children's books make use of "*interpolation* to signal the variety of ways through which Indigenous subjects exercise agency in textual production" (Bradford 54, emphasize in original). Within children's literature, interpolation and agency are expressed in the usage of Indigenous language, be it glossed or un-glossed. In the Inuit books included in this essay, words in Inuktitut range from "ulu" (Renaud n.p.) having the reader decipher from the context of the scene that it is a traditional Inuit knife, to terms such as "aaka", "aapa", "ilitqusia" or "uqsruagnaq" (Edwardson n.p.) which are explained in a glossary. In Kusugak's *Arctic Stories* such a glossary can be found at the end of the book (Kusugak 40). Just as some of his *Arctic Stories*, also *Baseball Bats for Christmas* ends with the term "Taima" – however, no translation can be found in this book. The first page of Kusugak's *Northern Lights the Soccer Trails* (1993/2007), includes a line in Inuktitut which is not explained – the reader can only guess whether it is the translation of the title into Inuktitut, whether it is a dedication, or also an additional message to readers who read and understand Inuktitut. Such lines which are not explained or translated can also be found in the inside of the front and back covers of *Baseball Bats for Christmas*. Those terms and lines in Inuktitut can be regarded as evidence that Inuktitut is a language that exists, that is spoken, and that is also worth of being printed in books. As Schwartz also indicates, those examples "bring language to the page as a visual document of its existence and equal validity to English" (Schwartz n.p.). Although it is also true that it is rather challenging to publish in Inuit languages as those consist of many different dialects and do not have a writing standard (Schwartz n.p.), Edwardson's *Whale Snow*, for example, is available in an Inupiaq-only version as well. The inclusion of phrases in Inuktitut and the availability of *Whale Snow* in Inupiaq allow, at least partly, countering David's estimation that Inuit are presented as a collective identity, "as one undifferentiated people" (David 143) with respect to North America. For such a conclusion to be extended to the circumpolar region, however, further fiction books need to be included in a broader survey.

5. Spaces of authentic Inuit Personality

It cannot be disputed that using a phrase such as "authentic Inuit personality" in an essay on Inuit children's literature is a tricky endeavor. How can I, a white middle class German PhD student discuss such a complex aspect which calls to mind notions of appropriation and colonial discourses? Being aware of the problematic notion of this phrase and the discussion to follow, I would like to discuss observations I came across when preparing this essay and researching Inuit children's literature. In David's essay on the representation of Inuit in current Canadian and British non-fiction, the passage on existing stereotypes of Inuit reveals a rather condescending, if not discriminating view on Inuit. As a source David refers to Hugh Brody who summarizes the common view of Inuit as "an eternally happy, optimistic little figure; a round, furry and cuddly human with a pet name … [who] [g]orge themselves as they might on raw meat and blubber, a stereotypical Eskimo of the impossible north wages his battle against environment in astonishing good humor" (qtd. in David 141). In response to this reflection from the year 1987, David maintains that in children's literature Inuit appear as "simple, bold images that create a small number of powerful impressions" and that "[c]onsequently, Inuit are frequently depicted as a smiling, good-natured people, living in igloos, surviving by hunter-gatherer strategies and the ability to fashion hunting and domestic artifacts from natural materials, and eating raw meat in what southerners see as a hopelessly inhospitable landscape" (David 141). Using the children's books by Renaud, Edwardson, Ulmer and Kusugak as a foundation, this estimation can justifiably be challenged. In the face of threatening snowstorms, the sudden appearance of airships and instable ice on lakes and ocean, Inuit children are presented as worrying, scared and serious family members who fear the death of their beloved ones, unable to influence their fate during the hunting season. The battle against the sometimes unpredictable weather is deadly serious and certainly not handled with "good humor". Manufacturing goods from material available from the environment contributes to the Inuit's sustainable lifestyle, using knowledge that has been passed down from generation to generation. This can also be seen as remaining independent from Southern and Western economic circulation and not living a simple life. As Missuk's inability to sew and carve shows, these are no skills that Inuit automatically inherit and are born with, but which have to be learnt and practiced in order to be powerful and effective. If living in the North is to be affordable and livable, hunter-gatherer lifestyles need to be reliable, and, more importantly, are part of tradition and Inuit identity. At the same time, this obviously does not mean that Inuit are separated from "modern" developments, as the skidoos and the fully equipped kitchen reveal. Also Brody's observation that Inuit carry pet names is, luckily, no longer true, as the protagonists are called Missuk, Ukaliq or Amiqqaq. The fictional Inuit texts for children analyzed for this essay are counter examples to Brody's estimation. However, it comes as a surprise that David reflects upon the aspect of Inuit stereotypes and description of personality in a similar tone, as especially Kusugak's stories have already been published before the millennium and other texts were available. As he stated in an interview with the CBC, Kusugak often found books "filled with misconceptions, misrepresentation of traditions, [which] held a colonial view of the Inuit as a primitive culture" (Schwartz n.p.). But his books and especially also Edwardson's do no longer present Inuit as "timeless artifact[s]" (Sundmark 159). In those books, the protagonists discover and explore different geographical and temporal spaces, which usually pave the way towards occupying new spaces of self; paths on which a protagonist also "moves toward a more integrated sense of identity and, at some level, a new understanding of life" (West and Harris 77). Missuk, for example, was not able to sew or carve when her father left, but in leaving snow geese in the snow, she enters a geographical and psychological journey. She leaves imprints of herself on the land and, when guiding her father home, becomes aware that she learns to perform those craftworks if she believes in herself. Space which formerly caused frustration, now offers comfort, trust and self-esteem. In a similar sense also Ukaliq enters a journey of a "self-realization" (West and Harris 84).

6. Inuit children on heroic journeys

The Inuit children's books introduced in this essay can be seen as exemplifications of the "type of story offering an important threshold to be crossed on the journey on which every child must be a hero" (West and Harris 85) – a hero of life, not of struggling with stereotypical Inuit identity or a reduction to the hardships of living in the North. However, this journey does not "provide opportunities for the transplanted young protagonists to grow as the result of being in a new or defamiliarized environment, distanced in space and/or time from the character's home" (West and Harris 77), but rather as a result of being part of and actively contributing to the safety and good of home. Through engaging with the environment, being part of it and become repeatedly aware of the interdependency of human and nature, Inuit protagonists are able to connect to traditions and geographic and social space. What seems essential in this context is the fact that those child protagonists do not need to re-connect to their Inuit identity as they have never lost this sense of self; a motive that is often prevalent in First Nation children's fiction. In *Whale Snow*, *Missuk's Snow Geese* or *The Gift of the Inuksuk*, the main protagonists do not search for a balanced identity and sense of belonging, but rather need to actively support community and be responsible for re-establishing family ties. In that, those children's books are different to other First Nations fiction, in which the main protagonist sets out on a journey to reconnect missing links of past and present First Nation identity[7].

7. Transformation of bleak mental landscapes

The increasing representation of Inuit child protagonists in geographic, temporal and cultural spaces allows comparing those journeys to Campbell's entry of heroes to "zone[s] of magnified power" (Cf. West and Harris 77). Those result in mental "manifestation[s] of change" (West and Harris 49) as their representation moves beyond the good-humored, raw meat eating and furry little man (David 141). Inuit child protagonists transcend thresholds from the invisible and insignificant to active agents who occupy spaces of self-confidence and balanced identity. This is, however, only possible if Inuit children's books are read critically and when certain images are de-constructed, as was the case with Ulmer's *The Gift of the Inuksuk*. Certainly, the already mentioned official moves in recognizing Inuit presence in the North have contributed to successful journeys. The first essential of such moves was the establishment of Nunavut as a new Canadian territory in 1999, which not only declared the Inuit their own political space, but also recognized Inuit language and customs on an official level that in turn also justified the foundation of self-sustained Inuit media companies. This supports the increasing space

7 Despite those being most often addressed at an older audience, books such as Jeanette Armstrong's *Slash* often revolve around the young protagonist's quest for a balanced identity and sense of self. Within the body of children's books, titles such as *A Stranger at Home* or *When I was Eight* by Christy Jordan-Fenton and Margaret Pokiak-Fentonboth tell of a Inuvialuit girl's experiences and memories of her time at a residential school. This comment should, however and under no circumstances, be understood as an undermining of the horrors of residential school experience for children and the disastrous consequences for the Inuit and other Indigenous communities. Of course those need to be reflected, remembered and taught to younger generations. At the same time, Inuit identity does not stop there and Inuit children also deserve positive and life-enhancing images of self reflected in the books they read.

in bookstores occupied by Inuit voices and adds to multicultural bookshelves within Canada and abroad, not only in number but also in quality. Additionally, publications by Inuit writers and writers who can draw from extended experiences in the North for their stories with Inuit content claim space for Inuit voices within a literary canon. The usage of Inuit languages and the presentation of young Inuit heroines and heroes who connect to the land and landscape to save loved ones as well as the presentation of the North as a home support the perception of the Inuit as a part of Canadian society who exist in the present and base their contemporary life on knowledge of the past, by inscribing stories on the printed page and projecting their cultural well-being for the future. Thus, not only bleak mental landscapes are transformed (West and Harris, 82), but also "empty" spaces in bookstores when Inuit children find themselves authentically represented in books speaking in their own voice and enabling them to *shout of joyous things*.

Works cited

Angutingunrik, Jose. *The Giant Bear*. Iqaluit: Inhabit Media, 2012.

Bennett, John and Susan Rowley. *Uqalurait: An Oral History of Nunvaut*. Montreal: McGills-Queen's University Press, 2008. Print.

Bradford, Clare. *Unsettling Narratives: Postcolonial Readings of Children's Literature*. Waterloo: Wilfried Laurier University Press, 2007. Print.

Brody, Hugh. *Living Arctic: Hunters of the Canadian North*. Seattle: University of Washington Press, 1987. Print.

Campbell, Joseph. *The Hero with a Thousand Faces*. New York: MJF Books, 1949. Print.

Edwardson, Debbie Dahl. *Whale Snow*. Watertown: Charlesbridge, 2004.

David. Robert G. "Representing the Inuit in Contemporary British and Canadian Juvenile Non-Fiction." *Children's Literature in Education* 32.2 (2001): 139–154. Print.

Edwards, Gail and Judith Saltman. *Picturing Canada: A History of Canadian Children's Illustrated Books and Publishing*. Toronto: University of Toronto Press, 2010. Print.

Harry, Margaret. "Literature in English by Native Canadians (Indians and Inuit)." *Studies in Canadian Literature / Études en littérature canadienne* 10.1 (1985). Web. 22 June 2013.

Kaslik, Ibi. *Tales from the Tundra*. Iqaluit: Inhabit Media, 2010.

Kassam, Karim-Aly S. "North of 60°: Homeland or Frontier?" *Passion for Identity: Canadian Studies for the 21st century*. Ed. David Taras and Beverly Rasporich. Scarborough: Nelson Thompson Learning, 2001. 433–455. Print.

Kilabuk, Elisha. *The Qalupalik*. Iqaluit: Inhabit Media, 2011.

Kusugak, Michael. *A Promise is a Promise*. Toronto: Annick Press, 1988.

–. *Baseball Bats for Christmas*. Toronto: Annick Press, 1990/2006.

–. *Northern Lights, the Soccer Trails*. Toronto: Annick Press, 1993/2007.

–. *Arctic Stories*. Toronto: Annick Press, 1998/2010.

Lewis, Marion. *Kaugjagjuk*. Iqaluit: Inhabit Media, 2011.

Luke, Carmen. "Media Literacy and cultural studies." *Constructing critical literacies: Teaching and learning textual practice*. Ed. Sandy Muspratt, Alan Luke and Peter Freebody. Creskill, NJ: Hampton Press, 1997. 19–49. Print.

McKenzie, Andrea. "The changing faces of Canadian children: Pictures, Power and Pegagogy." *Windows and Words: A Look a Canadian Children's Literature in English*. Ed. Aida Hudson and Susan-Ann Cooper. Ottawa: University of Ottawa Press, 2003. 201–218. Print.

Mikkigak, Qaunaq and Joanne Schwartz. *The Legend of the Fog*. Iqaluit: Inhabit Media, 2011.

"Quill & Quire's Books of the Year 2011." *The Canadian Children's Book Centre*. Web June 23, 2013.

Qaunaq, Sakiasi. *The Orphan and the Polar Bear*. Iqaluit: Inhabit Media, 2011.

Qitsualik, Rachel. *Shadows That Rush Past*. Iqaluit: Inhabit Media, 2011.

Qitsualik, Rachel. *Under the Ice*. Iqaluit: Inhabit Media, 2012.

Renauld, Anne. *Missuk's Snow Geese*. Vancouver: simply read books, 2008.

Schwartz, Joanne. "Transmitting Oral Culture to the Page: the Emergence of Inuit Children's Books," International Board on Books for Young People. Online: http://www.ibby.org/index.php?id=1135, June 22, 2013.

Sundmark, Björn. "The Idea of the North in Canadian Children's Literature Today." *Jeunesse: Young People, Text and Cultures* 3.1 (2011): 152–162. Print.

"A conversation with Inuit storyteller Michael Kusugak." CBC radio, Friday, November 18, 2011. Web. June 22, 2013.

Ulmer, Mike. *The Gift of the Inuksuk*. Chelsea: Sleeping Bear Press, 2002.

Uluadluak, Donald. *Kamik: An Inuit Puppy Story*. Iqaluit: Inhabit Media, 2013.

West, Alan and Lee Harris. "Secrecy and Space: Glenn Gould and Tim Wynne-Jone's *The Maestro*." *Windows and Words: A Look at Canadian Children's Literature in* English. Ed. Aida Hudson and Susan-Ann Cooper. Ottawa: University of Ottawa Press, 2003. 77–86. Print.

Part II: Conflict, Governance and Citizenship

Andreas Huck
Faculty of Spatial Sciences, University of Groningen

Perceptions, Emotions and Conflict Resolution: The Northern Gateway case in British Columbia, Canada

Since colonial times, British Columbia (BC) has been subject to conflicts between Western settlers and First Nations, Canada's Indigenous population (Castleden et al.). Currently, the proposal of the Northern Gateway pipelines by Enbridge Inc., which are supposed to transport oil sands from Alberta to British Columbia's coast, are at the center of one of the biggest political debates in Canadian history. Pipeline proponents and opponents are involved in heated discussions about economic and environmental issues, issues of energy security and climate change, provincial justice between Alberta and British Columbia and international (Chinese) interference in Canada's (oil) industry, but, above all, about relations between First Nation communities, government and the oil industry.

This paper explores the nature of this conflict by splitting it up into two main levels: the perception level and the emotional level. I contend that the conflict between First Nations on BC's coast and Enbridge Inc. together with Canadian federal government is amplified by the way First Nations are involved in the project's review process, which aims to assess whether the pipeline can be considered to be in Canada's national interest. I will discuss some approaches from Social Impact Assessment theory that could be used for conflict resolution. However, it is found that these approaches will not be of great help as long as the present conflict is painted over with a neo-colonial overtone. With its roots deep in Canadian colonial history, the conflict runs the risk to escalate and to push Canada back in time by re-implementing colonial-related policy structures.

Argumentation is based on (1) media analysis of national and provincial newspapers to explore main points of the discussion and to gain an overview of arguments from pipeline proponents and opponents; and (2) video-based in-depth interviews with key stakeholders to reveal participants' perceptions on the conflict situation in general and on the review process specifically and to learn about people's feelings and emotions concerning the conflict. Interviews were restricted to members of the Heiltsuk First Nation. Neither government representatives nor Enbridge representatives were willing to give interviews about the issue. Thus, their argumentation is restricted to publicly available written material. Also (3) literature analysis in the field of Social Impact Assessment was conducted to reveal suitable theoretical approaches for solving the conflict in study.

In the following, geographical and historical background information of the proposed Northern Gateway pipeline and First Nation's involvement in assessment processes in BC is presented. Subsequently, the conflict situation is discussed by splitting it up into two levels of conflict: perceptions and emotions. Thereafter, approaches of Social Impact Assessment theory are assessed to find out to what extent they can theoretically contribute to conflict resolution. Finally, the results are brought together and it is discussed how the present conflict mingles with Canada's colonial past.

1. Geographical background

The Northern Gateway Pipelines Project proposes a 1,177 km twin pipeline between Bruderheim, Alberta and Kitimat, BC (Enbridge Inc. "Project Details"). It will carry 525,000 barrels of crude oil per day from the oil sands in Northern Alberta to a marine terminal in Kitimat, and 193,000 barrels of condensate per day in the opposite direction to thin petroleum products for the pipeline transport. From Kitimat, huge oil tankers will transport the crude oil to refineries in Asia. The project is estimated to be worth $5.5 billion (Enbridge Inc. "Project Brochure"). Van Hinte et al. estimate that the Northern Gateway project will have more significant impacts than other similar proposals due to entailed port and tanker activity and tanker routes along the Douglas Channel in BC. Indeed, this passage is so far designated as a tanker-free zone because of the risk of tanker accidents and environmental vulnerability (van Hinte et al.). At the time of study, the project was undergoing a review process as part of an impact assessment conducted by a federal joint review panel of the Canadian Environmental Agency and the National Energy Board. Hearings were held following the proposed pipeline route between January 2012 and June 2013.

Figure 1. Proposed Northern Gateway Pipeline (red) and tanker traffic (black).

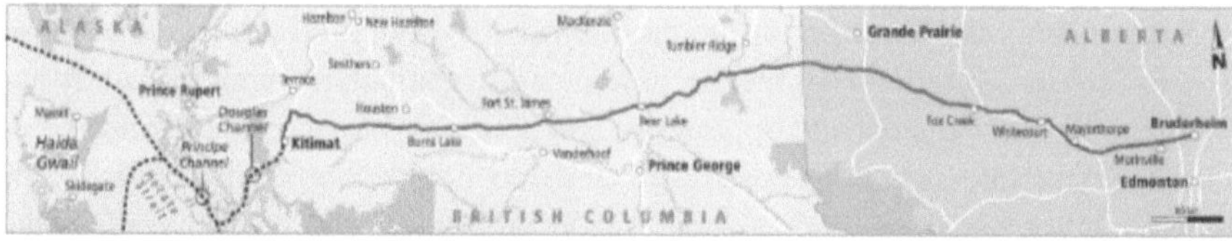

Source: *The Province "Residents deserve answers".*

The conflict this pipeline proposal implies has both provincial/interprovincial and national dimensions. Moreover, it has strong international implications. Crossing

Alberta and British Columbia, the pipeline touches interests of two provinces in Canada with Alberta as oil deliverer and British Columbia as passageway. Since the development of Alberta's oil sands is in the interest of the federal Canadian government and determines Canada's energy future, it is also a national issue. Chinese involvement in the Canadian oil industry and opening Canada's (oil) export market to foreign countries outside of the United States makes the issue internationally important.

Starting in Bruderheim, Alberta, the Northern Gateway pipelines will cross 773 active watercourses, of which at least 83 are deemed to be highly sensitive crossings (Enbridge Inc. "Pipeline Assessment"). Furthermore, the route crosses a variety of landscapes, including the Eastern Alberta Plains, Southern Alberta Uplands, Alberta Plateau, Rocky Mountains, Interior Plateau and Coast Mountains (Enbridge Inc. "Environmental and Socio-Economic Assessment: Discussion Guide"). The tanker terminal will be located in Kitimat, in the interior of the so-called Great Bear Rainforest (GBR). It is connected to the Pacific Ocean through tight and sometimes shallow watercourses. The rich diversity in the GBR includes rich human cultures because the area has been populated by 29 First Nations groups for over 10,000 years (Prescott-Allen). Smith and Sterrit point out that, historically, First Nations managed sustainably the natural resources based on Indigenous Knowledge (2). Nevertheless, since colonial times this area has been subject of conflict between Western settlers and First Nations (Castleden et al.).

2. Historical background

The conducted review process seems to fall in line with a series of failed First Nation participation processes in British Columbia. While Canadian First Nations are actually well considered in regulatory frameworks concerning Environmental Impact Assessment (EIA) and Social Impact Assessment (SIA)[1], participation procedures in BC regularly fail to meet minimum standards of SIA (see e.g. Armitage; Baker and McLelland; Booth and Skelton; Galbraith et al.; Hinte et al; Sinclair and Diduck).

---

1 First Nations' involvement is mandated by law (see e.g. Canadian Environmental Assessment Act, BC Environmental Assessment Act), by treaty obligations, and by a series of court rulings that adjudicated rights and title to certain lands to First Nations impacted by developments. First Nations must be "meaningfully" consulted by government (Canadian Environmental Assessment Act). However, the term "meaningful" has never been defined exactly by court and governments tend to pass their consultation obligation to the project developer (Booth and Skelton).

Booth and Skelton (52) argue that limitations in BC's Impact Assessment (IA) processes include a lack of mandatory First Nation criteria under current legislation, less aboriginal perspectives, inadequate resources, and a lack of cumulative assessment requirements. Similarly, Baker and McLelland argue that Environmental Assessment (EA) decision-making processes in BC reflect a poor integration of First Nations people and lack of openness, fairness, and objectivity. Besides others, access to such processes might be limited by language barriers, public review periods not suiting cultural timeframes, narrow project scoping, and on-going land claims (Baker and McLelland 582). Even the often positively highlighted assessment process in Mackenzie Valley, manifested in the Mackenzie Valley Resource Management Act (MVRMA) in 1998, has recently been criticised due to several weak points and issues, including jurisdictional complexity, less open and transparent processes, inappropriate use and control of traditional knowledge and power imbalances. Enbridge's corporate history in accommodating First Nations is subject to similar criticism. Dembicki (n.p.), for instance, refers back to a situation where Enbridge logged trees of spiritual values for the Haisla First Nation some years ago. This had become emblematic of Enbridge's failures to understand about people's way of life, their deep spiritual connection to the land, and their living sense of tradition and history (Dembicki).

The Northern Gateway assessment process has been subject to several reviews already. Thus far, evaluations do not reflect well on Enbridge and the regulatory body. For instance, van Hinte et al. reveal that the assessment procedure is inadequate in many points. Most important, "the responsible authority can make any decision regardless of the assessment without providing any clear rationale" (131). Moreover, stakeholder involvement processes are defined as adversarial and not collaborational. Also, despite the fact that the Canadian Environmental Assessment Agency (CEAA) provides the option for a collaborative mediated solution, it has never been used because of lacking legal pressure to negotiate Impact Benefit Agreements (IBA) with project opponents (131). Hinte et al. predict that, without addressing the detected deficiencies, the regulatory regime will not be able to ensure that the project is in the public interest. Sarah Panofsky assesses aboriginal engagement in the Northern Gateway Environmental Assessment in detail. She argues that there are serious limitations in the extent and quality of First Nations participation in the assessment process and that aboriginal rights and authority over their land are not acknowledged (6). Moreover, she argues that the joint review panel does not recognize aboriginal rights frameworks that have developed in Canada and internationally (38) and that aboriginal ontologies and epistemologies are excluded from the process (39).

Thus, the Northern Gateway review process illustrates once more the inability of the Canadian industry and state to 'meaningfully' accommodate First Nation's interests. This historical perspective is crucial for the following discussion because it frames the conflict and influences people's perceptions and feelings. Indigenous people have learned to expect little that is positive, and much that is negative, from state action, policy, institutions and processes thus far (O'Faircheallaigh). That state institutions guide the formal review process for the Northern Gateway proposal might be a reason in itself for distrust and conflict in BC.

3. Situating the conflict

> Canadians and especially British Columbians will be at each others' throats. There will be violence, God only knows how serious. (Mair n.p.)

The highly delicate political situation emerging out of the controversy between proponents and opponents of the pipeline proposal becomes obvious in the facts that more than 68,000 people signed a petition to ban tankers from the province's northern ports (Whittington n.p.) and roughly 4,500 people have asked to be heard by the national panel reviewing the pipeline proposal (Audette n.p.). Around 60,000 people have sent messages opposing Northern Gateway to BC Premier Christy Clark, while another 40,000 have emailed Enbridge President Patrick Daniel (Burgmann n.p.). George Hoberg, professor of environmental and natural resource policy and governance at the University of British Columbia, calls this conflict "a battle for the soul of Canada"[2].

The conflict can be divided into two main levels. First, there are different perceptions about the project itself, including differences in perceived benefits and threats. These perceptions are based on facts about the project and grounded in different value systems of groups of individuals. Second, the emotional level includes feelings of (dis)trust and (dis)respect. Emotions define relationships between different parties, here: coastal First Nations on the one side and Enbridge Inc. and the Canadian government on the other side.

The Perception Level

Of course, there are differences between First Nations bands and between different individuals within each band in terms of attitude towards the pipeline proposal. However, with 61 First Nation bands signing the "Save the Fraser Declaration," many of them built a strong unit (Drews n.p.). Argumentation is based mainly on

---

2 Interview: Vancouver, 23 Jul. 2012.

environmental risks and negative ripple effects on First Nation's culture and livelihood. The subscribers of the "Save the Fraser Declaration" point to the importance of river systems for their life and culture and therefore:

> in upholding our ancestral laws, Title, Rights and responsibilities, we declare: We will not allow the proposed Enbridge Northern Gateway Pipelines, or similar Tar Sands projects, to cross our lands, territories and watersheds, or the ocean migration routes of Fraser River salmon (Save the Fraser Declaration n.p.).

Fear for an oil spill is high. The Exxon Valdez disaster in 1989 is still in mind and opponents of the pipeline point to 610 recognised spills of other Enbridge pipelines between 1999 and 2008 (Nikiforuk n.p.). Recently, on 26 July 2010, 3,785,411 liters of crude oil spoiled into the Kalamazoo River in Michigan (Panofsky 21). ENGOs point to the importance of the area in terms of biodiversity and carbon storage, while First Nations focus on their dependence on natural resources and a healthy environment. With more than 50,000 jobs in this area, BC clearly depends on coastal fishing and tourism (Heymann n.p.). Kitimat chief councillor Ellis Ross summarises:

> We don't agree with the project. That's set in stone because we haven't seen any technology out there that can guarantee that, No.1, there won't be a spill, and, No. 2, if there is a spill, that it can be (cleaned) up (Meissner n.p.).

Amongst the proponent side, generally speaking, one can number Enbridge Inc. and the Canadian federal government. Their arguments basically turn on the creation of jobs and the importance of the project for the Canadian economy. A published section of the Environmental and Socio-Economic Assessment by Enbridge Inc., e.g., states:

> Construction in the three British Columbia regions will require 10,335 person-years while 3,535 person-years of employment will be required to construct the Alberta portion of the Project. The Project is expected to generate 15,675 person-years of direct, indirect and induced employment for residents of the six regions (Enbridge Inc. "Environmental and Socio-economic Assessment (ESA)-Human Environment, Section 4.4").

In simplified terms, it becomes clear that pipeline opponents perceive the project to be a threat to their livelihood and ecology, while proponents perceive the pipeline as a chance for economic growth. The crucial point is that their argumentation is based on entirely different facts and circumstances. They literally are not on the same page. This discrepancy can be explained by different value systems and different world views. Different perceptions, for instance, become visible in discussions about landscape and environment. On the one hand, pipeline proponents point to data and technical analyses they conducted to minimise the risk. They also calculate how much money it would cost to clean up after an oil spill. They perceive the landscape and the environment as natural resources, as something that can be quantified and transferred into monetary value, and, in the end, as something clearly separated from the human. On the other hand, the interviews showed that the Heiltsuk view is entirely different. Talking about the same issue, they point to the danger of losing their livelihood, of losing their basis of existence, of losing part of what they are. They perceive the environment as part of their selves, as a part of their identity. In this view, the landscape and the human cannot be separated. Jessie Housty, Director of Traditional Knowledge in Qqs (Eyes) Projects Society explains:

> Everything that we rely on as people is linked to the health of our waters. [...] Our language is very descriptive and it is tied to specific places. Our names that we hold are tied to place names, our traditional stories are located out on the landscape of our territory, and really the entire history of our people is a narrative that is written on the landscape and seascape of our territory. [...] It's all holistic, it's all integrated [...] and that's something that you can't put a price on. That's our identity and that's our history. That's something that you can't quantify. (Interview: Bella Bella, 16 Aug. 2012)

It becomes clear that different perceptions are closely linked to different value systems. For instance landscape, as a subject of discussion, is valued in entirely different ways: its meaning skips back and forth between various definitions. While pipeline proponents perceive the landscape to be something that you can quantify and compensate in economic terms, the Heiltsuk understanding of landscape is inextricably linked with their identity and, thus, cannot be put to discussion, not to mention to economic calculation. Instead, an attack on their lands is rather perceived as an attack on their own existence. Thus, a key point of the conflict lies in the inability to understand and accept different worldviews than one's own and in the omission to find a common definition of the most important subjects of the conflict.

The Emotion Level

An analysis of newspaper articles between December 2011 and July 2012 reveals three main mechanisms which heat up the discussion in emotional terms: name calling[3], arousing distrust by legislative and regulative changes[4], and disrespectful

3 Canada's Natural Resource Minister Joe Oliver caused a huge discussion by publishing an open letter in which he branded environmental organizations as "radical groups (...), who threaten to hijack [the] regulatory system to achieve their radical ideological agenda" (Natural Resources Canada n.p.). Also, former Prime Minister Stephen Harper has claimed that pipeline opponents are "foreign funded puppets" and are trying to slow down the process on the costs of Canadian public (Loon and Mayeda n.p.; Krause n.p.).

4 While the review process has been started already, Canadian government changed regulations of such review processes in general on legislative base. These changes include a time

treatment of First Nations in the review process. This lifts the factual discussion about potential benefits and risks of the proposed pipelines to another level where power relationships between different participants and emotional implications weigh more than pure facts. Thus, from a sociological perspective, the last mechanism is of greatest importance.

The review process shows the most direct impact on the nature of the relationship between pipeline proponents and opponents, respectively between Enbridge Inc. and the Canadian federal government on the one side, and Coastal First Nations on the other side. Taking Heiltsuk Nation's consultation as an example, the newspaper analysis reveals a plethora of conflict points on the emotional level. In-depth interviews with Heiltsuk Nation members confirm this perception.

Hearings in Bella Bella (Heiltsuk territory) were scheduled for four days in April 2012. The review panel was welcomed in time by peacefully protesting Heiltsuk members at Bella Bella airport. Due to safety concerns, however, the panel decided to shorten the hearings by one and a half days. Two days later, they announced logistical issues to be the reason for the delay (Stoymenoff n.p.). In July 2012, the lost time was made up by a hearing in Shearwater, a village across the water from Bella Bella.

Newspaper articles from April 2012 show how British Columbia's public perceived the joint review panel's attitude and behaviour. Reviewed articles use emotional expressions like "disrespectful treatment", "frustrated First Nations" (Hager n.p.), "disheartening" (Hunter n.p.), and "there's no honour" (The Province n.p.). As a consequence of the joint review panel's decision to shorten the hearings in Bella Bella, a neighbouring community, the Nuxalk Nation, even withdrew from the hearings (The Province: "Nuxalk pull out of compromised pipeline review." n.p.).

Interviews with participating members of Heiltsuk First Nation about the hearings in Bella Bella reveal a deeply emotional conflict. This includes feelings of inferiority, mistrust, helplessness, exasperation, and being disrespected. Harvey Humchitt, hereditary chief of Heiltsuk Nation, said: "It's a sad feeling. (…) I don't feel that there's a fairness in the hearing [process] itself. It's contrived by people that aren't from the coast and that are involved in oil". (Interview: Bella Bella, 14 Aug. 2012). Even though the national review panel is supposed to be an independent body that makes independent recommendations to the federal government, they

---

limit of 24 months for hearing processes, financial limits for ENGO's actions concerning review processes, elimination of the National Round Table on the Environment, and, most importantly, a transfer of power to make a final decision for huge infrastructure projects, like the Northern Gateway, to the federal government (McCarthy n.p.).

are perceived as being biased and prejudiced by participants of the hearings. Jessie Housty, director of traditional knowledge of Qqs (Eyes) Projects Society, states:

> Our relationship with the panel has been fraught with difficulties. (...) Throughout the whole process we really felt antagonised by the panel members. They were constantly interrupting our speakers, they were very dismissive of the evidence that was presented to them, we actually had several of our elders stand up and walk off in protest, because they felt that they have been so disrespected by the panel members that they weren't even willing to continue telling their stories. It was an incredibly disheartening thing. And it left a lot of unresolved hurt and anger in the community (Interview: Bella Bella, 16 Aug. 2012).

It is clear that Heiltsuk Nation members do not only oppose the Northern Gateway project itself, but, first and foremost, struggle with the way they are treated in the review process. These negative feelings amplify people's negative notion about the project itself and, in addition to that, reconstitute negative perceptions within the relationship between First Nation members and Canadian government. William Housty, director of Coastal Guardian Watchmen in Bella Bella, explains:

> Stephen Harper and their government have already made up their mind about what they wanna do. So that's really where the fight is. It's not really the National Energy Board, it's our own government who is doing this to us (Interview: Koeye Island, 11 Aug. 2012).

William Housty's statement shows that perceived negative treatment in the review process impacts Heiltsuk Nation's relation to state authority on a wider scale. Jessie Housty draws the same conclusion in stating that "in the whole process, (...) there isn't a huge emphasis on respectful engagement. (...) That's not a dialogue, that's not participation, that's not engagement, and certainly not consultation" (Interview: Bella Bella, 16 Aug. 2012). The National Energy Board's behaviour at Heiltsuk territory clearly demonstrates power imbalances and thus adds fuel to the flames of a deeply emotional conflict.

Interactions of perceptions and emotions

The sections above make clear that emotions play a crucial role in assessing the relationship between Coastal First Nations and Canada's federal government alongside the review process for Northern Gateway. The two levels of conflict interact with each other in the way that negative feelings (emotions) amplify perceived differences in opinions (perceptions) and disseminate the conflict to a broader level. Thus, with an inadequate review process, which is perceived to be conducted in a disrespectful way, the discussion gets widened to an extent reaching issues of human rights, colonization, and First Nation's treatment in Canada in general. An official statement by the First Nations Summit Task Group verifies this assumption:

> We are deeply concerned that our government has already determined the outcome of the controversial Enbridge pipelines proposal even before the panel responsible for assessing its impacts has commenced its hearings. This, in our opinion, has the real potential to completely undermine the independence and impartiality of the Panel, its report and recommendations. (First Nations Summit Task Group n.p.)

Without a doubt, the Northern Gateway assessment and review process failed to accurately accommodate First Nations. The conflict is not restricted to the actual subject of the conflict. And the conflict is not restricted to the actual scope of the Northern Gateway project. Rather, the conflict turns into what George Hoberg calls "a battle for the soul of Canada"[5].

Some interviewees, like Dallas Smith, Director of Nanwakolas First Nations, indicate that the treatment of First Nations by the government and economic players in this conflict is perceived as continuation of a dominant government style. Experiences from the past play a crucial role in how the conflict is perceived today:

> I think, in the end of the day, it's just gonna get pushed through like so many other pieces of bad policy have been. [...] I'm very embarrassed to be a Canadian sometimes when you look at how the federal government treats First Nation's people (Interview: Nanaimo, 25 Aug. 2012).

But what could a fair review process look like? What would Social Impact Assessment look like that truly accommodates Canada's Coastal First Nations? Could such a process even play a part in healing some of the deeper wounds of Canadian colonial history? Social Impact Assessment theory offers some approaches that can be of interest. The following section shortly introduces some of these approaches and relates them to the Northern Gateway case.

4. Theoretical approaches from the field of Social Impact Assessment

In 2007, van Hinte et al. recommended that "proponents, First Nations, and regulatory bodies at the federal and provincial levels of government should establish collaborative decision-making processes" (133). Furthermore, they suggested that all parties should establish a permanent relationship based on open communication, collaboration, and trust. External parties should provide information and clear decision-making criteria should be established (134). Improvement could also be achieved by asking the participants which participation techniques they prefer, minimizing potential for preferential treatment of certain groups, providing

5 Interview: Vancouver, 23 Jul.2012.

sufficient and intelligible information, and incorporating concepts like cultural diversity, social self-determination and equity and social justice (Baker and McLelland). However, the conducted interviews in BC and research by Panofsky reveal that all this has not been achieved adequately.

Referring to Christenson and Briassoulis, Sinclair and Diduck point out that "in circumstances characterized by conflict, uncertainty and change, a transactive [planning] model is often the appropriate choice" (132). In particular, environmental conflict mediation, conflict-sensitive impact assessment, community-based agreement making, Indigenous social development, and the recognition of the International Principles for SIA and human rights offer the chance for conflict resolution; at least in theory.

Environmental conflict mediation

Reasons for the conflict are grounded in emotional anger, fear and opportunism (Barrow), power imbalances and historical incidences (Panofsky) and different worldviews, religious beliefs, morals, and political outlook (Barrow; Panofsky). Although the Canadian IA system offers explicitly the possibility for external mediation, this chance has not been taken (Hinte et al.).

Environmental conflict mediation refers to attempts to solve disputes or episodes of conflict. It is related to the concept of joint decision-making, offering potential for collaborative planning and cooperative decision-making processes (Sairinen et al.). In particular, its practical orientation helps to resolve conflicts in constructive ways and might be useful for the case described above[6].

External conflict mediation offers approaches to solve both levels of conflict. First, it can help to solve the conflict on the perception level by fostering real dialogue in the sense that the two parties discuss about the same issues. As shown above, highlighting possible economic benefits cannot diminish the fear of possible oil spills. Rather it is necessary to discuss the risk and consequences of an oil spill separately. Second, external mediation and voluntary negotiation (Ross) can help to solve the emotional level of conflict. Name-calling and feelings of distrust might be attenuated once a real dialogue gets started and the parties start to talk

6 Techniques, that could be used, include "conflict mapping," in which the emphasis is rather on needs and fears of different parties than on stated positions, to support such processes (Ross), and "conflict assessment," where interviews with stakeholders about their main concerns, their perceptions of other stakeholders, their involvement in the conflict, and their concerns about the assessment process itself are conducted (Sairinen).

to each other in face-to-face meetings. In these meetings the parties would meet eye-to-eye, which diminishes feelings of suppression and superiority.

Conflict sensitive impact assessment

The approach of conflict sensitive impact assessment is based on the recognition that the very presence of a company can be a cause of conflict between them and their stakeholders as well as between different parties in the community itself (Kapelus et al.). It calls for a "management approach that understands the dynamics of the conflict, the triggers and root causes, and appreciates that managing and avoiding the escalation of conflict must be achieved by building and maintaining trust with stakeholders" (Kapelus et al. 288).

In this case it is particularly important to understand land rights and title (including social cultural and legal aspects), to appreciate basic rights of Indigenous people and marginalisation of their communities, and to recognise that any infringement of the rights of effected communities could heat up the conflict. Also the described history between First Nations and Enbridge Inc. has to be considered. Since trust building is one of the most important features of conflict management, it is important to use local knowledge, contextual analysis and participatory methodologies for data gathering and evaluation.

Conflict sensitive impact assessment can support solution finding on both levels of conflict. Understanding the conflict and its roots makes it possible to understand perceptions of the other party (perception level). This can serve as a baseline, setting the ground for dialogue. Since emotional reactions arise mainly out of misunderstanding and distrust, a common understanding of what the conflict is about will automatically diminish emotional reactions (emotional level).

Community-based agreements

Community-based agreements offer the possibility to respect community identities and de-politicise the process. They provide opportunities to improve approaches of incorporating local knowledge and concerns, defining local participation, and securing continuing involvement of communities in development processes (Nish and Bice)[7]. Hereby, the process itself plays the most important role. Politicisation of the Northern Gateway case generates an environment where

7 Outcomes can be Impact Benefit Agreements (IBA), Participation Agreements, or other agreements and contracts on the basis of equal partnerships.

negative impacts are neglected and where incorporation of local knowledge and concerns is limited (cf. Nish and Bice 61).

Potentials for solving the perception level are based on the acknowledgement of community needs and community self-determination. De-politicisation might also offer potential help for solving the emotion level, since the identified mechanisms that heat up the conflict (name-calling, legislative and regulative changes, and disrespectful treatment of First Nations in the review process) come from the Canadian federal government itself. However, given its active role in the process and its obvious interest in the Northern Gateway pipeline, de-politicisation is hard to imagine.

Indigenous social development

The approach of Indigenous social development is based on the perception that big infrastructure projects often include negative impacts for Indigenous peoples, because they often reinforce power imbalances by marginalising affected aboriginal communities (O'Faircheallaigh). O'Faircheallaigh's statement below explicitly reflects the situation of the Northern Gateway case:

> [A] proposed development will not be judged favourably on the basis that its economic and social benefits are expected to exceed its costs if it leaves underlying economic and social conditions unchanged and if corporate proponents and government regulators show no awareness of the need to address these conditions in fundamental ways (O'Faircheallaigh 138).

O'Faircheallaigh points to the importance of considering First Nation's history of dispossession and economic and political marginalisation leading to today's economic and social disadvantages. He states that Indigenous people have learned to expect little that is positive, and much that is negative, from state action, policy, institutions and processes. The Northern Gateway review process neglects local knowledge and concerns and treats First Nations in disrespectful ways.

A focus on Indigenous social development offers potentials for solving both levels of conflict. First, the perception level is addressed by focussing the discussion on social development in First Nation communities, acknowledging the real needs of each community. Second, the emotion level is addressed indirectly by supporting a better understanding of First Nation community needs and by acknowledging Canadian colonial history and past government-First Nations-relations.

Recognition of the International Principles for SIA and human rights

The *International Principles for SIA* highlight key features such as fairness, equity, transparency, participation, accountability, empowerment and the equal treatment of disadvantaged groups of people (Vanclay). Potential impacts have to be seen in the context of peoples' way of life, their culture, their community, their political systems, their environment, their health and well-being, their personal and property rights, and their fears and aspirations (Vanclay). MacNaughton and Hunt notice the close relationship of human rights and the International Principles by Vanclay[8].

The discussion above demonstrates that the question whether human rights are recognised in the case of study is more than justified. Panofsky shows that the Northern Gateway assessment process has not adequately addressed International Principles for SIA so far. Furthermore, van Hinte et al. argue that the Canadian/BC assessment framework cannot adequately address SIA guidelines.

The recognition of the International Principles for SIA and human rights are a fundamental baseline that has to be considered. Any action, concerning one or both of the two levels of conflict, has to recognize and seriously consider these basic principles and guidelines. As such, they offer the potential for setting the ground to solve both conflict levels. Concerning Hinte et al.'s statement, however, this has to include changes in Canadian/British Columbian legislation, land rights, and titles.

5. Discussion

The Northern Gateway Pipeline proposed by Enbridge Inc. causes a massive conflict in British Columbia between Enbridge Inc. and the Canadian federal government on the one side and coastal First Nations (supported by NGOs, and others) on the other side. Media analysis and in-depth interviews demonstrate that the conflict takes place on two main levels: the perception level and, sometimes even more important, the emotion level. At least partly, this conflict can be ascribed to inadequate (Social) Impact Assessment procedures, respectively, inappropriate First Nations involvement in the review process. Looking at Social Impact Assessment theory, it becomes clear that theoretical possibilities for solving the conflict were available but largely neglected. The following statement by Bruce Harvey reflects the situation:

8 Particularly connections can be drawn to the Universal Declaration of Human Rights, which states that (1) human rights are universal, (2) they must be protected by the rule of law, (3) everybody has the right to social and international order protecting these rights, (4) peace, freedom of fear and want, and participation in community life are essential components of human rights, (5) people have the right to take their part in governance, and (6) local cultures and traditional knowledge has to be taken into account by government policy and programs (MacNaughton and Hunt).

> SIA as currently approached simply fails to meet the new requirements of resource developers and communities [and] in the context of development at the frontier, disinterest can give way to deliberate expropriation under the banner of national interest (Harvey xxxi–xxxii).

This article shows that the conflict about the Northern Gateway project is neither restricted to the actual subject of the conflict nor to the actual scope of the Northern Gateway pipelines. There is deep distrust between pipeline proponents and opponents which can, at least partly, be traced back to past occurrences and general treatment of First Nations in Canada in the past. The review process is perceived by some First Nations as ongoing colonisation and, in this sense, as a reinforcement of the legacy of colonisation. Hence, conflict solving gets aggravated because the present mingles with the colonial past.

Taking the outcome of this study into account, it becomes clear that the conflict cannot be traced back solely to inadequate impact assessment but first and foremost to a more general notion of ongoing colonisation in Canada. Hence, Impact Assessment on its own will not and cannot ensure sustainable outcomes (Aucamp et al.). In British Columbia, it would need the political will of the Canadian federal government to rethink the country's neo-colonial attitude towards Indigenous populations, to truly acknowledge First Nation's self-determination, and to critically reflect First Nation-government-relations against the background of Canada's colonial past.

Works cited

Amos, Gerald. "No apology forthcoming". *Terrace Daily* 8 Jan. 2012. Web. 31 Mar. 2012.

Armitage, Derek R. "Collaborative environmental assessment in the Northwest Territories, Canada". *Environmental Impact Assessment Review* 25.3 (2005): 239–258. Print.

Aucamp, Ilse, Stephan Woodborne, Jan Perold, Anita Bron and San-Marié Aucamp. "Looking beyond impact assessment to social sustainability". *New Directions in Social Impact Assessment*. Ed. Frank Vanclay and Ana Maria Esteves. Cheltenham, UK: Edward Elgar Publishing Limited, 2011. 38–58. Print.

Audette, Trish. "Alberta voices will be drowned out at pipeline panel". *Edmonton Journal* 9 Jan. 2012. Web. 31 Mar. 2012.

Baker, Douglas C. and James N. McLelland. "Evaluating the effectiveness of British Columbia's environmental assessment process for first nations' participation in mining development". *Environmental Impact Assessment Review* 23.5 (2003): 581–603. Print.

Barrow, Christopher J. "How is environmental conflict addressed by SIA?" *Environmental Impact Assessment Review* 30.5 (2010): 293–301. Print.

Booth, Annie L. and Norman W. Skelton. "Improving First Nations' participation in environmental assessment processes: recommendations from the field". *Impact Assessment and Project Appraisal* 29.1 (2011): 49–58. Print.

Burgmann, Tamsyn. "First Redford, Bacon anti-oil crusaders Enbridge pipeline drama". *The Hoook* 11 Jan. 2012. Web. 15 Feb. 2012.

Castleden, Heather, Theresa Garvin and Huu-ay-aht First Nation. ""Hishuk Tsawak" (Everything Is One/Connected): a Huu-ay-aht worldview for seeing forestry in British Columbia, Canada". *Society and Natural Resources* 22.9 (2009): 789–804. Print.

Dembicki, Geoff. "How Enbridge Sawed Off Good Relations with BC First Nations". *The Tyee* 16 Jan. 2012. Web. 31 Mar. 2012.

Drews, Keven. "First Nations leaders say they are closing B.C. borders to Gateway pipeline". *Edmonton Journal* 1 Dec. 2011. Web. 15 Feb. 2012.

Enbridge Inc. "Environmental and Socio-economic Assessment (ESA)-Human Environment, Section 4.4: Regional Social and Economic Effects (New Material)". Oct. 2010. Web. 2. Apr. 2012.

–. "Enbridge Northern Gateway Pipelines: Project Details". 2012. Web. 01 Apr. 2012.

–. "Enbridge Northern Gateway Pipelines: Project Brochure". 2012. Web. 01 Apr. 2012.

–. "Enbridge Northern Gateway Pipelines: Pipeline Assessment and First Response Plan". 2012. Web. 01 Apr. 2012.

–. "Enbridge Northern Gateway Pipelines: Environmental and Socio-Economic Assessment Discussion Guide". 2012. Web. 10 Jan. 2012.

Esteves, Ana Maria and Frank Vanclay. "Social development needs analysis as a tool for SIA to guide corporate-community investment: Applications in the minerals industry". *Environmental Impact Assessment Review* 29.2 (2009): 137–145. Print.

Esteves, Ana Maria, Mary-Anne Barclay, David Brereton and Daniel Samson. "Enhancing the benefits of projects through local procurement". *New Directions in Social Impact Assessment*. Ed. Frank Vanclay and Ana Maria Esteves. Cheltenham, UK: Edward Elgar Publishing Limited, 2011. 233–249. Print.

First Nations Summit Task Group. "Open letter regarding hearings into proposed Enbridge pipeline". *Rossland Telegraph* 17 Jan. 2012. Web. 15 Feb. 2012.

Galbraith, Lindsay, Ben Bradshaw and Murray B. Rutherford. "Towards a new supraregulatory approach to environmental assessment in Northern Canada". *Impact Assessment and Project Appraisal* 25.1 (2007): 27–41. Print.

Hager, Mike. "First Nation frustrated over shortened pipeline hearings". *Calgary Herald* 3 April 2012. Web. 31 Mar. 2012.

Harvey, Bruce. "SIA from a resource developer's perspective". *New Directions in Social Impact Assessment*. Ed. Frank Vanclay and Ana Maria Esteves. Cheltenham, UK: Edward Elgar Publishing Limited, 2011. xxvii–xxxiii. Print.

Heyman, George. "Demonization of environmentalists stifles debate". *Vancouver Sun* 16 Jan. 2012. Web. 31 Mar. 2012.

Hinte, Timothy van. *Managing Impacts of Major Projects: An Analysis of the Enbridge Gateway Pipeline Proposal*. Thesis (MA). 2005. Simon Fraser University, Burnaby. Print.

Hinte, Timothy van, Thomas I. Gunton and Jon C. Day. "Evaluation of assessment process for major projects: a case study of oil and gas pipelines in Canada". *Impact Assessment and Project Appraisal* 25.2 (2007): 123–137. Print.

Hunter, Justine. "Pipeline review process hits another snag". *The Globe and Mail* 6 Apr. 2012. Web. 31. Mar. 2012.

Kapelus, Paul, Emily Richards and Hope Sherwin. "Conflict-sensitive impact assessment". *New Directions in Social Impact Assessment*. Ed. Frank Vanclay and Ana Maria Esteves. Cheltenham, UK: Edward Elgar Publishing Limited, 2011. 288–305. Print.

Krause, Vivian. "Foreign funding skews oil debate". *Vancouver Sun* 6 Jan. 2012. Web. 31 Mar. 2012.

MacNaughton, Gillian and Paul Hunt. "A human-rights based approach to social impact assessment". *New Directions in Social Impact Assessment*. Ed. Frank Vanclay and Ana Maria Esteves. Cheltenham, UK: Edward Elgar Publishing Limited, 2011. 355–368. Print.

Mair, Rafe. "Tube the Pipelines, All Three". *The Tyee* 23 Jan. 2012. Web. 15 Feb. 2012.

Meissner, Dirk. "Northern Gateway hearings start in Kitimat, B.C. on $5.5 billion oil pipeline proposal". *The Canadian Press* 8 Jan. 2012. Web. 31 Mar. 2012.

Natural Resources Canada. "An open letter from the Honourable Joe Oliver, Minister of Natural Resources, on Canada's commitment to diversify our energy markets and the need to further streamline the regulatory process in order to advance Canada's national economic interest". *The Media Room* 9 Jan. 2012. Web. 15 Feb. 2012.

Nikiforuk, Andrew. "The Enbridge Dirty Dozen". *The Tyee* 31 Jul. 2010. Web. 2 Apr. 2012.

Nish, Simon and Sara Bice. "Community-based agreement making with land connected people". *New Directions in Social Impact Assessment*. Ed. Frank Vanclay and Ana Maria Esteves. Cheltenham, UK: Edward Elgar Publishing Limited, 2011. 59–77. Print.

O'Faircheallaigh, Ciaran. "Social impact assessment and Indigenous social development". *New Directions in Social Impact Assessment*. Ed. Frank Vanclay and Ana Maria Esteves. Cheltenham, UK: Edward Elgar Publishing Limited, 2011. 138–153. Print.

Panofsky, Sarah. *Managing Lessons from the Canyon: Aboriginal Engagement in the Enbridge Northern Gateway Environmental Assessment*. Thesis (MA). 2011. University of British Columbia, Vancouver.

Prescott-Allen, Robert. "Coast Information Team: review report". *Government of British Columbia*. 2005. Web. 21 Jun. 2011.

Ross, Helen. "Environmental mediation". *The International Handbook of Social Impact Assessment*. Ed. Henk A. Becker and Frank Vanclay. Cheltenham, UK: Edward Elgar Publishing Limited, 2011. 296–314. Print.

Sairinen, Rauno. "Environmental conflict mediation". *New Directions in Social Impact Assessment*. Ed. Frank Vanclay and Ana Maria Esteves. Cheltenham, UK: Edward Elgar Publishing Limited, 2011. 279–287. Print.

Sairinen, Rauno, Chris Barrow and Timo P. Karjalainen. "Environmental conflict mediation and social impact assessment: Approaches for enhanced environmental governance". *Environmental Impact Assessment Review* 30.5 (2010): 289–292. Print.

Save the Fraser Declaration. n.d. Web. 02 Apr. 2012.

Sinclair, A. John and Alan P. Diduck. "Public involvement in EA in Canada: a transformative learning perspective". *Environmental Impact Assessment Review* 21.2 (2001): 113–136. Print.

Smith, Merran and Art Sterritt. "From Conflict to Collaboration: The Story of the Great Bear Rainforest". *Forest Ethics*. 2007. Web. 30 Jun. 2011.

Stoymenoff, Alexis. "Enbridge Northern gateway protest in Bella Bella was "absolutely peaceful" ". *The Vancouver Observer* 2 Apr. 2012. Web. 17 Nov. 2012.

The Province. "Residents deserve answers to oil plans". *The Province (Editorial)* 29 Feb 2012. Web. 1 Apr. 2012.

–. "Nuxalk pull out of compromised pipeline review". *The Province* 8 Apr. 2012. Web. 17 Nov. 2012.

Vanclay, Frank. "International Principles For Social Impact Assessment". *Impact Assessment and Project Appraisal* 21.1 (2003): 5–11. Print.

Whittington, Les. "Titanic clash looms over proposed Northern Gateway pipeline". *The Star* 8 Jan. 2012. Web. 31 Mar. 2012.

Kim van Dam
Arctic Centre, University of Groningen

Inuit Governance in Nunavut: How to "Inuitize" a Public Government

Canada's newest Territory, Nunavut, was created in 1999 following years of negotiation between Inuit – the aboriginal people living in the eastern Arctic of Canada – and the Canadian Federal Government. Since the 1970s, the Federal Canadian Government had been negotiating unsettled land claims with its aboriginal peoples: First Nations and Inuit. In general, there is great variation in the way these negotiations have been conducted, the time span involved and in the results that were achieved. Still, over the years many land claims have been settled (Bone 193). These so-called comprehensive land claim settlements or "modern-day treaties" (Muir in Saku et al. 110) define new relationships between the aboriginal people of Canada and its federal, provincial and territorial governments (Saku et al. 110). In principle, these comprehensive land claims all involve clauses that allow aboriginal people to govern internal affairs and to assume greater responsibility in the use and management of land and wildlife (Bone 193). The Nunavut Land Claims Agreement between the Inuit of Nunavut and Canada, signed in 1993, is considered to be one of the most extensive and successful examples of such agreements (e.g. Hicks 21–53). What was particularly unique to this land claim was the provision made for the creation of a new territory, Nunavut, and the establishment of a territorial Government.[1] The Nunavut Territory and Government are public jurisdictions not based on ethnic principles, but since approximately 85% of the population is Inuit, Nunavut is generally referred to as the Inuit Homeland or Inuit Territory. In practical terms, the creation of Nunavut means that the Inuit have gained a form of self-government. In return for this, the Inuit have surrendered their aboriginal title to land and any rights to further land claims (Henderson 5–24).

It is not very often that new regions emerge. In that respect, Nunavut offers us "a rare opportunity to explore the creation of a new political jurisdiction within an established democratic state" (Henderson 7). In political geography and adjacent fields, regionalism receives much attention, as there are plenty of examples of regions within a certain nation state that strive for different levels of independence varying from having more say in e.g. cultural issues to complete autonomy

1 This land claim is the NLCA: the Nunavut Land Claims Agreement (1993).

or independence from the nation state (cf. Johnston et al; Paasi; Cresswell; Van Dam). What is unique in Nunavut's case is that the creation of a new region happens within the context of aboriginal population and their endeavour to obtain self-government (Van Dam 47, Légaré 65–89). The particularity of Nunavut is that aboriginal self-government is linked to the formation of a new geopolitical entity, the Territory of Nunavut, and a new political jurisdiction – the Nunavut Government. The latter is rooted in the Euro-Canadian political system, while the former – Inuit self-government – suggests a typical aboriginal form of government, based on traditional practices of "government," leadership and decision-making. The challenge of Nunavut's Inuit Leaders, then, is to make this duality work in practice as they not only have to build a new regional government, but more fundamentally, with Nunavut they are expected to create a place that does justice to Inuit culture and society (White 57, 58).

This paper aims to discuss what Inuit Governance entails in the context of the Inuit of Nunavut. How is Inuit self-government implemented in Nunavut's regional government, what has been done to do justice to Inuit culture, and what are the results of this? As such, it presents a case study of Native or aboriginal self-representation in the political theatre. This may be an example to other aboriginal peoples, but also has its limitations. First, I will provide a brief overview of Nunavut's political organisation and governance structure that is perhaps less straightforward than may be expected. Second, I will discuss one of the flagships of the political system in Nunavut and Inuit Governance in further detail: Nunavut Government. How has this institute of public government, which is not a government based on ethnic principles, given shape to Inuit Governance? I will consider some fundamental innovations to the mainstream political system that are based and inspired on Inuit culture, and as such have a direct relation with the majority population, the Inuit. After discussing some of the most obvious characteristics of Inuit Governance, this paper will end with some reflections on the limitations of this form of aboriginal self-government.

1. Governance structure: the institutes of government

On April 1, 1999, with ceremony and flag, Nunavut Territory and Government were officially launched. It marked the start of Inuit Governance in Nunavut, one that is essentially based on the principles of the Nunavut Land Claim Agreement, sometimes referred to as the second "constitution" of Nunavut (Jull 120–125). However, when discussing the case of Inuit Governance in Nunavut, it is not enough to just consider the territorial government. In fact, outsiders and novices to Nunavut may be surprised to find that "governance in Nunavut is remarkably complex, encompassing not only the territorial, but also the Federal Government, an extraordinary powerful aboriginal government, a set of constitutionally protected co-management boards dealing with wildlife and environmental regulation, and a full array of local community governments, all operating within the framework of the extensive governance provisions of a comprehensive land-claim agreement" (White 58). Indeed, on close inspection, self-government in Nunavut has led to an interesting mix of institutes and organisations, all with different powers, responsibilities and resources.

The first entity to consider when discussing Nunavut's political organiational structure is the Nunavut Government. Strictly speaking, the Nunavut Government is a public government and not an Inuit government (Hicks 22; Van Dam and Lucardie 23). According to many observers, the Inuit's willingness to accept a public government rather than an aboriginal self-government has been a decisive factor in the negotiations with the Canadian Federal Government (Hicks 22). The Inuit did not opt for a new type of organisation, so the government itself is rather conventional, much similar to any Canadian organisation (White 61). On the political level there is an elected parliament, while the administrative organisation or the bureaucracy is inherited from the pre-1999 Northwest Territories. Two new departments were introduced: the Department of Culture, Language, Elders and Youth (CLEY) and the Department of Sustainable Development. These two departments were one of the "institutional innovations" or "unique design feature" of NG, "explicitly designed to foster Inuit priorities" (White 62).

The second organisation to consider in the context of Inuit Governance is the Nunavut Tunngavik Incorporated (NTI). NTI is "the extraordinary powerful Aboriginal government" (White) in the aforementioned quote. Where Nunavut Government has to serve all of Nunavut's residents, regardless of ethnicity, NTI is exclusively representing the rights and interests of Inuit. In fact, some academics, such as for instance Légaré, Henderson and White, consider NTI to be the main representative of Inuit Governance. While NTI does not have the same powers as the territorial government, they are the representatives of all Inuit beneficiaries in Nunavut. The main difference with Nunavut Government is that NTI controls and manages land, namely the land that is collectively owned by the Inuit.[2] These

2 The Inuit, defined as "all those members of the aboriginal people, sometimes known as Eskimos, that has traditionally used and occupied, and currently uses and occupies, the lands and waters of the Nunavut Settlement Area" (NLCA 1993: 4), signed the land claim. To be an Inuit beneficiary an Inuit enrolment list was established, by a Designated Inuit Organisation, identified in the Land Claim, to enrol the names of all persons who are entitled to enrollment and as such entitled to benefit from the Agreement. For

Inuit Owned Lands, that were appointed in the NLCA, account for about 17% of the total land area of Nunavut Territory and include lands to which Inuit have sub-surface rights (2%); the remaining 83% are owned by the Crown (Federal Government) that also holds sub-surface rights to the remainder of the area. One important consequence of the collective land ownership is that future royalties that may come with resource development on these lands are channeled via NTI to the Inuit beneficiaries.

Thirdly, Nunavut's creation and the Inuit land claim have also resulted in the establishment of Nunavut's co-management bodies for wildlife, land use planning, water management, land rights and impact review. These co-management bodies are intermediate institutes between the different organisations that work in Nunavut, and they were established to "guarantee Inuit meaningful involvement and participation in decisions relating to the preservation and future development of lands within the Nunavut Settlement Area" (Nunavut Wildlife and Management Board). They are funded through the Federal Government but take directions from the Nunavut Land Claims Agreement. The boards of these institutes are composed of the regional Inuit organisations, the Nunavut Government, the Federal Government and an independent chair. In principle, half of the members of these boards must be Inuit, and at least half of the members must live in Nunavut. Unlike any of the other three organisations considered here, these co-management bodies do not have any political decision-making capacity, nor do they have independent resources or land ownership; however, they do reflect the dual nature of Nunavut or are unique to Nunavut's organisation – as it combines the public character with the ethnic – Inuit government.

Finally, also the Federal Government of Canada is an important factor in Nunavut's government structure. Given the status of a territory, the Federal Government has certain responsibilities in Nunavut.[3] Despite the fact that the Inuit – after signing the land claim – have ownership of part of the land, most of the land of Nunavut Territory (83%) is still in the hands of the Federal Government. This is directly related to Nunavut's present status as a Territory. More fundamentally, the implication is that most of the land of Nunavut Territory is "public land" or Crown land, owned and managed by the Federal Government of Canada. As this question of land ownership is fundamental to the future development of Nunavut, any discussion on

this procedure, a list of requirements is enclosed in the NLCA (Article 35: Enrolment) (NLCA 1993: 4, 5, and 235–239).

3 The Nunavut Act – often referred to as the constitution of Nunavut – is a Federal statute (Legislative Assembly of Nunavut n.d.) This means for example that only the Federal parliament can amend the Nunavut Act.

the future development of Nunavut has to include the Federal Government. Thus the Federal Government is an important partner for the Nunavut Government and Nunavut Tunngavik Incorporated. At a high political level this partnership is effectuated in negotiations about the implementation of the land claim and in the further devolution of powers. In the day-to-day government of Nunavut, the Federal Government is a partner in all the co-management bodies. This way, the Canadian Government is for example represented in the environmental assessments executed by the Nunavut Impact and Review Board.

With all these governmental bodies, the "Nunavut project" (Légaré 336) has resulted in a complicated governance structure and a complicated mix of powers, responsibilities and resources distributed between the different agencies. Just because of the separation of the "ethnic" and the "public" character in government, there are now a public territorial government, an Inuit organisation, and many intermediate organisations. And because of the territorial status of its government, powers and resources of the regional government are limited, requiring more presence of the Federal Government in the Territory than in any other Canadian jurisdiction.

Of all these bodies, it is in particular the birthright organisation NTI that truly brings in another dimension to governance in Nunavut. In effect, some say there are two political systems in Nunavut, creating a duality in political life (Henderson 138). On the one hand, there is the elected public government, the Nunavut Government, which is there for all (Canadian) residents of Nunavut, and on the other hand there are partly elected Inuit organisations for Inuit beneficiaries.

Finally it is worth noting, as Légaré does, that the duality that characterizes Inuit Governance in Nunavut is also reflected in the organisation structure of these institutes of governance themselves (74). The internal organisation of the Nunavut Government and NTI is inspired by the Euro-Canadian mode of organisation and as such they do not reflect Inuit traditions or customs (Légaré 75). According to Légaré this has helped dealing with other organisations, such as the Federal Government and – in the case of NTI – with the Territorial Government. However: "this highly centralized and bureaucratized mode of operation is foreign to Inuit traditional decision-making and has raised some concerns among Inuit beneficiaries" (75).

2. Inuit values in political organisation

In this complex organisational structure, the Nunavut Government is – perhaps more than NTI – most often associated with Inuit self-government and self-determination. For many, the Nunavut Government is synonymous with Inuit Governance. However, the duality of being a public government, serving a majority of Inuit population, is also reflected in the Nunavut Government itself.

One of the key challenges of the Nunavut Government – as defined by the Inuit Tapirisat of Canada – is to adhere to Inuit cultural values and perspectives. How does Nunavut Government then enable the Inuit to control their own political, social and economic agendas?

In general, the parliament and government organisation of Nunavut functions like any other territorial or provincial government in Canada. The true task of Nunavut Government has been to bring Inuit values and culture into a system that is quite foreign to these values and culture (White 58). In order to do so, Nunavut Government has introduced some variations to the conventional Euro-Canadian style of government. This section will first discuss three of these Nunavut "twists" to Canadian public government: the principle of consensus, decentralization and Inuit representation in government. Although these are principles (consensus, decentralization, representation) that are relevant ingredients in most governments, the Nunavut project adds a typical Inuit-inspired flavour to this. Second, the principle of Inuit Qaujimajatuqangit ("what Inuit know") will be considered, as this has become the principle in Nunavut's political arena.

2.1 Consensus, decentralisation and representation

The first eye-catching adjustment to the Euro-Canadian style of Government is the introduction of consensus as the decision-making principle in parliament (Henderson 112–113). While Nunavut's parliamentary system and the constitutional principles are based on the Westminster model of parliament (Hicks and White 30–116), it has been adapted to fit the traditional culture of the Inuit by introducing consensus (O'Brien). Generally, this is linked to traditional decision-making in Inuit society that was based on consensus (Vlessidis 118–127, Mitchell 299; Henderson 112). The Inuit did not have a collective leader for all Inuit: decision-making was done mainly within the family groups and was prompted by the practical demands of daily life (Bennett and Rowley 95–98). Law and rules were passed in the oral tradition, and in particular Elders were responsible for seeing that laws were adhered to (Nuturak).[4] The tradition of consensual agreement and the goal of restoring harmony in the community or group was an important Inuit cultural trait (Grant 19). For the survival of the collective, it was important that there were no disputes, and people consented to and supported any decision that was made. It is this trait that has been linked to the running of Nunavut Government.

---

4 Elders have a row of seats in the Chamber directly behind the Members of the Assembly. This symbolically recognizes the important role of Elders in Inuit society.

One profound difference of this consensus style with the conventional parliamentary system is the absence of political parties in the Legislative Assembly of Nunavut. All members of the Legislative Assembly (MLAs) represent their constituency as an independent member: decisions are made based on consensus of the majority of its members, and not along party political lines. Another central concept to the consensus government in Nunavut is the fact that the Premier, the Ministers (together forming the Executive) and the Speaker are chosen from the 19 elected Members of the Assembly.

Nunavut's consensus government is referred to as fitting the people of Nunavut and more in particular: the Inuit. It is said to be in line with "Aboriginal values of maximum cooperation, effective use of leadership resources and common accountability" (Nunavut Government). At the same time, this consensus type of government is combined with more general objectives of modern democracies such as openness, accountability and transparency. In this way, the Nunavut style of consensus government roots the modern governmental practices in the contemporary Inuit society. By focusing on the links to traditional Inuit values and decision-making, this modern practice is embedded in Inuit traditions. This is an important process, as the parliamentary system itself is indeed foreign to traditional Inuit life. The underlying principles are inspired by important Inuit values that give this special Nunavut flavor: working together, cooperation, consensual decision-making based on compromises that everyone can feel comfortable with, and avoiding direct confrontation. These values are brought into a system that may have been foreign to traditional Inuit society, but the consensus trait helps to root this alien system in Inuit society of today.

A second trait of Nunavut's government is decentralization. As with the principle of consensus, the decentralization of the Nunavut Government has been a key issue for Nunavut's first Government. According to White, it was one of the unique design features of government (57–83). The key principle was that not only regional offices were to be spread around in the Territory, but also the so-called headquarter functions, typically located in capital cities, had to be dispersed into the communities of Nunavut (White 57–83). The main motivation for doing so was that it would better serve and reflect the people of Nunavut, which is a territory where people have always lived in localized small groups. Although less explicitly than with the consensus principle, the decentralization policy too was said to be rooted in Inuit ways of doing as it better suited the traditional Inuit political culture, which was locally based (Hicks and White 30–116). As Nunavummiut still live in relative isolation from other communities, including the capital Iqaluit, it was felt by Nunavut Government that the organisation should be decentralized so that as many communities as possible could benefit from the creation of the government. A major motivation for a decentralization policy was based on economic arguments: decentralization would bring government jobs to the communities thus increasing employment and training opportunities. This would help to diversify the economies and would enhance building capacity (Nunavut Government). Another motivation was the need to overcome the great distances within the territory, and as such decentralization was partly rooted in Nunavut's physical features. To have the territorial government in the communities would limit the necessity for job seekers to relocate in order to find work and in addition, the spreading of government over the communities would improve access by local people to programs and services and motivate the Inuit to participate in the administrative system (Hicks and White 30–116). In short, decentralization would bring the government to the people (Hicks and White 30–116). In addition, a major impetus for decentralization was the idea that not only jobs, but also power would be transferred to the regional and local level.

About 400 jobs were to be decentralized; in 2004, 68% of the decentralized positions had indeed been filled.[5] Certainly in absolute numbers decentralization is progressing into the communities, both by people being transferred with their departments to communities and by new employees hired in locally. Although as White states it may be too early to draw any final conclusions on the success of decentralisation (2009), the efforts of the Nunavut Government have been heavily criticised, also publically by the editor of the regional newspaper Nunatsiaq News (Bell). The criticism focused on the lack of planning, the fact that highly specialized jobs were hard to decentralize, and the inadequate housing facilities for staff. Also, decision-making power has not been truly transferred. Finally, although there have been many centrifugal effects with organisations moving out of the capital city Iqaluit, also some centripetal forces have worked much in favor of Iqaluit. This has led some critics to say that Iqaluit is well on its way to

---

5 Based on: Return to Written Questions No. 26–2 (2), asked by Mr. Peterson March 1, 2005, Status of Decentralization; tabled April 26, 2005 (Legislative Assembly of Nunavut 1999). There is an unexplained discrepancy of 4 positions in the data provided in the Return. The number of vacancies is 143; implying that 316 positions are filled. However, in answer to an additional question relating to the type of contract (indeterminate or term basis), 312 positions are considered (Legislative Assembly of Nunavut Hansard: March 1, 2005).

becoming another Yellowknife[6] now it is "successfully re-colonized by Nunavut's social and political elite" (Bell).

A third unique variation to the conventional public government design is that of Inuit representation. As stated in the Nunavut Land Claims Agreement, the Nunavut government was to be a representative government, meaning that in the political and the bureaucratic organisation 85% should be Inuit (Nunavut Land Claims Agreement). From the start in 1999 onwards, politically, the composition of the Legislative Assembly of Nunavut reflected the majority population of Nunavut. Inuktitut is frequently spoken in the House, and all the official documents, including the report of debates in the House, are available in Inuktitut. Politically then, measured by the number of politicians or elected members, the Nunavut Government is a representative government, communicating in the language of the people. But being a representative government also means that 85% of the workforce of the Nunavut Government and its agencies should be Inuit, a principle that was at the heart of the land claims agreement (Berger iii). Although there has been an increase in absolute numbers and a slight increase ratio-wise, the current Inuit representation level has stayed behind the 85% required for a representative government. The level of representation has been more or less stable at approximately 45%, with over-representation in administrative functions and under-representation in higher management jobs. That the numbers are not increasing is according to observer Berger not caused by the Nunavut Government not hiring enough Inuit employees but rather by the fact that the supply of qualified Inuit is exhausted (Berger iii). The Government requires qualified Inuit for executive, management and professional positions –positions currently taken by non-Inuit – but there are not enough Inuit that have these qualifications. Many Inuit have the skills and capacity that are needed in a modern Euro Canadian bureaucracy such as being a specialist or having experience. However, their number is too low, and there is a strong competition with other organisations such as NTI and the Federal Government for qualified Inuit (White 57–83). According to Berger, the present educational system in Nunavut, and especially the level of language development, limit Inuit chances of accessing a job in government (Berger iii). One of the consequences of the fact that many jobs are taken by non-Inuit is that the dominant language spoken in administration is English. This potentially creates an obstacle not only between the non-Inuit workforce and the Inuktitut

6 When Nunavut was still part of the Northwest Territories, Yellowknife was also "their" territorial capital. As such, Yellowknife came to be synonymous for the territorial bureaucracy that was both in a physical and a mental sense set far away from the people of Nunavut.

speaking Inuit politicians, but moreover, for the Inuit who don't master English as a second language to enrol in government jobs (Berger iii).

2.2. Inuit Qaujimajatuqangit

The consensus style of government, the decentralisation efforts and the challenge of creating a representational workforce all have contributed – at least to some extent – to transforming the existing government structures to better fit the Inuit population. However, the Nunavut Government realized it needed more to create a government that was truly based on Inuit cultural values. In this respect, the concept of Inuit Qaujimajatuqangit needs to be considered. Inuit Qaujimajatuqangit literally means "that what has been long known by Inuit" or "the Inuit way of doing things". Often it is used exclusively to refer to traditional knowledge, but it is more properly defined as: "the Inuit way of doing things: the past, present and future knowledge, experience and values of Inuit Society" (IQ Task Force 4). Inuit Qaujimajatuqangit is also described as knowledge obtained from the knowledge of Inuit elders pertaining to language, culture, values and beliefs, survival skills, use of resources, humane and sustainable harvesting, and the understanding of society, ecology and the environment (Nunavut Government).[7] It refers not only to experience, the knowledge and values of the past, but also includes the present and future (IQ Task Force 4). Gradually, over the first decade of Nunavut Government's running, Inuit Qaujimajatuqangit has become the leading political principle, giving shape to Inuit Governance in Nunavut.

The origins of Inuit Qaujimajatuqangit (abbreviation: IQ) in Nunavut Government politics can be found at a workshop in Igloolik on traditional knowledge in Nunavut, organised by the Nunavut Social Development Council (NSDC) (Henderson 1003–1004). In these early years, Inuit Qaujimajatuqangit was mainly discussed in the context of Traditional Ecological Knowledge,[8] thus referring to matters of the environment. However, over the years, IQ has outgrown this pure

---

7 Powerpoint presentation entitled "Sustainable Development's Inuit Qaujimanituqangit" obtained from Nunavut Legislative Assembly Library (Nunavut Government n.d.-b). The Department of Sustainable Development proposed to use Qaujimanituqangit instead of Qaujimajatugangit; the first has less passive connotation.

8 Berkes *et al.* in their article "Rediscovery of Traditional Ecological Knowledge as Adaptive Management" (2000) interpret this as a cumulative body of knowledge, practices and representations that describes the relationships of living beings with one another and with their physical environment, which evolved by adaptive processes and has been handed down through generations by cultural transmission. As the notion is often referred to by the abreviation TEK, capital letters are used here.

ecological interpretation and its application has become more general, incorporating other areas of life as well. It became a highly politicized concept, symbolic on how well the Nunavut Government is introducing Inuit culture and lifestyle into politics. Right from the start (2000), the Nunavut Government has worked on polices to incorporating IQ into policies, programs and services of Nunavut government "...in order to best meet the requirements of the majority of the population served by the new Government" (Nunavut Government 2000 3). Minister Kattuk for instance stated: "[w]e believe that the values of Inuit Qaujimajatuqangit will enhance the identity, pride and self-esteem of Nunavummiut" (Kattuk). IQ should not only provide direction to government; it also reflects the expectations of Nunavummiut. This was not an easy task. In the mid 2000s, a special IQ Task Force was installed to make recommendations to the Government on how to incorporate IQ and they defined the four basic relationships that are central to Inuit culture as the starting points for this: the relationship with the land, the relationship with one's family, the relationship with one's own inner spirit and lastly the relationship with one's own social grouping (community, organisation) and between social groupings (see Table 1) (IQ Task Force 12,13).

Table 1: IQ principles and relationships in Inuit Culture (simplified) by IQ Task Force

Relationship	IQ principle
With the land	Avatittinnik Kamattiarniq ("environmental stewardship") Qanuqtuurniq ("improvise with what is at hand")
With family	Pijitsirnjiq ("service")
With own spirit	Pilnimmaksarniq ("learning through practice")
With own social grouping	Piliriqatigiinigiq ("collaborative relationships") Aajiqatigiingniq ("consensus decision-making")

In 2003, the Nunavut Government intensified the incorporating of IQ in organisation and policy as many departments, for example the Department of Sustainable Development, struggled with the question on how to do this (Van Dam). In order to do so, the Nunavut Government established the 'Inuit Qaujimajatuqangit Katimajiit' or Elders' Council, a group of people from outside government to advise and comment on IQ issues and an advisory body to assist the government to integrate Inuit traditions, values and vision into service delivery and operation[9] (Akesuk).

9 Akesuk, Minister Statement 142–1 (6) Legislative Assembly of Nunavut Hansard: March 24, 2003.

Also the "Tuqtarviit" was established, a group of people from the departments of Nunavut Government to work on IQ issues and initiatives.[10] Finally, all departments installed a "Tuqtarvik" or IQ co-ordinator within the department to deal with issues within the department. According to the Government, this is a significant step towards a cross-government coordinated approach to IQ (Nunavut Government). Beside these practical measures, IQ also became prominent in the main policy document, the Pinasuaqtavut 2004–2009. In this document, eight guiding principles of IQ are defined (see Table 2). With that, these IQ principles have become central to the policy of Nunavut Government.

Table 2: Inuit Qaujimajatuqangit in Pinasuaqtavut: 2004–2009

Guiding principle	English explanation
Inuuqatigiitsiarniq	Respecting others, relationships and caring for people
Tunnganarniq	Fostering good spirit by being open, welcoming and inclusive
Pijitsirniq	Serving and providing for family and/or community
Aajiiqatigiinniq	Decision making through discussion and consensus
Pilimmaksarniq Pijariuqsarniq	Development of skills through practice, effort and action
Piliriqatigiinniq Ikajuqtigiinniq	Working together for a common cause
Qanuqtuurniq	Being innovative and resourceful
Avatittinnik Kamatsiarniq	Respect and care for the land, animals and the environment

So, over the last ten years by introducing IQ into the government of Nunavut, Inuit culture and society has become leading in the political organisation and general policy of Nunavut Government. By doing so, the conventional Euro-Canadian type of government has clearly been "Inuitized." Of course, one of the difficult things is defining what traditional Inuit culture is (White 57–83). After all, considering the fact that "traditionally" Inuit lived in isolated, localized groups, Inuit culture has many local and regional variations. It is questionable if having one guiding principle does justice to these differences.

However, on a more fundamental level, the issue is how the rather broad general principles of IQ can be implemented and merged with the "culture and operation"

10 The members of Tuqtarviit are the Tuqtarvik or Coordinators of all Departments of Nunavut Government (Terms of Reference in: Nunavut Government (2003).

of an essentially Euro-Canadian bureaucracy (White). White argues that symbolically, allowing people to go out hunting and to introduce Elders in development and have staff members go on an IQ workshop is fine, but it will not fundamentally change the nature of government. Many aspects of modern bureaucracy – such as hierarchy, formal rules and such – are completely alien to key elements of Inuit culture. This ethno-cultural motivated issue continues to be a major challenge for the public government that Nunavut Government is (White 57–83). A challenge Nunavut Government has to face in order to comply with the agreements set out in the land claim, and to do justice to the largest segment of its population.

3. Discussion and conclusion

This paper sketches how the Inuit of Nunavut have built the territory and the region as an example of aboriginal self-government in the context of a new geopolitical jurisdiction. All things considered, it is safe to say that Nunavut is one of the most far-reaching examples of how aboriginal people have regained power within their nation states. The Inuit have done this in a unique way. Instead of asking for self-government, they have chosen to fulfil these ambitions with a conventional public government with a mandate common for these types of government. A few observations can be made.

First of all, Nunavut Government is only one of the many institutions that play a role in Inuit Governance. In fact, at close inspection Inuit Governance is rather complicated, with a complicated mix of power, responsibilities and resources shared by these organisations. Strictly speaking, Nunavut has no aboriginal self-government – the Inuit have never asked for that as such. Because of the distinction between "ethnic" and "public" there are now a public government, an Inuit organisation, and many intermediate organisations. Added to that is the territorial status of its government, limiting the powers and resources of the regional government and requiring more presence of the Federal Government in the territory than in any other Canadian jurisdiction. Another difference with other aboriginal forms of self-government in Canada is that this is mostly organised at the local level – it is usually local government. The paradox in Nunavut is that although for the Inuit the local level is very important, there is no aboriginal or Inuit self-government present on the local level (White 57–83).

Second, Nunavut Government and NTI are not designed following traditional Inuit governance structures and leadership. In essence, it is miles away from that. Nevertheless, Nunavut Government has successfully introduced new Inuit elements into the conventional Euro-Canadian government structure. The three values discussed here – consensus, decentralization and representation – are based on Inuit values and culture. Although these principles are familiar or common in democracies and government policies, in Nunavut they are redefined and referred to as "typically Nunavut". As such they have become important markers that have helped to unify Nunavut by linking the state to the cultural identity of the majority population. This is an important argument used to root the further non-traditional form of government among the people. Although still much needs to be done on these issues, important steps to transform the non-traditional way of government have been made. In that respect, state building and region building have been quite successful in Nunavut. Rightly Légaré, a Canadian geographer, notes: "undoubtedly though, to this day, Nunavut's biggest success has been its contribution in creating a civic regional identity consciousness among the Inuit of the Canadian Central and Eastern Arctic." (41).

Third, despite these "Nunavut twists" to conventional Euro-Canadian government, many observers note, time and again, that the governance system is in essence foreign to traditional Inuit culture and society. With Inuit Qaujimajatuqangit as the main leading principle, Nunavut Government has introduced important Inuit values into the governance system. Over the first decade of Nunavut's existence as a region, Inuit Qaujimajatuqangit has become the main guiding policy concept. In many ways, Inuit Qaujimajatuqangit has become the politicized version of what was earlier referred to as Inuit culture, lifestyle and knowledge. It brings together "all that all Inuit know" in the format required to make policy: in defined guiding principles that government organisations can work with, and in a meeting and consultation structure to involve Inuit. One of the consequences of this is that it works to unify and create a collective system of knowledge. In this political version of Inuit Qaujimajatuqangit, regional or local differences in "what Inuit know" disappear. It remains to be seen if with the introduction of IQ the Nunavut Government has succeeded in "incorporating itself in Inuit culture" as was suggested by a group of Inuit experts. But, as it is now formulated as the main guiding principle for most important policy documents, the concept of Inuit Qaujimajatuqangit may be the "best scenario" to reach the desired "Inuit corporate culture of government". It is too soon to tell if this successfully transforms the organisation and policies to better fit Inuit culture, – you don't change corporate culture overnight – but it certainly offers many interesting new leads into doing just that. In that respect, the limitations of Inuit governance are set by the hard standards of today's Nunavut society. Serving about 32.000 people living in an area as big as half Europe, in an Arctic climate, is challenging for any government. Due to the size of the territory, in combination with a small dispersed population and the physical Arctic circumstances, Nunavut

Government faces – for instance – exceptionally high health, fuel and energy costs. Added to that is the overall financial position of Nunavut Government. As a territorial government, depending on a Federal grant and with a low revenue and tax base (Légaré 134), Nunavut Government has little spending room.

However, ultimately the success of the Nunavut project will be weighed against the vitality of the present and future Inuit population. Nunavut's society has some serious issues that need to be addressed as soon as possible. For instance, there are a number of urgent social problems, and the economic base is very small and weak. As Légaré argues, having a territorial government alone is not enough to meet all the challenges that Nunavut's population faces (144). Nunavut's fiscal dependency and its weak economy are both affecting the successful implementation of the NLCA. All considered, political autonomy and self-government does not secure the lives of Inuit, and economic development is much needed to meet all the ambitions set in the policy documents of Nunavut Government (Légaré 23–56). In that respect, much is expected of future resource development: Nunavut is rich in natural resources, and exploitation of these may bring the much-needed economic revenues.

And that finally brings us to Nunavut's territorial status within Canada, including issues of land ownership and resource development. With provinces Nunavut shares many powers (health, education and so on), but there are important differences that should be acknowledged. Due to the territorial status, Nunavut Government owns no land, and thus collects no revenues from any resource development. Except for the 18% Inuit-owned land, as the main landowner, the Federal Government is still in control of land and resource development. This means that all the revenues of development on these lands will flow directly to the Federal Government in Ottawa, while the revenues of the remaining 18% Inuit-owned land flow to the Inuit organisation NTI. The financial situation of the Nunavut Government then is that they have very little power over their budget. What the Territory receives comes directly from Ottawa, and thus Nunavut's spending basis is limited. In the mid-00s, negotiations were to start concerning the devolution of powers from the Federal Government to the Nunavut Government on issues like land ownership and resource development. This is linked to the territorial ambition towards being able to deliver full service to its population and thus further self-reliance and self-sufficiency. However, the Government in Canada did not proceed with these negotiations (Légaré 135) and left the devolution process "dormant" (Nunatsiaq News). In 2012, with the appointment of a chief negotiator, the former Harper government re-started and opened the process (Nunatsiaq News).

In conclusion, the great paradox of Nunavut is that future resource development revenues – much needed to overcome the social and economic problems in the Territory – flow to the main Inuit organisation, NTI, an organisation that does not have the same governmental powers and responsibility as the territorial government. And this in a situation in which the institute that has this power, Nunavut Government, does not have the means to deliver what the Inuit population needs. In this case, it seems that the deliberate choice for making a clear-cut distinction between the public (Nunavut Government) and the ethnic (NTI) side of Inuit governance may actually backfire on the Inuit.

Works cited

Bennett, J. and S. Rowley, eds. *Uqaluriat. An Oral History of Nunavut.* Montreal and Kingston: McGill-Queen's University Press, 2004. Print.

Bell, J. "Book review: a Starry-eyed egghead's view of Nunavut. A Review of Nunavut: Inuit regain control of their lands and their lives". *Nunatsiaq News* 11 May 2001. Web.

Bell, J.. "Go slow on devolution, report urges. Okalik's reaction lukewarm, but he says it's a good start". *Nunatsiaq News* 15 June 2007. Web 23 July 2012.

Berger, T.R.. *The Nunavut Project: Conciliator's Final Report. Nunavut Land Claims Agreement Implementation Contract Negotiations for the Second Planning Period 2003–2013.* Web 24 November 2006.

Bone, R.M.. *The Geography of the Canadian North: Issues and Challenges.* 2nd Edition. Don Mills: Oxford University Press, 2003. Print.

Creswell, T. *Place, a Short Introduction.* Malden: Blackwell Publishing. Print.

Grant, S. *Arctic Justice: on Trial for Murder, Pond Inlet 1923.* Montreal and Kingston: McGill-Queens University Press, 2002. Print.

Henderson, Ailsa. "Inuit Qaujimajatuqangit". *Encyclopaedia of the Arctic.* Ed. M. Nuttall. New York: Routledge, 2003. Print.

–. "Northern Political Culture? Political Behaviour in Nunavut". *Études/Inuit?Studies* 28.1 (2004): 133–154. Print.

–. *Nunavut: rethinking Political Culture.* Vancouver: UBC, 2007. Print.

–. "Lessons for Social Science in the Study of New Policies: Nunavut at 10". *Journal of Canadian Studies* 43.2 (2009): 5–24. Web 25 Jan. 2012.

Hicks, J. "The Nunavut Land Claim and the Nunavut Government: Political Structures of Self-government in Canada's Eastern Arctic". *Dependency, Autonomy, Sustainability in the Arctic.* Ed. H.K. Petersen and B. Poppel. Aldershot: Ashgate, 1999. 21–53. Print.

Hicks, J. and G. White. "Nunavut: Inuit self-determination through a land claim and public government?" *Nunavut. Inuit regain control of their lands and their lives.* Ed. J. Dahl, J. Hicks and P. Jull. Copenhagen: IWGIA Document No.12, 2000. 30–116. Print.

IQ Task Force. *The first annual report of the Inuit Qaujimajatuqangit (IQ) task force.* Legislative Assembly of Nunavut: tabled document 97–1 (6), tabled 24 March 2003. Print.

Johnston, R. J., D. Gregory, G. Pratt and Michael Watts eds. *Dictionary of Human Geography.* 4th Edition. Oxford, Malden: Blackwell Publishers. Print.

Jull, Peter. "The World looks North". *Nunavut 99.* M. Soublière. Iqaluit: Nortext Multimedia, 1998. 120–125. Print.

Légaré, André. "Canada's Experiment with Aboriginal Self-Determination in Nunavut: from Vision to Illusion". *International Journal on Minority and Group Rights* 15 (2008): 335–367. Print.

–. "The Construction of Nunavut. The Impact of the Nunavut Project on Inuit Identity, Governance, and Society". Diss. University of Saskatchewan, 2010.

–. "Le Nunavut: entre le rêve et la réalité. Bilan de dix années d'autonomie gouvernementale inuite et prospective socio-économique". *Journal of Canadian Studies* 43.2 (2009): 23–58. Web 24 Jan. 2012.

Mitchell, M.. *From talking chiefs to a native cooperate elite. The birth of class and nationalism among Canadian Inuit elite.* Montreal and Kingston: McGill-Queen's University Press, 1996. Print.

Nunatsiaq News. *Ottawa names Nunavut devolution negotiator.* 22 May 2012. Web 23 July 2012.

Nunavut Government – a. *Information Sheet Consensus Government.* n.d. 19 Nov. 2008. http://www.gov.nu.ca/english/about/cg.pdf.

Nunavut Government – b. *Sustainable Development's Inuit Qaujimajatuqangit.* Obtained from Nunavut Legislative Assembly Library. Iqaluit, n.d. Powerpoint Presentation.

Nunavut Government. *Report from the September Inuit Qaujimajatuqangit Workshop, Niaqunngnut, Nunavut, September 29–30, 1999.* Tabled Document 72–1 (3), tabled on 11 April 2000. Print.

Nunavut Government. "Inuit Qaujimajatuqangit guideline document released". *Nunavut Government News Release.* 24 July 2000. Print.

Nunavut Government. *Building Nunavut through Decentralization: Evaluation Report* Millennium Partners. Tabled document 18–1, 2 May 2002.

Nunavut Government. *Inuit Qaujimajatuqangit in the Government. First Report 1999–2003.* Tabled Document 174–1 (6), 4 December 2003. Print.

Nunavut Land Claims Agreement. *Agreement between the Inuit of the Nunavut Settlement Area and Her Majesty the Queen in the right of Canada*. Ottawa: Ministry of Indian Affairs and Northern Development and the Tunngavik, 1993. Print.

Nunavut Wildlife and Management Board. Web. 27 July 2012.

Nutarak, J.. "Parliamentary development from footprints in the snow." *Canada: a federation of democracies*. London: General Council of the Commonwealth Parliamentary Association, 2004. Print.

O'Brien, K.. "Some thoughts on consensus government in Nunavut". *Canadian Parliamentary Review* 16.4 (2003): 6–10. Print.

Paasi, A. "Europe as a Social Process and Discourse. Considerations of Place, Boundaries and Identity." *European Urban and Regional Studies* 8.1 (2001): 7–28. Print.

Saku, J.C., R.M. Bone and G. Duhaime. "Towards an institutional understanding of comprehensive land claim agreements in Canada". *Études/Inuit/Studies* 22.1 (1998): 109–121. Print.

Van Dam, K. and P. Lucardie. "Territorial and Ethnic Identities in Canada: Nationalism in Nunavut and Quebec". *Re-exploring Canadian Space/Redécouvrir l'espace canadien*. Ed. J. den Toonder and B. van Hoven. Groningen: Barkhuis Press Groningen, 2012. 13–26. Print.

Van Dam, K.I.M. *A Place called Nunavut. Multiple Identities for a New Region*. Diss. University of Groningen 2008. Print.

Vlessidis, M.. "Public Government". *Nunavut 99*. M. Soublière. Iqaluit: Nortext, Multimedia, 1998. 118–127. Print.

White, Graham. "Governance in Nunavut: Capacity vs. Culture?" *Journal of Canadian Studies* 43.2 (2009): 57–83 Web 25 Jan. 2012.

Merel de Buck
Department of Cultural Anthropology, Utrecht University

Contesting Citizenship: Educational Practices in an Indigenous Mixtec Community in Mexico

The rise of multicultural, neoliberal states in Latin America since the 1990s made room for Indigenous peoples to redefine the meaning of citizenship (Jackson and Warren 2005, Mattiace 2003, Postero 2007, Van Cott 2005, Warren 1998, Yashar 1999). Whereas before Indigenous peoples had to sacrifice their cultures to become part of homogenous nation-states, nowadays struggles are waged for an alternative citizenship model in which Indigenous identities are recognized and economic and social resources redistributed (Jackson & Warren 2005, Mattiace 2003). As a result, Indigenous movements face a new dilemma of how to reconcile inclusive national citizenship with special, Indigenous rights.

Caught in this dilemma, Indigenous movements contest the boundaries and practices of citizenship. A key field where this contestation takes place is that of education. In Mexico, various social movements have taken education into their own hands as a response to the partial exclusion of Indigenous peoples from the public education system and their unequal treatment within it. Alternative educational projects are often inspired by the vibrant tradition of popular education in Latin America, which explicitly links education to social and political transformations that favor popular classes.

Education and schooling is often understood in terms of a citizenship factory (García 2005: 12). In this logic, education institutions promote particular identities and orient moral conduct for group life. What does that mean for social movements' engagement in the field of education? Spindler (1987) expressed long ago that from an anthropological perspective, all education is citizenship education. As such, alternative educational projects inherently foster the consolidation of alternate identities and societies, which would make them counter-hegemonic citizenship projects.

In this article, I examine the "liberating education" [*educación liberadora*] project of CACTUS, a civil society organization active in Oaxaca, Mexico. In 2007, the group founded a preparatory school in the Indigenous community of Santos Reyes Tepejillo. For CACTUS, the school was a response to the right of Indigenous people to education, but also served as an instrument to trigger emancipatory processes in the community. Accordingly, the educational model and organizational structure of the school cultivated notions such as autonomy, social critique and the strengthening of Indigenous identity, knowledge, language and communal ways of life. I analyze this micro-political phenomenon to gain insight into how Indigenous movements engage with larger dilemmas of national versus Indigenous citizenship demands, hence I study the project as an integral part of social struggles over the meaning of citizenship and the reconfiguration of Indigenous peoples' relationship to the state.

Following in the footsteps of Lazar (2010), my intention is to contribute to the ethnographic work that explores citizenship as social practice (García 2005, Holston 2008, Lazar 2010, Ong 2006, Postero 2007). Of particular relevance is Ong's (1999) argument that citizenship is a dual process of self-making and being-made within power relations linked to the state and its subjects. In this logic, I envision the school as a field of encounter and conflict: a place where the contestation and negotiation of the meaning of citizenship takes place between the state, social movements and local community. More specifically, I examine the social practices of teachers to show what kinds of citizens, with what kind of knowledge, values, political agency and dispositions they seek to shape and how this intersects with the distinct aspirations and practices of schooling employed by students and parents (Levinson 2011).

This article starts by exploring the scholarly debate on social struggles between Indigenous movements and contemporary Latin American states. After that, I examine discussions on citizenship formation as social practice inside and outside the classroom. In the ethnographic account that follows, I assess these theoretical discussions by analyzing the social dynamics of the schooling project of CACTUS in the Mexican state of Oaxaca.

1. Contesting citizenship and neoliberal multicultural states in Latin America

Struggles over the meanings of citizenship are a recurrent theme in the recent literature on neoliberal and multicultural states in Latin America (Fischer 2009, Postero 2007, Yashar 2005). In the twentieth century, Latin American states promised citizenship to Indigenous peoples in exchange to relinquishing their customs, lands and languages. This nationalizing and homogenizing project attempted to assimilate Indigenous people into a mainstream *mestizo* society (Stavenhagen 2002: 28). Since the beginning of the 1990s, the terms of this project altered when various states adopted forms of multiculturalism in an effort to enhance the participation of Indigenous people in politics and to remedy histories of ethnic and racial domination. However, several scholars agree on the failure of the constitutional reforms to profoundly change unequal power relations (Hale 2002, Postero 2007, Rockwell 2010). Rockwell (2010: 165) writes about a "depoliticized version of multiculturalism" when referring to the new multicultural states, where cultural difference is recognized in a way that restricts actual possibilities for land reform, local autonomy and material justice in Indigenous communities.

Throughout the 1980s, the implementation of neoliberal reforms and democratization by Latin American states opened up new spaces for activism and created conditions for new Indigenous identities (Yashar 2005). Citizenship has been articulated in new ways by Indigenous movements which demand a redefinition of their relationships with the state. They seek to rework the meaning of citizenship so that cultural difference is no longer a criterion for exclusion, but one of inclusion in a multicultural political community (García 2005: 165). Indigenous movements articulate Indigenous citizenship on the basis of cultural identity and a differentiated organization within a country. Several scholars have studied the tensions that accompany these new articulations of citizenship which center on the conflict between enhancing political inclusion in the nation on the one hand and preserving difference on the other (De la Peña 1999, Fischer 2009, García 2005, Jackson & Warren 2005, Mattiace 2003, Postero and Zamosc 2004, Smith 2007, Yashar 2005). Gustafson (2009: 232) refers to "the paradoxical stance of indigenous movements": movements make claims on the basis of special, Indigenous citizenship, while demanding state resources based on the notion of regular citizenship rights. The underlying anthropological debate revolves around the question of how to reconcile inclusive national citizenship with multiculturalism and measures of autonomy. In this article, I analyze how this dilemma plays out in the politics and citizenship claims articulated by CACTUS in their community-schooling project.

2. Citizenship education as social practice

While many social theories pay particular attention to rights and responsibilities in accounts of state-citizen relations, I would like to connect to those studies that approach citizenship primarily as social practice (Holston 2008, Lazar 2010, Ong 2006, Postero 2007). Ong has made substantial contributions to the field when she analyzed citizenship by emphasizing agency as well as broader power relations: "cultural citizenship is a dual process of self-making and being-made within webs of power linked to the nation-state and civil society. Becoming a citizen depends on how one is constituted as a subject who exercises or submits to power relations" (1999: 264). In this article, I draw further on the work of scholars who approach citizenship in a processual manner and conceptualize it as a bundle of practices constituting the relationship between individuals and the state (Lazar 2008: 5).

The study of citizenship has become a prominent topic in political anthropology, but less so in the anthropology of education. Since all education constructs identity and orients moral conduct for group life, the study of the relationship between citizenship and educational processes becomes essential (Spindler 1987). Levinson defines citizenship education as "(…) efforts of societies and social groups to educate their members to imagine their social belonging and exercise their participation as (democratic) citizens" (2011: 284). He urges anthropologists to focus on the broader political implications of schooled identities by raising several questions: "what kinds of citizens, for what kind of democracy, with what kinds of intercultural sensibilities, deliberative competencies and political agency are being shaped in schools?" (2011: 283). This argument underlies broader educational debates in which schools are understood as arenas of conflict. Apodaca and Rockwell (2012) examine the conflictive nature of schools with a constructivist approach and argue that school cultures and governing structures are reproduced, resisted or re-elaborated in practices and social relations. Teachers, directors, parents, authorities and students each propose and contest the meanings and representations of schooling, thereby leading to multiple school realities (Apodaca and Rockwell 2012: 73). In this study, I look at the school established by CACTUS as an arena of social conflict, and I analyze what the divergent social practices that are employed at this particular school can tell us about citizenship formation and contestation.

3. Alternative citizenship formation by education

The engagement of Indigenous movements with the formation of alternative models of citizenship through schooling has been widely studied (Gustafson 2009, García 2005, Bertely 2009, Lazar 2010). Gustafson (2009: 216) illustrates how bilingual intercultural education programs in Bolivia constitute a platform for the production of alternative models of citizenship by the Indigenous Guarani people. Significant in this context is Holston's (1999: 167) concept of insurgent citizenship: "(…) these are forms found in organized grassroots mobilizations and in everyday practices that, in different ways empower, parody, derail or subvert state agendas. They are found, in other words, in struggles over what it means to be a member of the modern state (…)". In the case of Bolivia, intercultural education lays the foundation for Indigenous forms of citizenship by the acceptance of cultural differences and the encouragement of the construction of Indigenous identities.

Whereas Gustafson (2009) studied formal school programs, Bertely (2009) examined an autonomous educational project aimed at strengthening Indigenous forms of citizenship in Maya communities, defined as "democratic communitarian citizenship models". The *bien comun* [communal well-being] has a central place in this citizenship model associated with communitarian forms of democracy and Indigenous forms of organization. Lazar (2008: 8–13) taps into this discussion by identifying the tension between an individual sense of citizenship centered on individual interests, and a collective sense of citizenship based on a relational and communitarian self guided by responsibilities to a collective. What is more, Lazar (2010) introduces the notion of "critical" citizenship as encoded in critical pedagogy: the ability of students to criticize their social and political context. She questions if the practices of political socialization in a school in Bolivia enable or stifle critical citizenship. In the ethnographic analysis of this article, I address the concepts employed by these scholars in an attempt to gain insight into the broader meaning of educational practices in the particular rural context of Oaxaca.

4. Methodology

I spent a total of five months living in Santos Reyes Tepejillo, an Indigenous municipality located in the mountain range of the Mixtec Baja in Oaxaca. My research participants consisted of former and contemporary members of CACTUS, the students enrolled in the preparatory school and their parents who supported the project. The preparatory school was small: there were four, five and ten students respectively in the first, second and third group. I collaborated as teacher at the school and as such took part in all school activities like celebrations, field trips, community assemblies and internal meetings. I chose this participatory approach to secure my contribution to the project and to be at the heart of school activities, which made participant observation and informal conversations a constant activity. In addition, I conducted open ended, in-depth interviews with my participants and also with local intellectuals of other educational projects to broaden my horizon and to situate the project in more regional social-political dynamics.

In view of the small size of the schooling project, I was able to gain deep understanding of the social dynamics at play. This is presented in the ethnographic analysis that follows. First, I introduce the organization CACTUS and their involvement in regional struggles. After that, the particular context of the schooling project will be provided by an account of Santos Reyes Tepejillo. Then, I will unravel the complex workings of educational processes in this locality by focusing on the curriculum, pedagogy and organizational structure of the preparatory school. In the conclusion, I elaborate on how these local educational processes intersect with larger debates about citizenship and Indigenous struggles and what it tells us about the dilemmas faced by Indigenous movements.

5. Politics and citizenship claims of CACTUS

In 1998, the civil society organization CACTUS was founded to change the situation of poverty and marginalization endured by Indigenous peoples in the mountainous Mixtec Baja region, where extremely dry land and scarce water resources made for harsh agriculture conditions. A few years into its existence, the organization changed radically when a militant Indigenous woman, Bety Cariño, appeared to the scene. She introduced Zapatista ideals and transformed the development-oriented organization into an organization that worked for Indigenous rights and autonomy.[1] In 2006, CACTUS participated in the Other Campaign of the Zapatistas and in the vigorous Popular Assembly of the Peoples of Oaxaca (APPO) which both substantially impacted regional politics.[2] As such, CACTUS became part of the so-called "new politics" of social movements that developed in response to neoliberalism. These autonomy-based projects advocated the inclusion of Indigenous peoples into pluricultural nations (Dinerstein 2010, Monteagudo 2011, Stahler-Sholk *et al.* 2007, Stahler-Sholk 2007).[3]

CACTUS offered various Mixtec communities workshops about community radios, savings banks and agricultural projects. In a context where the government fails to address basic necessities like food, education, health and information, CACTUS members described their efforts as "the exercise of rights". In this logic, their

---

1 An Indigenous social movement based in Chiapas who since 1994 are involved in a low intensity war against military, paramilitary and corporate incursions in Chiapas. The Zapatistas struggle for the recognition and protection of Indigenous rights and autonomy in Mexico. Autonomy is central in their struggle since they demand the right to govern themselves locally and regionally according to traditional laws, to control the resources essential for their livelihoods, and to enjoy the recognition of Indigenous customs, traditions and spirituality (Mattiace 2003, Bertely 2008).

2 In 2006, the EZLN started a caravan called The Other Campaign [*La Otra Campaña*] through Mexico to meet various organizations and groups to unite forces against neoliberalism and capitalism. The APPO [*Asamblea Popular de los Pueblos de Oaxaca*] is a combination of various organizations that assembled in response to the repressive political situation in Oaxaca in 2006.

3 These new oppositional politics are distinguished by their emphasis on autonomy from political parties and other institutions, decision-making through participatory and horizontal processes and a quest for solidarity that goes beyond classes (Dinerstein 2010, Monteagudo 2011, Stahler-Sholk *et al.* 2007, Stahler-Sholk 2007).

workshops served to put the constitutional rights of national citizens to basic necessities into practice (De La Peña 1999, Fischer 2009, Mattiace 2003). At the same time, the community workshops functioned as a way to enter Mixtec communities and to promote struggles for the defense of Mixtec culture, language and autonomy. This line of work coincided with the broader hemispheric resurgence of Indigenous movements who struggle for Indigenous rights (Gustafson 2009).

In 2007, CACTUS extended its politics to the classroom in the form of two communitarian preparatory schools. The members view state-run schools as tools of statist control. One of them, Jairo, expressed CACTUS' stance clearly: "A child goes to school to become a worker, they learn to obey, to keep silent and to not criticize. They are being domesticated".[4] Although public schools are seen as spaces for domination, the activists upheld the view that schools can become a space for liberation and empowerment by practicing alternative forms of education (Pollock and Levinson 2011: 6). Popular education has guided the work of CACTUS in its aim to empower the oppressed to take control of their own learning and to effect social change (Kane 2000). In fact, members of CACTUS intended to educate new leaders for Indigenous resistance. Often referred to as "the making of political cadres [*cuadros políticos*]", CACTUS members nourished insurgent forms of citizenship: citizens who could subvert state agendas in struggles over what it means to be a member of the modern state (Holston 1999).

Besides the objective to educate new leaders, CACTUS members also advocated the strengthening of communal identities and conduct in their schools. In activist discourse, Indigenous communities are often associated with communal forms of living and communitarian identities and interests (Gustafson 2009: 112). Intellectuals in the region of Oaxaca define this notion as *comunalidad* which has been described as: "the essence of being Indian, the will to be collective and to conceive of life and social organization in this manner" (Maldonado 2002: 30). Other scholars associate this with the perspective in which the communal well-being has a central place, in contrast to a liberal worldview based on individual interests (Apodaca 2008, Lazar 2008). Indeed, members of CACTUS aspire to promote "a communitarian sense of citizenship" (Bertely 2009). For instance, they often proclaimed that their work should "strengthen *lo comunitario* [the communal]" to enhance Indigenous identities associated with communal forms of social life but also to satisfy their personal longing for a sense of community.

This portrayal of the politics of CACTUS shows the way in which the organization is entangled in new politics of social movements and how the field of

---

4 Interview Jairo 12-12-2011 Huajapan de León.

education became their center stage of struggle. Furthermore, I have pointed out how their politics are determined by specific ideological understandings that in turn intersect with diverse citizenship models. Next, I turn to an in-depth analysis on how CACTUS' practices play out in the local realm of the preparatory school in Santos Reyes Tepejillo.

6. The schooling project in Santos Reyes Tepejillo

The municipality of Santos Reyes Tepejillo counts an estimated population of 1200 inhabitants, all *Ñuu Savi* [Mixtec people] of whom 890 speak the Mixtec language. The total area of the municipality covers 89.31 km^2 and is located at a height of 1940 meters.[5] The level of marginalization in the Mixtec region is considered very high according to measurements of income and access to basic services like housing, education and public healthcare systems.[6] Tepejillo is no exception. The harsh agricultural conditions have forced many inhabitants to migrate to Northern Mexico or the United States. While the majority of men find work as farmers or wage laborers, some inhabitants have gotten themselves involved in drugs trafficking.[7] As a result, remittances are substantially higher for some families in Tepejillo compared to their neighbors. This also explains the presence of a gas station, some impressive residential houses, paved streets and the large amounts of money spent on community festivities in the community. Nevertheless, conditions of poverty persist for the majority of the population.

Social life in Tepejillo is under heavy influence of migration. The cultural expressions of inhabitants are combinations of Mixtec traditions with American popular culture. Migration has also affected Indigenous forms of self-governance. In accordance with regional and historical trends, Tepejillo is governed according to *usos y costumbres*: self-governance structures associated with large amounts of autonomy, a strong sense of community solidarity and collective ways of life (Bertely 2008, Lazar 2008). However, migration has put this model of community organization under pressure by introducing values associated with money,

5 Enciclopedia de los Municipios de México, Oaxaca. Instituto Nacional para el Federalismo y el Desarrollo Municipal, Gobierno del Estado de Oaxaca.

6 POBREZA MULTIDIMENSIONAL Y DERECHOS HUMANOS: SITUACIÓN ACTUAL EN LA MIXTECA OAXAQUEÑA EN EL CONTEXTO DE LA POLÍTICA ECONÓMICA NACIONAL, Martín Carlos Ramales Osorio, Miguel Ángel Coronado Alcántara, Ricardo García Jiménez. Contribuciones a las Ciencias Sociales September 2014 http://www.eumed.net/rev/cccss/29/mixteca.html.

7 Information obtained through various informal conversations during fieldwork.

individualism and consumerism to the region (Pombo 2010: 153). With regard to modes of self-identification in Tepejillo, migration has only strengthened feelings of belonging to the community. In the Mixtec region, ethnicity is not usually a form of self-identification (Nagengast and Kearney 1990: 73). This holds true for Tepejillo's inhabitants who make little reference to Indigenous or Mixtec identity markers, but take pride in identifying as original inhabitants of Tepejillo.

In sum, the situation in which Tepejillo fares can be characterized by profound social-economic marginalization and heavy influences of migration. In this context, CACTUS founded the schooling project oriented toward improving educational conditions in the community as well as to encourage struggles for Indigenous autonomy. As the school lacked official state recognition and funding, the mothers of the students formed a committee to support the school. With this self-determination and self-sufficiency over education, the activists hoped to cultivate autonomous forms of organizing in the community. However, in the absence of Indigenous modes of identification and ethnic activism in Tepejillo, the school yielded conflicting expectations among community members and CACTUS activists.

Before the foundation of the schooling project, there was no preparatory school in Tepejillo. Remote villages in rural areas often lack access to public education institutions and sending the youngsters to school in nearby cities is often no option for parents, due to high living and traveling costs. As a result, girls normally got married and boys predominantly opted for migration after graduation from secondary school in Tepejillo. In this context, the schooling project of CACTUS offered new opportunities for the Indigenous youngsters to continue studying and hence facilitated the right to education. As such, the school responded to an unequal citizenship model in which the state differentiates between first- and second-class citizens: those who have access to education and those excluded (Holston 2008: 5).

Many students enrolled in the new preparatory school because higher education promises social mobility and job opportunities. The mothers of female students highlighted still other reasons for their daughters' enrollment. For many of them, going to preparatory school and subsequently finding a job served as strategy for their daughters to gain independence. Doña Camila explained her point of view:

> It is better to be able to decide what you want to do with your life. Not like a donkey, wait till your husband gets home or sends you money. Someone [the husband] who does not help you or care about you. I do not want her [her daughter] to become dependent of a husband, I want her to make her own life.[8]

8 Interview Doña Camila 26-10-2011 Santos Reyes Tepejillo.

In Tepejillo, the gendered reasoning of the mothers proved progressive since the prevailing tradition dictated that girls should "marry well," rather than study or find employment. Also for male students, enrollment in preparatory school exceeded the norm. The community's involvement in international migration contributed to a cultural milieu in which young males were expected to engage in foreign wage labor rather than in public education as a strategy for socioeconomic mobility (Dyrness 2012: 43). Thus, for both female and male students, going to preparatory school was quite exceptional.

While the students and parents involved in the schooling project went against the grain of local traditions, their expectations when it comes to schooling did not always match those of CACTUS. Whereas for community members, the school was an "ordinary" school that filled the gap in education, CACTUS members situated the school in broader Indigenous struggles. Consequently, the school developed into an arena of potential conflict (Apodaca and Rockwell 2012). In fact, the school can be understood as a local manifestation of the paradoxical stance of Indigenous movements: the school evoked both claims to national education rights and special Indigenous rights which provoked certain tensions in the locality (Gustafson 2009: 232). In the next sections, I explore how tensions and ambiguities unfold in actual educational practices and the way it effects the contestation of citizenship in the school project.

7. The curriculum and Indigenous identity formation

According to Rockwell (2010: 162), the standard curriculum taught in Mexican schools imposes subtle cultural meanings and practices identified with the western, white world, and thereby dispossesses Indigenous youth from their own culture, language and way of experiencing the world. In line with this stance, the teachers of CACTUS developed an alternative curriculum to contest the identities and dispositions normally learned in Mexico's public schools.

The curriculum of CACTUS includes topics on gender (in)equality, capitalist resource extraction, transgenic seeds and industrial agriculture, and climate change from a perspective that questions dominant ideas and encourages social critique. What is more, the curriculum addresses the history of Indigenous pueblos, Indigenous rights, and biology inspired by Indigenous cosmovisions, Mixtec literature and Mixtec writing courses. This highlights the objective to strengthen Indigenous identification and feelings of belonging, strongly related to the objective to nourish communal ethics and Indigenous forms of organization that are also included in the curriculum in the form of school assemblies and community service.

My observations during a Mixtec writing course illustrate the dynamic workings of the curriculum in practice. Many children in Tepejillo have given up speaking Mixtec and although the preparatory school students were still bilingual, they were unable to write in Mixtec. As the language is in danger of extinction, the teachers of CACTUS hoped that writing in Mixtec would enable a process of cultural revitalization and Indigenous identification. During the first class, students learned to write a variety of words in Mixtec by playing with syllables written on small pieces of paper. Under the sound of loud giggling, the majority of the students enthusiastically participated and some even proudly agreed with the teacher at the end of the class: "Indeed, we need to preserve our roots!".[9] However, other students refused to take part in this particular class. For instance, Beatriz justified her absence in the following terms: "I do not want to learn to write in Mixtec! Like I am ever going to use it…. As if anyone will ever ask for Mixtec as a job requirement?".[10] Beatriz was opposed to learn writing in Mixtec because it lacked usefulness for her, which points to her instrumental perspective of education (Lazar 2010: 195). In her view, it frustrated her dream of social mobility through proper employment, perhaps even in the United States. Rather than Mixtec, she often approached me for English classes, as it could help her to move up in the world. At a certain point, however, Beatriz learned about a government policy that offered scholarships to Indigenous students proficient in writing Mixtec. She soon returned to class.

This short description shows how different expectations and objectives of students and teachers clashed in the classroom. Whereas the teachers aimed to "make indigenous citizens" and many students appropriated these educational practices, Beatriz mapped out contradicting plans. Eventually, she only participated in the class after redefining the educational practices that then became meaningful to her. This leads to the acknowledgment that schools can propose civic identities that may deeply influence students, but alternative imaginaries and counterpublics outside the school often bring such identities into creative contradiction (Levinson 2011: 286).

8. Pedagogy and agency of resistance

A look at the pedagogy employed by CACTUS' teachers provides further insight into what kind of dispositions, local political agency and what kind of democracy is fostered in the school (Levinson 2011: 284). As the teachers criticize the pedagogy practised in conventional Mexican schools for cultivating uncritical and passive

9 Fieldnotes 13-10-2011 Santos Reyes Tepejillo.
10 Fieldnotes 13-10-2011 Santos Reyes Tepejillo

behaviour, their pedagogy is guided by the principle of anti-authoritarianism to create space for students to form their own opinions and act upon it. Exemplifying is a teachers' story about a history class:

> I let them [the students] listen to two songs about the violent north American expansion and the consequences for the Indigenous pueblos in our territories. After the students listened the songs, they stayed silent, there were no comments. I did not say "horrible Americans [*pinche gringos*], we have to fight them," nothing like that. I simply explained a historical process. [...] I kept silent and I saw that something was happening, something was moving in their hearts and minds.[11]

Without imposing an ideology or specific ideas, the teacher made efforts to arouse a critical awareness that would nourish a specific kind of agency. In contrast to agency described by Holston (2008: 13) that "reproduces entrenchment, persistence and inertia", the teachers foster an "agency of resistance" that can change oppressive societal structures. In this logic, weekly school assemblies served as spaces for students to develop these dispositions. For instance, they practiced in speaking in front of a public, learned to criticize school policy, defended their rights in conflicts with other students or community authorities, and organized and acted upon injustices. Some students confided their feelings of emancipation to me ever since they enrolled in preparatory school, as Juanita recounted:

> I used to be very quiet, even if I wanted to say something. In the preparatory school, I stopped being afraid. Even if it is someone of importance, it does not matter, now I perceive them as equal, and just say what I think. I learned this during conversations with my teachers.[12]

I observed how the educational practices employed by the teachers orientated at developing "agency of resistance" were adopted by some of the students. However, even though all students were offered space for participation in class and school politics, some students avoided active involvement and remained immune for the teachers' intentions. Thus, the educational practices that were meant to promote specific kinds of civic behavior actually turned out to be a fractured and incomplete process that developed through a dialectic whereby the subjects seemed to define the terms of its incorporation (Lazar 2008:6). This account emphasizes the dynamic nature of educational processes and the continuous negotiation between teachers and students in the classroom when it comes to inciting certain identities and behavior that facilitate social change.

11 Interview Jairo 12-12-2011 Huajapan de León.
12 Interview Juanita 10-11-2011 Santos Reyes Tepejillo.

9. Collectivity outside the classroom

The teachers of CACTUS also engaged in education beyond the walls of the classroom. In fact, educational efforts were not only directed towards students, but included their mothers. The mothers of the students formed a committee to support the school. For instance, by organizing festivities and selling food in the local park they collected money to cover school expenses and the material needs of teachers who worked on a voluntary basis. But most importantly, the committee held the responsibility to decide over school matters. Thus, rather than government institutions, a group of community members collectively controlled and organized the school. In this sense, the organization of the school was structured according to Indigenous self-governance structures defined as *usos y costumbres,* which are commonly associated with values of solidarity in which the communal well-being has a central place and the supreme value is social participation (Bertely 2009: 186). By encouraging the mothers to engage in this collective work for collective interests, the teachers hoped to strengthen autonomous practices, values of solidarity and a sense of collectivity.

On Sunday afternoons, the mothers were often to be found sitting together in one of the empty classrooms. The sound of chewing gum echoed around and some mothers were embroidering napkins while others were engaged in heated discussions. The meetings of the committee often took hours. Although disagreements often sparked tensions between the mothers, Doña Elbertina, the president of the committee, emphasized: "We are all part of the committee, even when I am the president that does not mean that I am the committee, we all work, we all bring the teachers tortillas, here we are all equal."[13] This kind of collective participation and sense of solidarity was exactly what the teachers aspired to encourage. I observed this collectivity expressed in their behavior as they for instance worked together to clean up the schools garden and all did their share of work.

The poor conditions of the school and lack of government funds made work urgent and compelled the mothers to work hard. Although the mothers also seemed to enjoy the collective work for the school, they all too often complained about the endless meetings and financial responsibilities. In addition to their responsibilities as heads of households, as most of their husbands worked in the United States, they experienced the work for the committee as hard, tiresome and often just too much to handle. This caused that the mothers experienced the maintenance of the school more as a burden than as a collective achievement to be proud of. In fact, they dreamed of a public school where the government would pay teacher

13 Interview Doña Elbertina 10-10-2011 Santos Reyes Tepejillo.

salaries and provide adequate classrooms, uniforms and educational material. As Doña Elbertina narrated: "A real school, how beautiful would that be, right?".[14]

Thus, whereas the teachers saw the collective organization of the school as an ideological structure that stimulated autonomy, the mothers only participated because no other options existed. This shows how the mothers negotiated the meaning of educational practices in the school setting. They embraced the committee work that was meant to promote collectivity and self-determination, but out of pragmatic reasoning rather than a belief in Indigenous autonomy. To the contrary, the mothers dreamed of a publicly funded school that would respond to the constitutional right of national citizens to education. Obviously, the modes of dynamism and negotiation that characterized educational practices inside the classroom also marked CACTUS' education outside the classroom.

10. Conclusion

This article explored the engagement of social movements in the contestation of citizenship through education. I examined how social movements engage in citizenship formation, in and outside the classroom, a field normally dominated by the state. More specifically, I aimed to explore how this process unfolded in the context of paradoxical stances of Indigenous movements who make claims on national as well as Indigenous rights. To gain insight into these broader social-political processes, I studied the local educational practices employed in CACTUS' school, defined as a counter-hegemonic project.

The account of CACTUS' political history showed that an activist organization can contest dominant citizenship models in Mexico in multifaceted ways and at various levels of their political activities. Furthermore, I showed how the involvement of CACTUS in Indigenous struggles and new politics of social movements laid the foundation for the civic identities and behavior promoted in their schooling project. The school in Santos Reyes Tepejillo, however, generated tensions because of divergent expectations and objectives among community inhabitants and activists. For community members, the school responded to the constitutional right to education, whereas members of CACTUS promoted Indigenous citizenship models consistent with struggles for autonomy. In fact, the school discloses how the paradoxical stance of Indigenous movements, demanding inclusion in the nation-state and simultaneously preserving difference, can manifest itself in a local context. The analysis of educational practices as expressed in the curriculum, pedagogy and

14 Interview Doña Elbertina 10-10-2011 Santos Reyes Tepejillo.

organizational structure of the school then illustrates how this shapes the process of citizenship formation among the different local actors.

The educational practices to shape Indigenous identities were sometimes embraced and appropriated by the students, but more often creatively contested and provided with new meaning. What is more, efforts to encourage "agency of resistance" were only incorporated by particular students, depending on specific persons and context. The same tendencies developed outside the classroom, where mothers also negotiated the educational practices aimed at promoting collective dispositions: they welcomed the collective work but simultaneously subverted its meaning from a pragmatic stance.

In the local realm of the school, different citizenship models were reproduced, negotiated, resisted and re-elaborated in everyday educational practices. These processes followed the logic of Ong's (1999) theory of citizenship; as produced in negotiations and understood as dialectically determined by the state and its subjects. In the communitarian preparatory school, I observed educational encounters in which certain elements were embraced by parents and students, while simultaneously efforts were made to modify or redirect these in ways that responded to people's own interests and aspirations.

What does this article about a particular project, in a specific community, tell us about Indigenous struggles over the meaning of citizenship? By making the paradoxical claims of Indigenous movements tangible in a particular place, time and context, we learn how experiences of citizenship are part of permanent negotiations between local actors, social movements and states that follow a creative logic. Furthermore, my ethnographic study stresses the complexities and inconsistencies of local realities and people engaged in everyday practices of social transformation. This makes me conclude that we cannot think about Indigenous struggles over the meaning of citizenship in unequivocal ways. Rather, it requires the unique perspective of the anthropologist to understand the connections between the often-abstract goals of social movements or states with regard to citizenship, and local social processes where contesting citizenship can take on unexpected forms.

Works cited

Apodaca, Erika G.. *Los profesionistas indios en la educación intercultural: etnicidad, intermediación y escuela en el territorio mixe*. Mexico, D.F.: Universidad Autónoma Metropolitana, 2008. Print.

Apodaca, Erika G., and Elsie Rockwell. "Anthropological research on educational processes in Mexico". *Anthropologies of Education: A Global Guide to*

Ethnographic Studies of Learning and Schooling. Ed. Kathryn M. Anderson-Levitt. New York: Berghahn Books, 2012. 71–92. Print.

Bertely, María. "Educación intercultural para la ciudadanía y la democracia activa y solidaria. Una crítica de la Otra educación al multiculturalismo neoliberal y comunitarista". *Multiculturalismo, educación intercultural y derechos indígenas en las Américas*. Ed. Gunther Dietz, Rosa G. Mendoza Zuany, and Sergio T. Galván. Quito: Ediciones Abya-Yala, 2008. 267–302. Print.

–. "Education for Intercultural Citizenship: The Maya Teachers of Chiapas in the Construction of Alternate Citizenships from below". *Interamerican Journal of Education for Democracy* 2 (2009): 197–210. Print.

Böhm Steffen, Ana C. Dinerstein, and André Spicer. "The (Im)possibilities of Autonomy. Social Movements in, against and beyond state, capital and development". *Social Movement Studies* 9 (2010): 17–32. Print.

De La Peña, Guillermo. "Territorio y ciudadanía étnica en la Nación Globalizada". *Desacatos* 1 (1999): 13–27. Print.

–. "A new Mexican nationalism? Indigenous rights, constitutional reform and the conflicting meanings of multiculturalism". *Nations and Nationalism* 12 (2006): 279–302. Print.

Dyrness, Andrea. "Contra Viento y Marea (Against Wind and Tide): Building Civic Identity among Children of Emigration in El Salvador". *Anthropology & Education Quarterly* 43 (2102): 41–60. Print.

Fischer, Edward F. *Indigenous peoples, civil society, and the neo-liberal state in Latin America*. New York: Berghahn Books, 2009. Print.

Freire, Paulo. *The Pedagogy of the Oppressed*. London: Penguin, 1999 [1970]. Print.

García, María E.. *Making indigenous citizens: identities, education and multicultural development in Peru*. Stanford: Stanford University Press, 2005. Print.

Giroux, Henry. *Schooling and the Struggle for Public Life. Democracy's Promise and Education's Challenge*. 2nd edition. Boulder, CO: Paradigm, 2005. Print.

Gledhill, John. *Power and its Disguises. Anthropological Perspectives on Politics*. London: Pluto Press, 1994. Print.

Gustafson, Bret. *New languages of the state: indigenous resurgence and the politics of knowledge in Bolivia*. London: Duke University Press, 2009. Print.

Hale, Charles. "Does multiculturalism menace? Governance, cultural rights and the politics of identity in Guatemala". *Journal of Latin American Studies* 34 (2002): 485–524. Print.

Holston, James. "Spaces of Insurgent Citizenship". *Cities and Citizenship*. Ed. James Holston. Durham, NC: Duke University Press, 1999. 155–176. Print.

–. *Insurgent Citizenship. Disjunctions of Democracy and Modernity in Brazil.* Princeton: Princeton University Press, 2007. Print.

Jackson, Jean, and Kay Warren. "Indigenous movements in Latin America, 1992–2004: controversies, ironies, new directions". *Annual Review of Anthropology* 34 (2005): 549–573. Print.

Kane, Liam. *Popular Education and Social Change in Latin America.* London: Latin American Bureau, 2009. Print.

Lazar, Sian. *El Alto, rebel city. Self and citizenship in Andean Bolivia.* Durham, NC: Duke University Press, 2008. Print.

–. "Schooling and Critical Citizenship: Pedagogies of Political Agency in El Alto, Bolivia". *Anthropology & Education Quarterly* 41 (2010): 181–205. Print.

Levinson, Bradley. "Citizenship, Identity, Democracy: Engaging the Political in the anthropology of Education". *Anthropology and Education Quarterly* 3 (2005): 329–340. Print.

–. "Towards an Anthropology of (Democratic) Citizenship Education". *A Companion to the Anthropology of Education.* Ed. Bradley A. U. Levinson and Mica Pollock. West Sussex: Blackwell Publishing Ltd, 2011. 279–298. Print.

Maldonado, Benjamín. *Los indios en las aulas. Dinámica de dominación y resistencia en Oaxaca.* INAH, Col. Etnografías de los pueblos indígenas de México, Oaxaca, 2002. Print.

Mattiace, Shannan L.. *To see with two eyes: peasant activism & Indian autonomy in Chiapas, Mexico.* Mexico City: University of New Mexico Press, 2003. Print.

McLaren, Peter. *Life in Schools. An Introduction to Critical Pedagogy in the Foundations of Education.* Boston: Pearson Education, 2007. Print.

Monteagudo, Graciela. "Neoliberalism, Democracy, and Contemporary Social Movements in Latin America". *Latin American Politics and Society* 53 (2011): 151–160. Print.

Nagengast, Carole, and Michael Kearney. "Mixtec Ethnicity: Social Identity, Political Consciousness and Political Activism". *Latin American Research Review* 25 (1990): 61–91. Print.

Ong, Aihwa. 1999 "Cultural Citizenship as Subject Making". *Race, Identity and Citizenship.* Ed. Rodolfo D. Torres, Louis F. Mirón, and Jonathan X. Inda. Oxford: Blackwell Publishers, 1999. 262–294. Print.

–. *Neoliberal as Exception: Mutations in Citizenship and sovereignty.* Durham. NC: Duke University Press, 2006. Print.

Pollock, Mica, and Bradley Levinson. *A Companion to the Anthropology of Education.* West Sussex: Blackwell Publishing Ltd., 2011. Print.

Pombo, María D.. "Youth Identities and the Migratory Culture among Triqui and Mixtec Boys and Girls". *Migraciones Internacionales* 5 (2010): 140–164. Print.

Postero, Nancy. *Now we are citizens, indigenous politics in post multicultural Bolivia*. Stanford: Stanford University Press, 2007. Print.

Postero, Nancy, and Leon Zamosc. *The struggle for indigenous rights in Latin America*. Brighton: Sussex Academic Press, 2004. Print.

Rockwell, Elsie. "Resistance and Cultural Work in Times of War". *New World of Indigenous Resistance*. Ed. Lois Meyer, and Benjamín Maldonado. New York: City Lights Books, 2010. 161–178. Print.

Scott, James. *Weapons of the Weak: Everyday Forms of Peasant Resistance*. New Haven: Yale University Press, 1985.

Smith, William. "Multiculturalism, Identity and the Articulation of Citizenship". *Latin American Research Review* 42 (2007): 238–251. Print.

Spindler, George D.. *Education and Cultural Process: Anthropological Approaches*. 2nd edition. Prospect Heights, IL: Waveland Press, 1987. Print.

Stahler-Sholk, Richard. "Resisting Neoliberal Homogenization, the Zapatista Autonomy Movement". *Latin American Perspectives* 34 (2007): 48–63. Print.

Stahler-Sholk, Richard, Harry E. Vanden, and Glen D. Kuecker. "Globalizing Resistance: The New Politics of Social Movements in Latin America". *Latin American Perspectives* 34 (2007): 5–16. Print.

Stavenhagen, Rodolfo. "Indigenous Peoples and the State in Latin America". *Multiculturalism in Latin America: indigenous rights, diversity and democracy*. Ed. Rachel Sieder. Hampshire: Palgrave, 2002. 24–44. Print.

Stephen, Lynn. *Transborder Lives. Indigenous Oaxacans in Mexico, California, and Oregon*. Durham and London: Duke University Press, 2007. Print.

Van Cott, Donna L. *From Movements to Parties in Latin America: The Evolution of Ethnic Politics*. Cambridge, UK: Cambridge University Press, 2005. Print.

VanWey, Leah, Catherine M. Tucker, and Eileen Diaz McConnell. "Community Organization, Migration, and Remittances in Oaxaca". *Latin American Research Review* 40 (2005): 83–107. Print.

Warren, Kay. *Indigenous Movements and their Critics: Pan-Maya Activism in Guatemala*. Princeton, NJ: Princeton University Press, 1998. Print.

Yashar, Deborah. "Democracy, Indigenous Movements and the Postliberal Challenge in Latin America". *World Politics* 52 (1999): 76–104. Print.

–. *Contesting Citizenship in Latin America: the rise of indigenous movements and the post liberal challenge*. New York: Cambridge University Press, 2005. Print.

Part III: Tradition, Representation and Cultural Expression

Wil Pansters
*Centre for Mexican Studies, University of Groningen,
and Utrecht University*

The Politics of Indigenous Identity and Representation in Twentieth-Century Mexico

In 2001, Fernando León de Aranoa made a beautiful documentary called *Caminantes*.[1] Situated in the heart of the Purépecha region in the western Mexican state of Michoacán, it tells the story of how a small Indigenous community prepared for the arrival of the march of a large group of Maya Indians and their followers, the so-called Zapatistas, who had rebelled against the state at the beginning of 1994, and who had departed from the southern state of Chiapas some time before and were meandering through the country on their way to Mexico City. The march of the Zapatistas was the outcome of an invitation of president Vicente Fox, who in 2000 had chased the erstwhile revolutionary ruling party out of power after more than seven decades, and who had offered the Zapatistas to come to Mexico City and discuss their demands.[2] The documentary shows how a local musical *banda* rehearses for the welcoming ceremony, how people make plans and build a huge podium, how a local teacher writes a speech to be delivered in front of the leader of the Zapatista delegation, subcomandante Marcos, and the other leaders of Indigenous groups from Southern Mexico. Another teacher writes and rehearses a small play with the school children, called *Caminantes*.

While the moving documentary zooms in on the efforts of ordinary Indigenous people, children, grown-ups and elderly, filled with pride about the impending visit, it is also a window on the complexity of the processes of Indigenous identity formation and social mobilization at the local level and their deep connections with social and political transformations, both nationally and globally. The documentary is therefore a useful starting point to make some initial arguments about Indigenous identity and representation in Mexico. In the following section I will point to Indigenous mobilizations in Mexico, their socio-economic context and

---

1 Fernando León de Aranoa is an award-winning Spanish screenwriter and film director. *Caminantes* was released at the end of 2001 in Spain. "Caminantes" means "walkers" or "those who walk."

2 This was the consequence of his campaign promise (or bravado) that in office he would resolve the Chiapas problem in "just 15 minutes."

the discourse of Indigenous rights. The next section then deals with revolutionary nationalism and changing citizenship regimes as major factors in explaining the contemporary politics of Indigenous identity and representation. I will use a broad historical perspective here. The last section looks at the shifting relationships between class and ethnicity in popular mobilizations and links them to political theories of multiculturalism and rights. I conclude with some brief reflections on how certain developments and practices of Indigenous organizing and demand-making in Mexico can shape the terms of political theorizing.

1. Zapatismo, international migration, and Indigenous rights

Firstly, the moment of engagement in the purépecha village of Nurío that features in the documentary is a direct consequence of the extraordinary dynamics caused by what could be called the second wave of Zapatista activism in Mexico, after the first wave following the original armed uprising at the beginning of 1994. The movement in Chiapas gave a tremendous boost to demand-making by Indigenous groups across Mexico, but also inspired and set an example for Indigenous leaders elsewhere in Central and South America and even beyond the continent. It was the beginning of what Olesen called "international zapatismo" in his study first published in 2004. This wave of nationwide Zapatista-inspired Indigenous activism faded out somewhat after December 1996, when the reform project that came out of the long negotiations between the Zapatistas and the state was turned down by the federal executive. The second wave, in contrast, was part of the immediate aftermath of the historical defeat of the revolutionary party (PRI) that had ruled Mexico for decades at the federal elections of 2000, and the ascendance to power of the flamboyant Vincente Fox of the center-right National Action Party. This turn of events opened up spaces for new arrangements, and most of all, it triggered the hope among Mexicans of all walks of life that major transformations were about to come. The new president had made numerous promises about how he would dismantle the authoritarian system of priísta rule and put an ending to major disputes and controversial legacies. An important pending problem was the Zapatista conflict in Chiapas that had ended up in a stalemate and the wider issue of Indigenous rights. And hence Fox invited the Zapatistas to the negotiation table again in Mexico City. And so on the 24 of February 2001, the Zapatistas began their March that would also bring them to Michoacán's purépecha communities.

Processes of Indigenous organizing and demand making in different parts of Mexico have their own local and regional histories, profoundly shaped by the specificities of regional social and political developments. Groups in northern Mexico, such as the Yaqui in Sonora or the Tarahumaras in Chihuahua, have trajectories different from the Otomís in Veracruz, the Nahuas in Hidalgo, the Mixtecos in Oaxaca and the diverse Maya communities in southern Mexico. Even so, the Zapatista struggle that emerged in the forests of Chiapas had a deep impact on the politics of Indigenous activism all over Mexico. The documentary *Caminantes* demonstrates how the purépecha community sees itself as part of a national Indigenous movement that, it is hoped, will be able to bring about significant reform. It chronicles a hopeful moment on the eve of the eventual failed attempt to introduce an Indigenous Law in Michoacán, and then, instead, of the adoption of a new set of laws concerning community justice that disallowed an autonomous exercise in the resolution of conflicts within purépecha communities. In response, alternative projects of communal citizenship subsequently emerged in different municipalities in the region, aimed at exercising *de facto* forms of autonomous governance on the basis of new participatory political practices and ideas of communal cohesion.[3] In many ways, much of what was about to happen in the purépecha region in the following years would also occur in the southern region of Chiapas where their Zapatista visitors originated from.

Secondly, the documentary lays out the context in which Indigenous identity formation and representation are embedded. Gone are the days in which Indigenous communities were believed to be "closed and corporate," almost disconnected from wider social and economic systems. One of the dramatic scenes in the documentary is about the children in the local school preparing for a play to be performed in front of the Zapatista delegation. In this context, the teacher tells about the broken families in which the children grow up, in some cases parentless families, due to widespread international migration. In an exercise the teacher teaches the children to write a letter. The climax of the scene is when the boys and girls, some with great difficulty, read out loud the letter they have written, mostly to their absent fathers, sometimes to both of their parents. The heartbreaking scene in which children struggle with reading their own lines and with their emotions symbolizes a fundamental social reality in many Mexican Indigenous communities: the profound impact of (international) migration on the community and family life. There can be little doubt about the destructive consequences of absent parents for children's social and emotional development. But migration also has deep cultural and political consequences. In the documentary, a purépecha activist speaks about the dangers of migration for the reproduction of social and cultural

3 For an excellent analysis of these developments in Michoacán, see Ma. Del Carmen Ventura Patiño, *Volver a la comunidad. Derechos indígenas y procesos autonómicos en Michoacán*, 2010.

Indigenous institutions (language is very important in this respect), which are otherwise seen as significant sources for social mobilization and solidarity.

On the other hand, the work of Gaspar Rivera-Salgado and others has emphasized the constructive processes taking place in the contact zone between international migration and ethnic political projects (Rivera-Salgado & Fox 2004, Stephen 2007). The innovative study of Velasco Ortiz about the Mixtecos from the state of Oaxaca examines the emergence of several transnational Indigenous organizations in what she calls the "greater Mexico-US border" through the construction of social and political identities that no longer conform to identities associated with "sending" or "receiving" societies. The groups she studied operate on both sides of the border and maintain strong links with the communities in the Mixteca region. She finds how new ethnic identities are formed under conditions of international migration, which result in the emergence of organizations and leaderships, such as the Binational Oaxacan Front, and become ethnic agents of change. The outcome is a new transnational ethnic consciousness built on experiences of a community that constantly crosses the border. The international dispersion of Indigenous community members and the risks this entails for family relations and communal institutions find their counterpart in the formation of politicized migrant networks that have generated both hometown associations (in Mexico) and transnational pan-ethnic organizations. Another recent study about changing politics and social institutions in San Miguel Tlacotepec, Oaxaca, shows how migration has contributed to organizational and political experiences in Mexico and the US, and how these have come to play a role in upsetting local political hierarchies and breaking the hold on power by old cacique families. The Binational Indigenous Front of Oaxaca, the formation of which was at least partly inspired by the 1994 Zapatista uprising, played an important role in this (Curiel). International migration is an important, but by no means the only way in which globalization affects Indigenous communities. In fact, processes of agrarian transformation and modernization deeply influence the survival strategies of Indigenous communities – as they did at the end of the nineteenth century – and constitute the main forces behind contemporary impoverishment and exclusion, pushing local Indigenous producers into new markets or economic sectors, often for the worse.

Finally, the documentary makes abundantly clear how the language of Indigenous rights has penetrated "México profundo" ("deep Mexico"). Several people interviewed in this purépecha village speak about their condition as a "pueblo indígena" that struggles for a range of cultural, social, economic and territorial rights. Their identification with their "brothers" from southern Mexico appears immediate and unproblematic. In essence this discourse of rights is directed at the state, in the sense that the latter is supposed to support Indigenous communities and protect their interests. At first sight this may appear self-evident. After all, Indigenous people constitute a significant proportion of Mexico's current population, around 10%, which amounts to more than ten million people. The large majority of Mexico's population is mestizo, which means that by definition the Indigenous is deeply present in Mexican society and culture. In this respect, Mexico differs substantially from countries like Argentina, Chile and Uruguay, which have much less marked Indigenous legacies, both demographically and culturally. Moreover, Mexico's impressive pre-Colombian civilizations form part of the country's proud self-image and a key ingredient of Mexico's global marketing strategy to attract mass tourism. Despite all this, the public and political articulation of Indigenous identity and the concomitant representation of Indigenousness in Mexico, which occur and are accepted widely nowadays, are not self-evident processes, much less so framed by the global discourse of human and/or collective rights. What then explains the rise to prominence of neo-Indigenous (identity) politics in Mexico and, for that matter, the rest of Latin America, most prominently Bolivia and Ecuador, but also Guatemala? Moreover, what are the key concepts in this form of politics and mobilization? I will briefly examine these questions in the next section by making a few key observations.

2. Nationalism, citizenship regimes and Indigenous identity

My first key argument relates to understanding the broad socio-political transformations that enable us to understand the emergence of neo-Indigenous politics in Mexico in recent decades. It is important to observe that the historical logic of the relationships between state, nation and Indigenous people in Mexico differs strongly from developments in Canada and the US. The links forged through migration of Indigenous peoples across North America are of relativly recent origin. When Deskaheh, the leader of the six Indigenous nations of Canada, appealed to be heard at the League of Nations in 1923–24 because of what he saw as the undermining of the sovereignty of the nations by the Canadian state, due to hidden policies of assimilation, Indigenous people in Mexico were just becoming the subject of an increasingly complex and broad package of policies aimed at incorporating them in the project of postrevolutionary nation-state building. While Deskaheh was convinced that the original granting of sovereignty to the six nations gave them the right to join the League of Nations on their own, the Mexican state was moving in the direction of an ideology of racial hybridization or mestizaje. Thinking of "Indian nations" within the confines of the independent Mexican state was impossible as it brought back memories of colonial "repúblicas de Indios" (which were perceived to potentially pose serious threats to the national unity of a country with deep regional divisions). As it turned out, Deskaheh was unsuccessful in overcoming the state-centered discourse of the League of Nations, which was, moreover, wary of anything that smelled of intromission in internal affairs of member states (Niezen). The fundamental tenets of this discourse would only gradually start to change after World War II.

Instead of "Indian nations", the dominant framework in the making during the 1920s in Mexico was that of a "nation without Indians" (24), as Rodolfo Stavenhagen once put it. In the case of Mexico, the emergence of this framework can only be seen against the background of the Mexican revolution. From 1910 to 1917 (and beyond), Mexico was the site of an armed struggle between peasant armies and government troops, and especially between rival revolutionary factions, about social, economic, and political reforms. After the bloody civil war, the country was characterized by deep fragmentation in every societal domain. The 1917 Constitution, that was extremely progressive at the time, marked the end of the civil war and the start of a period of approximately twenty-five years during which repeated efforts were made to overcome the deep divisions and fragmentation and to construct a new unity and consensus. The need to think about reconstruction also "triggered … a preoccupation with the meaning of Mexico" (Schmidt 98). But after years of revolutionary struggle, transforming military, political, and ideological power relations into a new social order was no simple matter.

In politics, an important step towards unification was taken in 1928, when one large national party was founded as a response to enduring factional political violence. The party later became the *Partido Revolucionario Institucional* (PRI), which ruled Mexico at the national level until 2000. In the 1930s, the party was modelled along corporatist lines. In ideological terms, the political system was structured around reform and nationalism. In fact, revolutionary nationalism became the ideological adhesive of the Mexican political system, at least until the 1980s. Postrevolutionary Mexican nationalism, founded on a particular interpretation of national identity, had an anti-imperialist connotation and legitimated the formation of a strong national state that could serve as a buffer against foreign political and economic influences, while redefining Eurocentric development aims. An active state role was to regulate the market so as to favor the national community, which could best be served by an all-powerful party that represented the various social sectors in a hierarchical and corporatist fashion (Morris).

What is the subject of Mexican nationalism, and how was the underlying notion or essence of Mexican-ness, or *mexicanidad*, defined? At the beginning of the twentieth century, these questions were mostly framed by an analysis of the country's racial relations; that is, between *criollos*, *mestizos*, and Indians. Although the Revolution had not produced an explicit and self-conscious Indian project, if compared to the explicit *campesino* or peasant identity and project, many Indians nevertheless had taken part in the social and military upheavals and conflicts (Boyer). The "Indian question", the position of Indian communities within society and the Mexican nation, was incorporated into the official discourse of the state and became known as state-led *indigenismo*. The aim was to integrate the multifarious Mexicos and shape a new unity where the Indian communities would also be given a proper place, and not simply be relegated into separate corporative spaces. The fact that there was space in the new nationalism for Indian symbols, myths, and history did not deny the importance of "European" culture in Mexico. On the contrary, it was the process of cultural and social mixing that was emphasized. This is how a break was made with the Eurocentric ethos of the nineteenth century anciėn regime. Historian Knight has made the following comment on this important change: "According to the emerging orthodoxy of the Revolution, the old Indian/European thesis/antithesis had now given rise to a higher synthesis, the *mestizo*, who was neither Indian nor European, but quintessentially Mexican" (84–85). The response given by important thinkers to the question regarding the subject of the new Mexican nationalism was unambiguous: the authentic Mexican is a mestizo (or ought to be), the official protagonist of the nation and history.[4]

In short, the core of the ideology of the Revolution was a combination of social reform and nationalism, particularly *mestizo* nationalism. This ideology, and its concomitant policies, supported the strong state and the corporatist party (PRI), whose aim was to include the entire society and represent it as one entity. Education policies, for example, were not only used to support peasants and persuade them to take part in land reform operations and state-led social organizations; they were also used, and perhaps to an even greater extent, to promote national integration and cultural homogeneity (Vaughan). There is not much room for (political, cultural or ethnic) pluralism in this mind-set. The cultural logic of homogeneity, racial *mestizaje* and "imposed unity" corresponds with the political logic of the corporatist one-party regime (Morris 395).

What we observe then in the decades following the Mexican revolution is the consolidation of a corporatist citizenship regime, a process that has been examined

4 There is an interesting bibliography about what has been called "mestizofilia." See e.g. Agustín Basave Benítez, *México mestizo: análisis del nacionalismo mexicano en torno a la mestizofilia de Andrés Molina Enriquez*. Mexico City: Fondo de Cultura Económica, 1992; Kelley Swarthout, *"Assimilating the primitive": parallel dialogues on racial miscegenation in revolutionary Mexico*. New York: Peter Lang Publishing, 2004.

comparatively by Yashar for the Andean region, but that is relevant for Mexico as well. In fact, in Mexico some of the key features of corporatist citizenship regimes, especially in relation to Indigenous politics and identity, acquire their most developed form. Two aspects should be emphasized. First, the huge project of agrarian reform created a new massive infrastructure of state-supported new property relations (*ejidos*) and a whole range of supporting institutions and organizations that, despite all their shortcomings and eventual subordination to the imperatives of political control, provided space for the reproduction of rural (Indigenous) communities. The key social identity was that of the *campesino*. Second, with the combined policies and processes of *mestizaje* and *indigenismo*, the Indigenous population was incorporated in the national state, society and culture. In doing so they became largely "invisible," as they were primarily incorporated as Indigenous *campesinos*. They also tended to represent themselves in this way. Within the corporatist regime, ethnic identity was subordinated to class identity. But since corporatist arrangements provided protective mechanisms for local communities, it meant they also functioned as shields for the exercise of *de facto* autonomy of Indigenous communities. In other words, Indigenous groups benefitted from corporatist arrangements as they blended into a *campesino* identity, which gave them opportunities to sustain their communal practices and institutions, which, moreover, were supported by official *indigenista* policies.

Corporatist citizenship regimes in Latin America remained influential until the 1980s, when they were gradually replaced by what is called the neoliberal citizenship regime. Although this is not the place to amply examine the broader political economic context (nationally and globally) that is behind these changes, some points are in order. I will focus on the implications for state-Indigenous groups relationships and the nature of Indigenous demand-making and discourse. A key aspect in the transition towards the neo-liberal citizenship regime is that corporatist political and economic arrangements, that had been built under the aegis of the developmentalist state, implied a "state-heavy" system of institutions that in the framework of the emerging Washington consensus were perceived as contradictory to the logic of market reforms and the imperatives of deregulation and state downsizing. The implementation of the neo-liberal agenda hence implied the ending of a whole series of state protections, e.g. of agricultural products and services. Yashar has emphasized that whereas the corporatist citizenship regime privileged civil and social rights (less political rights) through class-based interests, the neoliberal citizenship regime privileges civil and political rights (much less social rights) partly through the dismantling of class-based interest organizations.

These developments directly affected Indigenous communities and meant that the institutional mechanisms responsible for some form of de facto autonomy disintegrated. Indigenous communities started to experience new forms of vulnerability, worsened by deepening inequalities and recurring economic crisis (during the 1980s and 1990s). In effect, these changes have dismantled and terminated the relationship between Indians and the state established during the decades following the Mexican revolution. In a way, the Zapatista uprising could be seen as a recognition by Indigenous communities themselves of the changing relationship with the state, and most importantly, as an expression of their decision to renegotiate it on their terms. The core message at the start of the armed uprising was: the project of *mestizaje* and subordinate integration has failed, but we are still here ("*Aqui estamos*!!").

Apart from real threats to de facto Indigenous autonomy, and the spread of new socio-economic vulnerability, there are other processes that have contributed to the emergence of powerful ethnic demand-making in Mexico and elsewhere in Latin America. All this is happening in a time when Mexico's political system is experiencing profound changes, that, however one may want to qualify them, substantially started to increase political associational spaces, of which also Indigenous organizations and activism benefitted. Changes were also taking place in the international context, most importantly the consolidation of a global rights discourse and the formation of global human and Indigenous rights communities and networks, with the use of modern technologies. In fact, the unprecedented exposure and media influence of the Zapatista rebellion within and outside of Mexico could not be disconnected from the use of modern communication technologies and the role they started to play in the emergence of transnational solidarity networks, even though the powerful (and surely seductive) image of *subcomandante* Marcos of the Zapatistas working online on his laptop in the Chiapas jungle was untrue (Ponsioen, Olesen 2004). Already some years ago, Nelson described activists who struggled for Indigenous cultural rights in Guatemala as "Maya-hackers". Similar to computer hackers, who though technically highly skilled operate in systems they do not control, Maya activists have also appropriated modern technology and knowledge and refused to become dissolved in mestizo society (Nelson). Local demands and movements for Indigenous rights were framed by global discourses about rights and multiculturalism and, with the use of digital technologies, thus converted into transnationalized phenomena (Sieder & Witchell).

3. Between class and ethnicity, or the pride of don Félix Serdán

The historical transformation of corporatist towards neoliberal citizenship regimes has thus been accompanied by a re-articulation of peasant (campesino) and Indigenous identities. As Yashar's comparative political analysis has convincingly shown for Latin America, the neoliberal citizenship regime has created a systemic context in which Indigenous political and cultural subjects have flourished (Yashar). Even so, at a deeper (experiential) level the campesino and Indigenous politics and identities are interconnected, thereby constructing a sense of continuity of popular struggles in twentieth century Mexico. I want to illustrate my overall point with a telling anecdote about the encounter with a man whose long life spans both citizenship regimes. In the summer of 2008, I visited, together with a journalist, an aging man in Jojutla, Morelos. We came to interview Félix Serdán, who was by then 90 years old. He was the last survivor of the regional peasant movement headed by Rubén Jaramillo in the 1940s and 1950s, which had rebelled and fought against the state in the heartland of Zapata, until Jaramillo was assassinated in 1962. The jaramillistas had struggled against what they considered the betrayal of the ideals of the Mexican revolution (land and justice). During our conversation, don Félix remembered with great detail episodes of his role in the troops of Jaramillo hiding out in the mountains of Morelos. But he also talked with great warmth and emotion about his commitment to the struggle of the present day Zapatistas, whom he had visited on numerous occasions. He spoke of the honor bestowed upon him when in 1996 he was named "honorary major" of the Zapatista forces in Chiapas, in many ways a world very different from Morelos. In that context he pointed to a large painting, in the typical Mexican muralist style, that depicted a "history of struggle." In the center of the painting are three historical references: in the middle is Rubén Jaramillo, to his left his famous predecessor Zapata – there are also references to their key proclamations, the Plan de Cerro Prieto and the Plan de Ayala respectively. To his right appears a reference to the Zapatista uprising and the Agreements of San Andrés from 1995. There is a strong sense of historical continuity and perseverance in this painting, in which Jaramillo connects the legacy of the old Zapata of the 1910s to the neo-Zapatistas in Chiapas of the 1990s. This is why don Félix went to Chiapas and spoke to subcomandante Marcos. There is, however, also a remarkable change embedded within this overall historical narrative: while in the 1910s through to the 1930s, and during the jaramillista uprisings in the 1940s and 1950s, the core organizing social identity was that of the *campesino*, who was recognized as a legitimate subject of the postrevolutionary state, although within clearly defined boundaries, in the 1990s it had shifted towards one of ethnic (Indigenous) identity.[5] Political language and the entire discursive as well as socio-political context had changed. Don Félix, however, wanted to emphasize the commonalities: in the end, what Zapata, Jaramillo, he himself, subcomandante Marcos and comandante Ramona fought for had not really changed[6]: land, freedom, and justice for the ordinary people of Mexico, some of which are Indigenous, others mestizo.

The shifting politics of identity in postrevolutionary Mexico is also the subject of an anthropological study of the small municipality of Nicolás Ruiz (Chiapas) conducted by Speed. In it she examines the historical trajectory of community identity formation that started with Indigenous identity (before the revolution), then moved into a campesino identity through the community's relationship with the postrevolutionary state agrarian and indigenista policies, followed by a radicalization of campesino identity as people grew frustrated in their interactions with the state, and finally a radical Indigenous identity as they engaged with new social organizations and movements in the context of the Zapatista uprising. In other words, the campesino identity emerged in a dialogical relationship with the state (as the main interlocutor in long lasting struggles about land), but ceded to a reemergent Indigenous identity as the state failed in this role, while rivalling actors and organizations, like the Zapatistas, burst onto the scene. Speed shows, as don Félix already suggested, that identity "is still based around their land struggles, but these struggles themselves have moved out of the realm of the "agrarian" and into the "ethnic" struggle" (114).

Indigenous politics and representation in modern Mexico are thus always about land and socio-economic interests, as well as about culture, language and identity. In the language of current political debates, neo-Indigenous movements are about the politics of redistribution and recognition. A decade ago Mattiace captured this point with the beautiful title of her book about the struggles of Tojolabal Indians in Chiapas: *To see with two eyes*, which, as the subtitle conveys, refers to the fact that contemporary Indigenous struggles are simultaneously about peasant activism and Indian autonomy. It is about the deep connections between class and ethnicity, economy and culture, politics, language and art. On

---

5 The best study of the jaramillista movement is Tanalís Padilla, *Rural resistance in the land of Zapata. The jaramillista movement and the myth of the pax priísta, 1940–1962*. Durham: Duke University Press, 2008.

6 Comandante Ramona was the most important female leader of the contemporary Zapatista movement from Chiapas. She played a key role during the tour of the Zapatistas through Mexico that passed through Michoacán, as it was she who addressed Mexican parliament in the nation's capital. She died of cancer in 2006.

the ground, struggles for Indian autonomy are integral to peasant politics and everyday struggles for survival (Mattiace). By its very nature then, and this my more general point, contemporary Indigenous mobilization is always a critique of state-sanctioned multiculturalism, which, as the American critic Russell Jacoby already observed many years ago, is a happy fellow traveler of economic neoliberalism, as it potentially leads to the fragmentation of class subjects and de-politicization, due to its reified emphasis on cultural difference (Jacoby 29–66).

The constitutive connections between radical politics and ethnic revivalism were already present in one of the most successful ethnic movements in Mexico before the Zapatista uprising of 1994. Underscoring this argument is not possible without reference to the Zapotec movement of the Coalición Obrera Campesina Estudiantil del Istmo (COCEI) from the Juchitán region in Oaxaca during the late 1970s and 1980s. COCEI was successful in wrenching political power from the PRI with a radical ethnic political strategy that combined class politics with cultural and ethnic revivalism. Social policies toward the rural and urban poor were wedded to a creative cultural program, which included the glorification and revitalization of Zapotec language, speech, poetry, humor and fiestas, its support for journals, radio, and art exhibitions in the local Casa de la Cultura. Several important studies have demonstrated that COCEI's ethnic cultural politics were a crucial element in explaining the political successes of the movement (Rubin, Campbell). For political philosopher Jung, these and other popular mobilizations and struggles in Mexico make clear that "indigenous identity offers a political alternative to peasant identity, arising as a strategic response to shifts in the political landscape that undercut the discursive leverage of a redistributive political paradigm at the same time that the international human rights regime has expanded to include collective and cultural rights" (11). The different Mayan communities in Chiapas, the Mixtecos and Zapotecos in Oaxaca, the Purépechas in Michoacán and many other Indigenous communities in Mexico can probably do without the language of the philosopher since they never forgot that identity never was one-dimensional nor static, but a political and social achievement conditioned by broader social and political developments.

Jung's analysis is interesting because it is an attempt to develop a more general theory of critical (political) liberalism that commits democratic government to active engagement with the claims of culture on the basis of an analysis of the Mexican Indigenous rights movement. For her, the moral force of Indigenous demand-making resides not in the existence or protection of cultural difference, but on the deeply rooted history of exclusion. She thereby wants to contribute to general political theoretical debates about multiculturalism, recognition, and minority rights, in which the contributions of Canadian political philosophers have been particularly influential. The major purpose of these debates was the elaboration of a liberal political theory that seeks to establish new standards for the relationships between individual and collective rights, as well as the relationships between culture, politics and rights. Scholars as Taylor and Kymlicka have deeply influenced these discussions not only in Canada, the US and Europe, but they have also shaped studies about Mexico and other parts of Latin America.[7] My main argument is that the conceptual propositions of the politics of recognition (Taylor) and multicultural citizenship (Kymlicka) have proven to be very useful in framing and understanding Indigenous identity politics in Mexico. However, by now the conceptual terrain has started to move on the basis of new insights produced by empirical work about Mexico, and, above all, by the creative political practices of Indigenous peoples themselves that has resulted in changing the terms of the debate altogether. A key example is the debate about the relationship between collective and individual rights, a thorny issue for liberal political theory. This debate has been particularly fierce when it comes to the study of the intersections between ethnic identity and gender. One just has to remember the polemical essay published by Susan Okin several years ago.[8] Behind the debate was the presumed contradiction between Indigenous communities' collective rights to maintain their culture and the rights of individual community members (especially women) that might be violated by those same cultural norms and practices. To resolve this tension the debate has for long centered on the question whether individual or collective rights should have primacy. It is interesting that recent work about Mexico has started to argue that the dichotomy, for which Kymlicka designed his distinction between internal and external protections, might at the end of the day be unproductive and obscure more than clarify. In this context, Speed has convincingly argued on the basis of her extensive anthropological fieldwork about the intersections of class, ethnicity and gender how Indigenous women's interpretations of gender rights are forged in dialogue with outsiders and then brought into dialogues inside their communities themselves. As gender demands are constructed in active engagement with discourses of individual and collective rights embedded in local understandings and practices, they help develop an alternative way of thinking "beyond binaries." In order to underscore the relevance for political theorizing of these practices, and, if I may add, the benefits of on the ground field research, she concludes that "we may see many indigenous women fostering potentially powerful

7 See Charles Taylor's essay in Amy Gutmann (ed.), *Multiculturalism and "The Politics of Recognition."* Princeton: Princeton University Press, 1992 and Will Kymlicka, *Multicultural Citizenship: A Liberal Theory of Minority Rights*. Oxford: Oxford University Press, 1996.

8 *Is Multiculturalism Bad for Women?* Princeton: Princeton University Press, 1999.

new ways of conceptualizing rights and of resisting oppressive power relations" (136). It might just be that some of the purépecha children from Nurío, who participated in the play *Caminantes* in front of the Zapatista leadership in 2001, will, in the near future, make their own contribution to the continuing and changing politics of Indigenous identity and representation in Mexico.

Works cited

Boyer, Christopher. *Becoming Campesinos: Politics, Identity, and Agrarian Struggle in Postrevolutionary Michoacán, 1920–1935*. Stanford: Stanford University Press, 2003. Print.

Campbell, Howard. *Zapotec renaissance: ethnic politics and cultural revivalism in southern Mexico*. Albuquerque: University of New Mexico Press, 1994. Print.

Curiel, Charlynne. *'En momentos difíciles nosotros somos un pueblo'. Haciendo política en la mixteca de Oaxaca: un estudio sobre el ritual, la pasión y el poder*. Diss. Wageningen University, 2010. Print.

Del Carmen Ventura Patiño, María. *Volver a la comunidad. Derechos indígenas y procesos autonómicos en Michoacán*. Zamora: El Colegio de Michoacán, 2010. Print.

Jacoby, Russell. *The End of Utopia: Politics and Culture in an Age of Apathy*. New York: Basic Books, 2000. Print.

Jung, Courtney. *The moral force of indigenous politics. Critical liberalism and the Zapatistas*. Cambridge: Cambridge University Press, 2008. Print.

Knight, Alan. "Racism, revolution and *indigenismo*, Mexico, 1910–1940." *The idea of race in Latin America, 1870–1940*. Ed. Richard Graham. Durham: Duke University Press, 1990. Print.

Mattiace, Shannon. *To see with two eyes. Peasant activism & Indian autonomy in Chiapas*. Albuquerque: University of New Mexico Press, 2003. Print.

Morris, Stephen D.. "Reforming the Nation: Mexican Nationalism in Context." *Journal of Latin American Studies* 31.2 (1999). Print.

Nelson, Diane. "Maya hackers and the cyber-spatialized forms nation-state: modernity, ethnostalgia, and a lizard queen in Guatemala." *Cultural Anthropology* 3 (1996): 287–308. Print.

Niezen, Ronald. "Recognizing Indigenism: Canadian Unity and the International Movement of Indigenous Peoples." *Comparative Studies in Society and History* 42.1 (2000). Print.

Olesen, Thomas. *International Zapatismo: The Construction of Solidarity in the Age of Globalization*. London: Zed Books, 2004. Print.

–. "The transnational Zapatista solidarity network: an infrastructure analysis". *Global Networks* 4.1 (2004): 89–107. Print.

Ponsioen, Arnout. *www.guerrilla.mx. Een onderzoek naar de elektronische strijd van de Zapatistas in Mexico*. Diss. Utrecht University, 1997. Print.

Rivera-Salgado, Gaspar & Jonathan Fox (eds.). *Indigenous Mexican Migrants in the United States*. La Jolla: Center for U.S.-Mexican Studies, 2004. Print.

Rubin, Jeffrey. *Decentering the regime: ethnicity, radicalism, and democracy in Juchitán*. Durham: Duke University Press, 1997. Print.

Schmidt, Henry C.. *The Roots of lo Mexicano. Self and Society in Mexican Thought, 1900–1934*. College Station/London: Texas A&M University Press, 1978. Print.

Sieder, Rachel & Jessica Witchell "Advancing indigenous claims through the law: reflections on the Guatemalan peace process." *Culture and Rights: anthropological perspectives*. Ed. Jane K. Cowan, Marie-Bénédicte Dembour, and Richard A. Wilson. Cambridge: Cambridge University Press, 2001. 201–225. Print.

Speed, Shannon. *Rights in Rebellion. Indigenous Struggles and Human Rights in Chiapas*. Stanford: Stanford University Press, 2008. 83–117. Print.

Stavenhagen, Rodolfo. "Indigenous peoples and the state in Latin America: an ongoing debate." *Multiculturalism in Latin America: indigenous rights, diversity and democracy*. Ed. Rachel Sieder. London: Palgrave MacMillan, 2002. 24–44. Print.

Stephen, Lynn. *Transborder Lives: Indigenous Oaxacans in Mexico, California, and Oregon*. Durham: Duke University Press, 2007. Print.

Vaughan, Mary K.. *Cultural politics in revolution: peasants and schools in Mexico, 1930–1940*. Tucson: University of Arizona Press, 1997. Print.

Velasco Ortiz, Laura. *Mixtec Transnational Identity*. Tucson: The University of Arizona Press, 2005. Print.

Yashar, Deborah J.. *Contesting Citizenship in Latin America: The Rise of Indigenous Movements and the Postliberal Challenge*. Cambridge: Cambridge University Press, 2005. Print.

Laurence Simard-Gagnon
Department of Geography, Queen's University

Caroline Desbiens
Department of Geography, Université Laval

The Social Life of Berries: Gendered Practices of Picking and Sharing in a Contemporary Context

> *Berry picking is not just about going berry picking, just to get berries...*
> (participant)
>
> *So I'm more of a berry picker than a fisher [or a hunter.] Some hate berry picking [...] I guess they're not patient people. Or they're more into, you know, doing things, moving.*
> (participant)

This paper aims to highlight the importance of berries, a product of women's territorial activities, within the cultural and social fabric of contemporary Inuit families and communities. The subsistence activities of Inuit women tend to be poorly documented, especially considering the enthusiasm generated by practices of men, hunting in particular. This lukewarm interest seems to be related to the fact that, in contrast to grandiose and spectacular perspectives of men's territories and experiences, subsistence activities of Inuit women tend to happen in other places, on a smaller scale and on a more regular basis. Nuttall, for example, states that:

> Hunting is differentiated from "work" in that it is shaped by immediate needs. [...] Whereas the hunter makes an effort to provide what is needed, a woman's role in subsistence activities falls within the category of "work." [Work] refers to "action," something that must be finished, in the sense of a task such as scraping sealskins. [...] Furthermore, there are usually several sealskins to be scraped and washed at a given time, thereby making women's work repetitive. (1991, 219)

According to this perspective, women's tasks are depicted as a sequence of actions that, even when finished, must always be started over again. These tasks are intertwined in an infinite whole – the everyday – through which the uniqueness of individual gestures is lost. Their repetitive, never-ending nature pushes these tasks to the background of life. It is then tempting to diminish the worth and impact of each gesture in terms of culture and identity.

Unsurprisingly, the long-standing academic enthusiasm towards Inuit territorial activities of subsistence has been focused mainly on the experiences of men – for instance the hunt of great marine mammals – such that these experiences tend to dominate representations and analyses of Inuit territoriality as a whole. These skewed depictions of activities and experiences of men – and women – are coherent with wider academic understandings of gendered identities, roles and spaces. Feminist geographers have highlighted the construction of dualistic identities and spaces based on gender (see Rose, Massey, McDowell, Domosh and Seager). One of the key structure underpinning such binary constructions is the divide between public and private spheres of activities. Understandings of gender centered on this binary division not only essentialize gender roles and identities, but also follow a hierarchical structure where experiences, spaces and practices associated with men and the masculine are always valorised over those associated with women and the feminine (Rose, Desbiens 2010).

Perspectives informed by these binary versions of gender overshadow the crucial role of Inuit women in maintaining food and cultural systems as well as territorial networks in general (Desbiens 2010). In this chapter, we argue that such an understanding of the activities of Inuit women is stifled within the closed binary conceptual framework that informs dominant academic visions of gender, including the gender breakdown of social, economic and cultural roles. Through our study of Inuit women's practices of berry picking and sharing, we aim not only to highlight the significance of women's contributions to Inuit subsistence, social cohesion and cultural continuity, but also to demonstrate the hindrance of binary and essentialist understandings of gender in recognizing and celebrating these contributions. We proceed first by underlining briefly the significance of berry picking as a contribution of Inuit women to territoriality. We then explore the importance of berry sharing in nurturing social and cultural belonging. We finally open up our discussion to elaborate on the limiting action of binary understandings of gender, and particularly the notion of complementarity, in apprehending Inuit women's experiences and contributions, especially in contemporary context.

This research was based on ethnographic work carried through semi-directed interviews and participatory observations during the summer and fall of 2011 with Inuit women in the community of Inukjuak. Inukjuak is one of the fourteen communities of Nunavik, the region of the province of Québec, Canada, located North of the 55th parallel. Nunavik is bordered by the Hudson Bay to the west, the Hudson Straight to the North, the Ungava Bay to the North East, and the Labrador to the North (see Figure 1). The community of Inukjuak is located on the East Coast of the Hudson Bay, at the mouth of the Innuksuak River. It officially became a Northern Village (NV of Inukjuak) in 1980, and now comprises over 1200 residents, mostly Inuit. Several berry producing species are found in the regions of Inukjuak. The ones most commonly harvested are cloudberries (*aqpik, Rubus chamaemorus*), blueberries (*kigutangirnaq, Vaccinium uliginosum*), redberries (*kimminaq, Vaccinium vitis-idaea*) and blackberries or crowberries (*paurngaq, Empetrum nigrum*).

Our work with women we met in Inukjuak highlights the implications of practices surrounding berry picking and use in the construction of these women's individual cultural and gender identity, but also in the cultural and territorial continuity of the community as a whole.

Figure 1. Permanent Inuit communities of Nunavik post-1950 (Nunavik government)

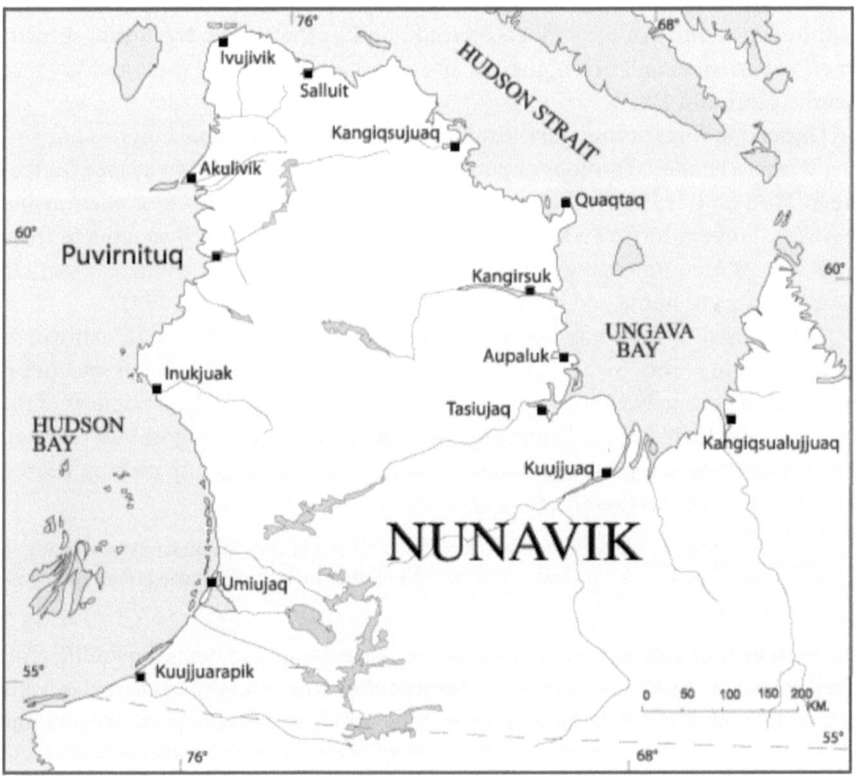

1. Berry picking and territoriality

Subsistence has long been a constant source of concern for the Inuit because of the scarcity of food (Lévesque, Bernier, et al.). The traditional economic system of Inuit hunter-gatherers rested heavily on cyclic migrations and movements of animals, as well as on the growth and production of wild plants – that is, on elements that fall outside of direct human control (as opposed, for example, to agriculture – see Ingold 61–76). Thus Inuit livelihood – and survival – was traditionally grounded on a direct relationship between territory and subsistence (see Saladin d'Anglure, Gombay). This relationship can be expressed through Bonnemaison's concept of territoriality – a concept that may be defined as "the social and cultural relationship that a group maintains with the framework of places and itineraries that make up its territory" (254). Territoriality is embedded within the identity of individuals as Inuit, and in that sense, territorial subsistence, experiences and belonging are all important markers of Inuit identity (see Searles 2001 and 2002).

Understandings of Inuit territoriality often follow conceptual binaries informing Western gendered notions of public vs. private domains of activity (see Bodenhorn 1990 and 1993). In that sense, experiences feeding this close relationship between human, territory and cultural identity are understood to emerge from activities of men unfolding out on the land, in opposition to women's practices tied to spaces of home and community (see for example Nuttall 1991).

For women in Inukjuak however, berry picking is very much an expression of territoriality. This "social and cultural relation" embodied in berry picking is established gradually, first during childhood, through repeated experiences of the territory and fruits. At the beginning, the reluctance – even disgust – of children towards picking is a generalized source of humour that spices up picking stories. One participant recalled that:

> I used to hate berry picking actually. Yeah, I hated it. And I couldn't understand why we had to berry pick and… it took a long time to fill that pail. Until I started to go on my own I guess…

Women in Inukjuak expound gleefully on issues related to bringing young children to pick berries: the children are fidgety, they stomp on the fruits and quickly ask to go back home – as for teenagers, they outright refuse to go berry picking. It could be tempting to attribute this reaction of children to the abrupt social and cultural changes experienced in the communities of Nunavik. However, it seems that this phenomenon is part of each individual's evolving relation to picking and berries. The women of Inukjuak themselves state that they only started picking "seriously" and appreciating it when they reached adulthood. One participant recalls:

> [I started to pick berries] when I was 18, 20, around there [...][when I was a kid] I wasn't interested to pick, I would just eat it before, now I want to collect it.

Adult women end up valuing picking because, in addition to ensuring access to berries, it evokes feelings and memories associated with family and territory. Throughout women's lives, picking represents events where concepts of identity, belonging and territory are constructed and interact with one another.

2. Seasonality, food emotions and territoriality

The importance of berries and berry picking within the territoriality of Inuit women, and of the community as a whole, is also evidenced by emotional responses to their availability or lack thereof. This availability, along with that of the different food products on the land, is determined by the seasonal cycle. The circular movement of time and seasons is an element through which the connection between territory, subsistence and cultural identity is strongly highlighted. For the Inuit, this connection is expressed through territorial emotions – more or less intense feelings of anticipation of coming seasons, and nostalgia of seasons past. These emotions are channelled in the memories and discussions related to the different foods harvested on the land. Lévesque and collaborators thus call them "food emotions" (Lévesque, Bernier, et al.).

As berries mature at the end of summer and through the beginning of fall, they are associated with the warmest, most luminous and abundant period of the year. The women of Inukjuak anticipate a sequence of environmental conditions that, like a climatic ritual, will lead to the full development of fruits: sun, "straight" rain, and thunderstorms for good measure. The "food" or "territorial" emotions associated with berries are significant: on the one hand, fruits mature during a period conducive to celebrations; on the other hand, berries are only available for a limited time.

This scarcity makes the berries valuable, particularly in the case of *akpiks* (cloudberries). They are the first berries to ripen and their picking period is relatively short as they spoil quickly. *Akpiks* are much appreciated, especially because of their rarity. For example, when asked "Which is your favourite berry?" a participant answered:

> Well akpiks, for sure, will always be, because they only have a certain time to grow and they finish at a very short time, so akpiks, they're kind of special. And black, blue, and red, you know you can pick them for longer time, so I like all of them.

Although *akpiks* are quite scarce – and very much appreciated – the picking period for all types of berries is limited, especially since pickers have the geese to compete with. The maturing of berries causes some excitement in the community:

> When it's berry-picking season, it's everywhere, when they start growing, you hear it all the time. And some take it very seriously. If they don't go berry picking they're moody.

The feeling expressed by the individuals unable to go picking goes beyond disappointment. Rather, it seems to resemble berry "cravings," which some women say they experience when they are deprived of them, for example at the end of winter when provisions are depleted. These "cravings" cannot be compared to cravings for store-bought food – like soft drinks or potato chips – because they evoke complex emotions related to the territory and the passing of seasons. "Craving" for territorial foods and the alternating availability and non-availability of these foods are part of a seasonal cycle that has long defined the diet of the Inuit (Lévesque, Bernier, et al., Lévesque, De Juriew, et al.). Although the women of Inukjuak indicated dreading berry "cravings", they also seemed to accept the situation with serenity and laughter: "Oh well, there's always next year…" Nonetheless, a frequent strategy used to meet berry needs in times of shortage is to appeal to the social – or the family – sharing network.

3. The social life of berries

Once picked, berries move through sharing networks formed within relatively extended family groups. This observation goes against the works of Guédon, Saladin d'Anglure and Labrèche who state that the output of women's territorial activities is consumed exclusively within the household. We understand such statements as echoing uncritical binary conceptualizations of gendered practices and spaces (as argued above), and we deplore their impact in limiting understandings of the significance and resonance of Inuit women's practices within a social and cultural canvass. In fact, to the best of our knowledge, researchers have not formally documented berry sharing within Inuit family groups in Nunavik. As the scope of our ethnographic research is too limited to paint a complete picture of these practices, the following discussion is based on meat sharing models in Inuit groups.

Although based on social and economic organizations from different regions (West Coast of Alaska, Baffin Island in Nunavut and East Coast of Greenland, respectively), the models developed by Bodenhorn (2000), Wenzel (1995 and 2000) and Hovelsrud-Broda (2000) show important elements of similarity between each other and the reality of berry sharing in Inukjuak. Therefore, they can be used as a basis for highlighting some aspects of women's berry sharing system in Inukjuak.

In all cases, sharing food is considered a central element of the identity of the Inuit. In the words of Bodenhorn, "The fact of sharing food is what makes one properly Inupiaq, not a proper relative" (Bodenhorn 1993: 47). In fact, even if most of the sharing is more or less mutual within the immediate family, the members of Inuit communities also feel an obligation to share unilaterally with the people who, for one reason or another, do not have as much access to the food of the land (Bodenhorn 1993).

In Inukjuak, the berry period is characterized by a series of radio requests from individuals who do not have access to berries. Indeed, the women of Inukjuak met through our project felt obligated to share with certain members of their extended family or their friendship network, without expecting anything in return. The two main factors explaining the necessity for such sharing were remoteness – especially in the case of individuals living north of Pivurnituq, where berries are scarcer – and sickness and/or invalidity. In the latter case, the need for berries does not appear so much to derive from the fact that the sick and/or invalid person cannot go out on the land, but rather that the berries will have a therapeutic effect on that person. Such therapeutic virtues of territorial food for the Inuit are discussed by several authors (for exemple, see Searles 2002; Lévesque, Bernier et al., and regarding plants see Ziegler and Joamie, Jones).

Bodenhorn (2000) underlines the fact that these cases of punctual and generalized sharing (without expecting something in return) are interspaced with more regular, reciprocal sharing. According to her, these events of "open" sharing fulfill the requirements of all Inuit towards their environment and are necessary to maintain the balance of relations with non-humans. Thus, generalized sharing ensures the proper functioning of the social system of regular subsistence and sharing which is focused, to a large extent, on the immediate family network (Bodenhorn 1993, Hovelsrud-Broda 2000, Wenzel 2000). Our interest with women's practices of berry picking and use lies within the day-to-day meanings and trajectories of berries within close networks of family and/or friendship.

Based on experiences and narratives of women we met in Inukjuak, the following section explores some aspects of the trajectories of berries and of the meanings assigned to them within immediate family networks. The discussion is structured around the stories of three families. Through each story, a particular theme or aspect of women's relationship with berries and sharing is highlighted. This structure was chosen for the sake of clarity; however, it is important to note that the experiences of the various families do not unfold in isolation from one another, and that elements highlighted in the narratives of one family are often echoed in those of the others.

Epoo[1] Family – the concept of center

As established above, the immediate family is at the heart of food sharing transactions for the Inuit. However, the meaning of "immediate family" depends on the context and the vision of the ethnographer. Hovelsrud-Broda (2000) presents the household, an almost-nuclear family focused on a man-woman couple, as the primary sharing unit in the Isertoq community in Greenland. Beyond the household, she describes regular sharing connections between households with similar resources and related through kin relations, i.e., an immediate family network. This sharing model is close to Bodenhorn's, who also associates regular sharing with networks between smaller families of similar socio-economic status. Based on the Barrow community in Alaska, Bodenhorn insists on the central role of a man-woman couple that would be responsible for the management and distribution of territorial products of subsistence in sharing networks (Bodenhorn 1990, 1993 and 2000).

Conversely, Wenzel describes sharing in Clyde River, Nunavut, as done mainly within highly hierarchical family networks, centered on one elder (see Wenzel 1995 and 2000). Those networks operate following the respect/obedience requirements that govern relations between the various family members, and are defined by unchanging status indicators such as gender and generational position. The family networks described by Wenzel, Bodenhorn and Hovelsrud-Broda all demonstrate sharing relations that revolve around a stable foundation made up of one person or a couple with strong family and social status. With respect to berries in Inukjuak, the story of the Epoo family suggests that the centre of sharing networks – or the central position of one person or more – can be determined in a more fluid fashion.

The four Epoo sisters (Suzy, Sarah, Elsie and Mary), their mother and a number of other people form a sharing network of berries and other territorial products. After getting to know Suzy – mainly through our children – during the summer of 2011, I (Laurence) had the chance to conduct an individual semi-structured interview with her in the fall, and to meet her three sisters in a group interview. As most of the Epoo sisters have adopted the name of their husbands, I did not realize the kinship between Suzy and her sisters until later, a fact that I found quite interesting.

Suzy is an enthusiastic picker, but her sisters prefer fishing. This preference tends to limit their picking efforts. Nevertheless, Sarah, Elsie and Mary like to prepare berry-based meals. They particularly like fish with berries, *suvallik* (a mixture of fruit, oil and fish eggs), and baked goods like pies or muffins. Elsie even developed her own blueberry muffins recipe. She explains:

---

1 All the names of the participants mentioned in this chapter have been changed.

> For me, I bake [berries] in muffins. I found this recipe on a Northern store calendar. And I baked it, almost every day, and made improvements on it, and now everybody wants it. Yes. I didn't use some of the ingredients that the recipe says, and added some of my own.

By developing knowledge that is hers alone, Elsie acquired a special status within her sharing family network: she is now recognized as the person capable of baking blueberry muffins, a food product appreciated by all. Consequently, Elsie has become a centre towards which the resources necessary for the preparation of her famous muffins converge. Given the fact that Elsie herself is not a particularly productive picker (compared to Suzy, for example), there is a certain obligation for the other members of the family network to provide her with berries. Thus, to the question "Have you picked a lot of blueberries this year?" Suzy answers:

> [Yes.] But my sister she makes blueberry muffins, so... We didn't have a chance to save some. [...] We eat them all with muffins *laugh*
> Thanks to her special knowledge, Elsie is responsible for receiving the berries from different members of her family network and redistributing them in a prepared form.

The story of Elsie Epoo places two elements in perspective regarding the concept of "authority" or "centre" of sharing networks. Firstly, Wenzel's model – according to which the obedience/respect relations with the person at the head of the family network would be based on status attributes like gender and generational position – cannot be applied in this particular case. In fact, as a woman and daughter of parents practising subsistence activities (fishing, hunting), Elsie would be in a subordinate position according to Wenzel's model, but such is obviously not the case.

Secondly, Elsie's story highlights the dynamic nature of the sharing systems within families. As Elsie developed a particular knowledge (ie. her own muffin recipe), the sharing network centered upon her, so that the whole of the family group can now access the products of this knowledge (the muffins) more easily. Bodenhorn, Hovelsrud-Broda and Wenzel present the concepts of status and productivity as constant attributes of the person or people at the center of sharing networks. Elsie's story suggests that this central role could be more fluid, at least concerning berries. Moreover, the story of the Epoo family does not mention the trajectories of other territorial subsistence products like meat or fish. It may well be that these do not converge towards Elsie and that, consequently, several "centres" exist within this family's sharing network.

Kokiapik Family – the idea of "shares"

In the Kokiapik family, the sharing of berries brings to mind the idea of *shares* developed by Bodenhorn (2000) in the context of whale hunting in the community of Barrow, Alaska. According to Bodenhorn, the idea of "shares" results from the fact that a series of contributions beyond the act of killing an animal by a hunter are needed to ensure the success of the hunt. The actions contributing to hunting are diverse, and each of the contributions would imply an inalienable right to a "share" of the animal hunted. Thus, this system allows any individual, through his or her contribution, to claim a right to the products of the hunt for him or herself, whether this contribution is directly related to hunting or not. According to Bodenhorn, the "shares" system takes place in both ad hoc situations – in which case acquiring a "share" does not necessarily imply a long-term relation between individuals – and in complex sharing systems that are extended through time, such as within a family. The example of berry sharing in the Kokiapik family illustrates the idea of "shares" insofar as it allows members who do not pick berries to have access to them through other contributions.

As far as can be assessed, the Kokiapik family's berry sharing network involves Louisa, her mother, her two sisters Nancy and Siasi, and their cousin. I (Laurence) met Nancy and Siasy through sewing and craft activities organized by the *Sungirtuivik* family centre. In October 2011, I was able to exchange with Louisa in a more structured way.

Nancy and Siasi Kokiapik and their cousin are enthusiastic pickers. Louisa tends to pick more with her adult niece and her production is less than her sisters'. Louisa's mother is the heart of the family-sharing network of small fruits. Louisa explains:

> [Two of my sisters and my cousin] they're real serious berry pickers. [...] They're just always going. Always, everyday they go. They give [the berries] to my mother to freeze them. So whenever I want berries badly I just go eat some at my mother's.

Sharing fruit in the Kokiapik family is close to the Wenzel's model described above in the sense that the central pillar of the network is an elder – Louisa's mother – who collects the resources and redistributes them to the family members who would not otherwise have access to them. It is also towards Louisa's mother that other resources and contributions converge – following Bodenhorn's concept of "shares." Louisa's testimony illustrates this:

> My mother loves to eat the berries, any kind of berries with *Dream Whip*. Yeah, so, I have to go to the store to get her *Dream Whip*. Because three of my sisters they go berry-picking a lot.

The fact that Louisa assigns herself the task of buying whipped cream for her mother highlights two things. Firstly, it illustrates the idea of interdependence at the centre of the descriptions and analyses of Inuit's subsistence systems. Indeed, Louisa, by her action, is completing the action of her sisters – intensive picking – so that the result of her actions – berries and whipped cream – can be combined into the food desired by the Kokiapik mother. Secondly, Louisa's story reflects Bodenhorn's idea that participation in food production is not hierarchized (see Bodenhorn 2000). In fact, it would be difficult to evaluate the importance of Louisa's and her sisters' contributions. They are both part of the actions that establish, and are established by, belonging to the sharing network, which in turn reflects belonging to the family.

Idlout family – the emotional gift

This last story demonstrates some emotional aspects of berry sharing. The point of view discussed here is that of Annie Idlout. Annie is in her early thirties and the single parent of a little boy and a teenager. Employed full time, she handles many demands on her time and energy. Annie's food sharing network is centered in her parents' home where she and her children eat most of their meals. Annie imparts a great deal of importance to territorial food, towards which she expresses a strong sense of attachment. She indicates how important it is from a perspective of well-being, and in terms of therapeutic values.

For various reasons, Annie could not pick *akpiks* (cloudberries) during the summer of 2011. However, she could obtain some through her mother:

> I didn't go picking *akpiks*. My mom [picked some], especially for my kids. [...]During winter time, when we have birthday parties, when the kids see the *akpiks*, the blackberries, they really want it. Well that's my kids, [they] really like it, when they see the berries, during winter time on the birthday parties.

Annie's words demonstrate the symbolic importance of berries, for herself as well as for her children. The fruits given are a symbol of the land and the emotional relations established around place and territory. The gift of berries from Annie's mother contributes to Annie and her children's sense of well-being, security and belonging. Beyond a redistribution of the family resources, this action appears to be to akin to "nurturing," a concept that includes the ideas of caring, feeding and loving.

This interpretation finds echoes within the work of Briggs, who states that "Inuit, when lonely and afraid, often crave the food that symbolizes care" (Briggs 1997, 229). In that sense, by feeding her children berries picked by her mother, Annie imparts the berries with symbols of family belonging. This emotional resonance is enhanced by the association of berries with particular rituals. Thus, as much as the presence of berries on the cake adds a specific value to the birthday, the birthday itself adds to the affective value of the berries. Briggs comments on this phenomenon: "It is emotionally charged personal experience that gives emblems their symbolic load and attach people to cultural identities or alienate them from these identities" (Briggs 1997: 233).

4. Berries and gender

The stories told by women in Inukjuak highlight a complex system of human relations nurtured by berry sharing – therefore undoubtedly a *social* system. This system challenges the commonly accepted assumption that berries – as female territorial products – are limited to the immediate household, and therefore necessarily private and *a*social. In fact, the existence of this system disrupts the accepted conceptual convention whereby segregation of gender necessarily implies segregation of space – including social and/or "public" space. This suggests that we cannot strictly mobilize the binary analytical structures of western academic thinking to establish an analysis of the gender-based organization and its significance to the Inuit.

The concept of complementarity

This said, the discussion presented thus far confronts us with certain paradoxes in relation to territoriality and gender, especially regarding the roles of men and the idea of complementarity. If men are not – or only nominally – mentioned in our discussion so far, it is because the women we met in Inukjuak mention them very little during conversations about berries. However, men are present, in the background, and except for women only outings[2], stories told by women about picking often take place during outings with male family members.

The fact that women and men often perform their activities together is recognized, but commonly (and deliberately?) forgotten in analyses of Inuit territoriality. Briggs noted almost 40 years ago that, even if Inuit men define themselves by great marine mammal hunting, the amount of time directly spent on this activity is actually limited – most of the time, men and women are together (Briggs 1974). It is precisely this fact that led Shannon (2006) to ponder the validity of the idea of a strict gender segregation among the Inuit. She finds this idea at odds with the numerous activities shared by men and women together – for example fishing. To the question "Do the men pick too?" an Inukjuak woman answered:

> Not really. *laugh* Well… if you're gonna spend all day out on the land then… might as well pick, so my dad sometimes picked. Sometimes. [But it's] more for women.

Therefore, men spend time with women: they operate the boat, hunt and fish, but usually do not pick. On the other hand, some women use a blueberry "picker," a kind of instrument shaped like a comb with metal teeth that allows them to pick faster.

2 It was not possible, during fieldwork, to assess the importance accorded to outings between women versus outings together as a family in the comprehensive picking activities of women.

Women who use it have all received it from a male relative, most often their father. By building these instruments, men are, in a way, contributing to women's picking.

This example meets the concept of complementarity that is the basis for discussions of gender in much of the literature of Inuit studies. Complementarity is understood by Guemple, among others, as the obligation of each gender to perform their tasks for members of the other gender – an obligation that, according to him, is the linchpin of gender identity among the Inuit. Other authors, like Trott, also see in the idea of complementarity the expression of the symbolic presence of one gender within the construction of the opposite – Trott compares this Inuit version of gender to the concepts of yin and yang. The idea of complementarity is present, for example, in the kayak – a symbol of masculinity which is "dressed" by women – and in the house – a place of femininity which is built by men (Collignon, Guemple, Thérrien). Like these two objects, the blueberry picker built by men is an example of complementarity.

And yet, an analysis of gender roles based on the idea of complementarity is not satisfactory in many ways. First, this idea can be akin to a conceptual broom used to sweep the gender question under the carpet in discussions of territoriality and Inuit cultural identity. For example, the question of complementary gender allows us to "complement" our understanding of Inuit realities (for example in Nuttall 1998) without having to reconsider the very validity of this understanding based almost exclusively on the experiences of men. The idea of complementarity also makes it easier to conduct an analysis based on binary analytical structures related to gender. As a result, the analyses of Inuit gender in contemporary and market-driven contexts lead to interpretations that are often incomplete. For some authors, the important presence of women in paid workplaces in Inuit communities is viewed as a form of emancipation; women thus have access to the public sphere which, from a western standpoint, is associated with masculinity and power (see Guay for exemple) and should therefore be "liberating" This outlook is particularly problematic when compared to the discourse of many aboriginal feminists who deplore the intrinsic patriarchal nature of colonialism (for example Martin-Hill, Eikjok, Green, Henning, Kuokkanen, Smith). These authors highlight the binding effects of a western understanding of identity and gendered roles embedded in binary and hierarchized conceptual structures. This understanding of gender tends to place representations of women's experiences in a static framework. It also tends to encourage power imbalances between genders, in which women's contributions are described as subordinate to men's.

Complementarity, gender and contemporaneity

Moreover, complementarity as a conceptual anchor to understanding and problematizing Inuit gender(s) is necessarily limiting because gender identity is neither experienced nor articulated in a uniform manner. Indeed, the concept of complementarity as a rigid basis of gender does not leave room to apprehend the multiple effects of contemporaneity, itself structured by colonialism, in the construction and appropriation of gendered identities. Inuit concepts of gender – as a social construction – are inevitably imbued with cultural change related to colonial encounters. For example, some authors consider the crystallization of gender roles among the Inuit under binary axes to be the result of Christianity (see Stewart) and western consumerism (Condon and Stern, Stewart). Kuokkanen, a Sami feminist author, discusses this point eloquently:

> Contemporary perceptions of and attitudes toward women in Sami society are [...] an entangled combination of influences of various origins and from different periods of time, making it rather difficult [to] trace back the traditional status and roles of Sami women (whatever is implied by the always problematic notion of "traditional"). (75)
>
> It would be misleading and naive to seriously believe that in some miraculous ways, Sami gender relations have remained entirely unaffected through the centuries-long colonizing process that changed every other aspect of the lives and cultural practices of our people. (84)

Within much of the academic literature concerned with aboriginal genders – as well as for many aboriginal people – the concept of "femininity" is constructed in a way that evokes a static and polarized understanding of "tradition" (Martin-Hill, Eikjok, Kuokkanen). Within Inuit studies, this is exemplified by contemporary depictions of female gender as linked with the abilities to perform "traditional" female activities, such as sewing or tending the oil lamp – abilities that, along with men's hunting activities, would meet the imperatives of a semi-nomadic land-based existence (see for example Guemple and more recently Trott).

We argue that conceptualizing gender based on a "traditionally" bound and static notion of complementarity creates particular constraints and dissonances for individuals whose experiences of gender are now embedded within the complexity of contemporary contexts (see also Eikjok). This argument resonates with the work of Kuokkanen who argues that contemporaneity means the combination of two kinds of expectations for aboriginal women. The first, as illustrated above, is related to static gender identities and is based in stereotypes related to the idea of tradition. The second is related to needs and life circumstances in a contemporary context, meaning capitalist and westernized.

For the Inuit, contemporaneity implies that connections between identity and subsistence now unfold in an increasingly globalized political and economic context. For example, Dahl describes the integration of capitalist structures and so-called "subsistence" structures in a community in Greenland to demonstrate the strong relationship between the two systems in contemporary economy. In this context, access to money becomes essential to subsistence. Speaking about the Inuit of Clyde River, Wenzel wrote:

> [...] it is the scarcity of money, or at least limitations on access to money, that, as much as weather or prey conditions, presently affect Clyde subsistence relations. (62)

Access to money requires integration into the capitalist economy, and it is often the women who make this integration through paid employment (McElroy, Dahl, Lévesque, Lussier, et al., Wenzel 2000, Searles 2001, Dowsley et al.). As Searles states: "The popular saying that 'every great hunter has a wife with a good paying job' alludes to the fact that many hunters are supported by their wives" (Searles 2001, 127). This observation undermines the idea of complementarity as the foundation of gender. Indeed the variety and complexity of circumstances related to contemporary experiences entails a multiplicity of roles and contributions for individuals of both genders, which makes it difficult to conceptualize male and female identities as being constructed in a neat mirror relation of complementary opposition. It is also evident – and perhaps the crux of the issue – as we contrast various stories of women in Inukjuak that the effects and circumstances related to contemporaneity have different meanings depending on individuals, experiences and circumstances. By imposing a rigid framework based on static understandings of "traditional" roles in readings and representations of gender identity, the idea of complementarity does not leave the latitude required to understand and acknowledge these various experiences, thus creating another insidious blind spot.

This is particularly significant in Inuit communities, where there frequently is a certain tension between individuals who are fully engaged in the market economy and those more intensively involved in territorial systems of subsistence (Wenzel 1995, Searles 2001 and 2002). These different engagements result in different combinations of experiences and constraints in relation to the ongoing practice of territorial subsistence activities. These engagements are mediated by circumstances facilitating or hindering territorial experiences such as: access to necessary resources (most importantly money), time constraints related to a paid job, extent of family networks, sense of belonging on the land, frequency of land-based picking/fishing/hunting activities, and access to a camp. Such circumstances have an impact on the ways in which gendered identities are built and perceived. Indeed, if the separation of labour between men and women – on which the idea of complementarity relies – is key to gendered identity, the primordial purpose of this separation is to be adaptive and to render life as easy and comfortable as possible (Desbiens 2007). This ultimate goal necessarily involves flexibility, given the wide variability in circumstances that define men and women's experiences (Briggs 1974).

This flexibility is discussed by Briggs, who points out that the most skilled individuals among the Inuit are the ones with the ability to do tasks not only associated to their gender, but also those of the opposite gender (Briggs 1974). The need for flexible gendered skills arises in the stories of some Inukjuak women. For example, to a question about safe picking strategies when a wolf is lurking about (a common occurrence), a woman answered:

> We bring a gun. Even if we're all ladies and we're craving for picking, even if there's wolves, we take the gun and go.

Therefore, even if individuals generally focus on roles traditionally related to their gender, circumstances of life on the territory can render specialization restrictive. Acquiring some skills related to the opposite gender increases mobility, thus competence. In addition, the fact of being capable of performing skills related to male activities can be experienced as a source of emancipation, as expressed by another woman:

> This summer, early summer we went fishing, there were five Hondas, and maybe seven ladies. It was lots of fun. Yeah… My Honda got stuck and I thought I was going to lose it to the ground and I was terrified and… these girls knew what to do. They got my Honda out. We put rocks under the tires. We just pulled it out. I said "Super women!" Yeah! Even if we were just only women. Even if we don't have men around we can do things.

In her story this woman clearly challenges the binary structures that drive her own perception of gender. This story, like the one about the wolves, implies that greater skills result from the ability of a person to transcend obvious gender categories, themselves related to notions of territory and traditional roles. However this idea of skills as being enhanced by transcending gender binaries cannot necessarily be projected in the same way into other contexts, even if these contexts are experienced by the same person. For example, the idea of transcending gender expectations that are based on complementary traditional roles cannot necessarily be projected in similar ways in a context of paid employment, where many women in Inukjuak spend much of their time. This is not because places of paid employment are not gendered – in fact, as noted by Kuokkanen, they include their own sets of stereotypes and expectations. What we can conclude from these narratives however is that gender is a multidimensional and inherently contextualized phenomenon that cannot be rigorously apprehended through the binary constraints of a notion of complementarity.

5. Conclusion

Our discussion about the idea of skills illustrates how the emphasis is placed on the complementarity of roles deemed "traditional" in gender construction and representation, creating a gender identity that cannot represent and embrace individuals' experiences, or at least their entire experience. For women, this dissonance between gender experiences and static notions and discourses of gender identity is amplified by the power imbalance between men and women – whether or not this is a result of colonialism. Eikjok (118), a Sami feminist author, writes eloquently that:

> "The Mothers" of Indigenous worldviews are being taken out of their original context and placed in the global political context of today in a show of resistance against "the western." The problem is that the definition of woman becomes narrow and loses any potential for change. This is not useful or functional for modern Indigenous women.

Reducing the representation and understanding of gender to a definition based on first the "separation," then the "complementarity" of male and female, public and private or "traditional" and "contemporary" activities is not helpful to understanding and acknowledging the multiplicity of women's experiences. This binary conceptual reflex is immobilizing for women at any time, and especially in the context of contemporary life.

Works Cited

Bodenhorn, Barbara. ""I'm Not the Great Hunter, My Wife Is" Iñupiat and anthropological models of gender." *Études/Inuit/Studies* 14.1–2 (1990): 55–74. Print.

–. "Gendered Spaces, Public Places: Public and Private Revisited on the North Slope of Alaska." *Landscape: Politics and Perspectives*. Ed. Barbara Bender. Providence: Berg, 1993. 169–203. Print.

–. "It's Good to Know Who Your Relatives Are but We Were Taught to Share with Everybody: Shares and Sharing among Inupiaq Households." *The Social Economy of Sharing: Resource Allocation and Modern Hunter-Gatherers*. Ed. George W. Wenzel, Grete Hovelsrud-Broda, and Nobuhiro Kishigami. Vol. 53. Osaka: National Museum of Ethnology, 2000. 27–60. Print. Senri Ethnological Studies.

Bonnemaison, Joël. "Voyage Autour Du Territoire." *L'Espace géographique* 4 (1981): 249–262. Print.

Briggs, Jean L. "Eskimo Women, Makers of Men." *Many Sisters; Women in Cross-Cultural Perspective*. New York: The Free Press, 1974. 261–304. Print.

–. "From Trait to Emblem and Back: Living and Representing Culture in Everyday Inuit Life." *Arctic Anthropology* 34.1 (1997): 227–235. Print.

Collignon, Béatrice. "Esprit Des Lieux et Modèles Culturels. La Mutation Des Espaces Domestiques En Arctique inuit//Sense of Place and Cultural Identities: Inuit Domestic Spaces in Transition." *Annales de Géographie* 110.620 (2001): 383–404. Print.

Condon, Richard G., and Pamela R. Stern. "Gender-Role Preference, Gender Identity, and Gender Socialization among Contemporary Inuit Youth." *Ethos* 21.4 (1993): 384–416. *CrossRef*. Web. 18 Dec. 2010.

Dahl, Jens. "The Integrative and Cultural Role of Hunting and Subsistence in Greenland." *Études/Inuit/Studies* 13.1 (1989): 23–42. Print.

Desbiens, Caroline. "Speaking the Land: Exploring Women's Historical Geographies in Northern Québec." *Canadian Geographer/Le Géographe canadien* 51.3 (2007): 360–372. Print.

–. "Step Lightly, Then Move Forward: Exploring Feminist Directions for Northern Research." *The Canadian Geographer/Le Géographe canadien* 54.4 (2010): 410–416. Print.

Domosh, Mona, and Joni Seager. *Putting Women in Place: Feminist Geographers Make Sense of the World*. New York: Guilford Press, 2001. Print.

Dowsley, Martha et al. "Should We Turn the Tent? Inuit Women and Climate Change." *Études/Inuit/Studies* 34.1 (2010): 151–165. Print.

Eikjok, Jorunn. "Gender, Essentialism and Feminism in Samiland." *Making Space for Indigenous Feminism*. Ed. Joyce Green. Trans. Gunhild Hoogensen. Black Point, Nova Scotia: Fernwook Publishing, 2007. 108–123. Print.

Gombay, Nicole. "Placing Economies: Lessons from the Inuit about Economics, Time, and Existence." *Journal of Cultural Geography* 29.1 (2012): 19–38. Print.

Green, Joyce. "Taking Account of Aboriginal Feminism." *Making Space for Indigenous Feminism*. Ed. Joyce Green. Black Point, Nova Scotia: Fernwook Publishing, 2007. 20–32. Print.

Guay, Hélène. "Socialisation et Emplois Salariés: Une Ethnographie Des Femmes Inuit d'Igloolik." *Culture* 9.2 (1989): 3–24. Print.

Guédon, Marie-Françoise. "Organisation Des Activités Féminines Dans La Communauté Esquimaude d'Ivujivik." Mémoire de maîtrise en anthropologie. Université de Montréal, 1967. Print.

Guemple, Lee. "Men and Women, Husbands and Wives: The Role of Gender in Traditional Inuit Society." *Études/Inuit/Studies* 10.1–2 (1986): 9–24. Print.

Henning, Denise K. "Yes, My Daughters, We Are Cherokee Women." *Making Space for Indigenous Feminism*. Ed. Joyce Green. Black Point, Nova Scotia: Fernwook Publishing, 2007. 187–198. Print.

Hovelsrud-Broda, Grete. "'Sharing', Transfers, Transactions and the Concept of Generalized Reciprocity." *The Social Economy of Sharing: Resource Allocation and Modern Hunter-Gatherers*. Ed. Grete Hovelsrud-Broda, Nobuhiro Kishigami, and George W. Wenzel. Vol. 53. Osaka: National Museum of Ethnology, 2000. 193–214. Print. Senri Ethnological Studies.

Ingold, Tim. *The Perception of the Environment: Essays in Livelihood, Dwelling and Skill*. New York: Routledge, 2000. Print.

Jones, Anore. *Plants That We Eat – Nauriat Niginaqtuat*. Fairbanks: University of Alaska Press, 2010. Print.

Kuokkanen, Rauna. "Myths and Realities of Sami Women: A Post-Colonial Feminist Analysis for the Decolonization and Transformation of Sami Society." *Making Space for Indigenous Feminism*. Ed. Joyce Green. Black Point, Nova Scotia: Fernwook Publishing, 2007. 72–92. Print.

Labrèche, Yves. "Variations Saisonnières et Échange-Don de Nourriture Chez Les Inuit Du Nunavik." *Études/Inuit/Studies* 30.2 (2006): 73–94. Print.

Lévesque, Carole, Dominique De Juriew, et al. "Between Abundance and Scarcity: Food and the Institution of Sharing Among the Inuit of the Circumpolar Region During the Recent Historical Period." *Sustainable Food Security in the Arctic – State of Knowledge*. Ed. Gérard Duhaime. Université Laval: Groupe d'études inuit et circumpolairs (GÉTIC) et Canadian Circumpolar Institute (CCI) Press, 2002. 103–116. Print. Occasional Publication Series 52.

Lévesque, Carole, Catherine Lussier, et al. "Changement Social, Culture et Alimentation Chez Les Inuit de La Région Circumpolaire." 1999: n. pag. Print.

Lévesque, Carole, Susie Bernier, et al. "Les Choix Alimentaires Des Inuit de l'Arctique – Une Enquête En Alaska et Au Nunavik." 2004: n. pag. Print.

Massey, Doreen. *Space, Place, and Gender*. Minneapolis: University of Minnesote Press, 1994. Print.

Martin-Hill, Dawn. "She No Speaks and Other Colonial Constructs of 'the Traditional Woman.'" *Strong Women Stories – Native Vision and Community Survival*. Ed. Kim Anderson and Bonita Lawrence. Toronto: Sumach Press, 2003. 106–120. Print. Women's Issues Publishing Program.

McDowell, Linda. *Gender, Identity, and Place: Understanding Feminist Geographies*. Cambridge: Polity Press, 1999. Print.

McElroy, Ann. "Canadian Arctic Modernization and Change in Female Inuit Role Identification." *American Ethnologist* 2.4 (1975): 662–686. *CrossRef*. Web. 18 Dec. 2010.

Nuttall, Mark. "Critical Reflections on Knowledge Gathering in the Arctic." *Aboriginal Environmental Knowledge in the North*. Ed. Louis-Jacques Dorais, Murielle Nagy, and Ludger Müller-Wille. Québec: GÉTIC, Université Laval, 1998. 21–35. Print.

–. "Sharing and the Ideology of Subsistence in a Greenlandic Sealing Community." *Polar Record* 27.162 (1991): 217–222. Print.

Rose, Gillian. *Feminism and geography: the limits of geographical knowledge*. Minneapolis: University of Minnesota Press, 1993. Print.

Saladin d'Anglure, Bernard. "Les Inuit Du Nunavik." *Le Nord: Habitants et Mutations*. Ed. Gérard Duhaime. Sainte Foy: Les Presses de l'Université Laval, 2001. 85–102. Print. Atlas Historique Du Québec.

Searles, Edmund. "Fashioning Selves and Tradition: Case Studies on Personhood and Experience in Nunavut." *American Review of Canadian Studies* 31.1–2 (2001): 121–136. Print.

–. "Food and the Making of Modern Inuit Identities." *Food and Foodways* 10.1 (2002): 55–78. Print.

Shannon, Kerrie Ann. "Everyone Goes Fishing: Understanding Procurement for Men, Women and Children in an Arctic Community." *Études/Inuit/Studies* 30.1 (2006): 9–29. Print.

Smith, Linda Tuhiwai. *Decolonizing Methodologies: Research and Indigenous Peoples*. 12th ed. Dunedin: University of Otago Press, 2008. Print.

Stewart, Henry. "Kipijuituq in Netsilik Society – Changing Patterns of Gender and Patterns of Changing Gender." *Many Faces of Gender – Roles and Relationships through Time in Indigenous Northern Communities*. Ed. Lisa Frink, Rita S. Shepard, and Gregory A. Reinhardt. Calgary: University of Calgary Press, 2002. 13–25. Print.

Thérrien, Michèle. *Le Corps Inuit (Québec Arctique)*. Paris: SELAF, 1987. Print.

Trott, Christopher G. "The Gender of the Bear." *Études/Inuit/Studies* 30.1 (2006): 89–109. Print.

Wenzel, George W. "Ningiqtuq: Resource Sharing and General Reciprocity in Clyde River, Nunavut." *Arctic Anthropology* 32.2 (1995): 43–60. Print.

–. "Sharing, Money, and Modern Inuit Subsistence: Obligation and Reciprocity at Clyde River, Nunavut." *The Social Economy of Sharing: Resource Allocation and Modern Hunter-Gatherers*. Ed. George W. Wenzel, Grete Hovelsrud-Broda, and Nobuhiro Kishigami. Vol. 53. Osaka: National Museum of Ethnology, 2000. 61–85. Print. Senri Ethnological Studies.

Ziegler, Anna, and Aalasi Joamie. *Working with Aalasi: An Introduction to Edible and Medicinal Arctic Plants*. Ed. Neil Christopher. Trans. Rebecca Hainnu. Toronto & Iqaluit: Inhabit Media, 2009. Print.

Martin Berger
National Museum of Ethnology, Leiden

The Importance of Tradition? Analyzing the Struggle for Survival of *Pelota mixteca*, an Indigenous Mexican Game

This paper explores the different ways in which the Mexican government has attempted to ensure the survival of the Indigenous Mexican handball game *pelota mixteca*, the reaction of the players of the game to the state's actions, and the possible impact of all these initiatives on the chances of survival of this Indigenous game in a globalizing world. Through an examination of government communication on the game and the initiatives taken by different Mexican local and state authorities to promote it, it is argued that the Mexican government treated this game as an Indigenous cultural tradition and a means of attracting tourism rather than appreciating its value as an Indigenous Mexican sport. These diverging visions on the (cultural) significance of *pelota mixteca* imply different future trajectories for the safeguarding of this sport for generations to come. The path that the Mexican state chose to follow made the Secretary of Culture and Tourism responsible for promoting the game, focusing on the cultural-historic value of the game. In contrast, the players of *pelota mixteca* themselves argued for a professionalization and detraditionalization of the game, taking *pelota mixteca* out of the sphere of cultural tradition and into the realm of professional sports. This way, more people would start playing the game, thereby enhancing the game's chances of survival.

Ultimately, the main issue that is explored in this chapter is the tension between the appreciation of Indigenous traditions as intangible heritage on the one hand and lived practice on the other. The "museumization" or "heritage canonization" of lived (Indigenous) traditions not only freezes them in time, but also confines them to a certain sector of society. On the other hand, the popularization of Indigenous traditions leads to detraditionalization, which in turn brings about a transformation of the original practice. The aim of this chapter, then, is to come to a better understanding of this apparent paradox in which the practitioners of a tradition argue for its detraditionalization while outsiders argue for its canonization as national patrimony.

1. Pelota mixteca

Pelota mixteca is a game that originated in the state of Oaxaca in southern Mexico. The game was and is mainly played by Mixtecs and Zapotecs, but also by members of the *mestizo* community and other Indigenous peoples. Whether or not *pelota mixteca* is a game of pre-Columbian origins is a matter of debate among archaeologists. While most researchers, as well as most of the players, think that the game is of pre-Columbian origin, others have argued for a European origin of the game. Lack of space does not permit a reproduction of the discussion on the origins of the game here. However, for sake of clarity it should be noted that, since the rules of *pelota mixteca* are exactly the same as those of traditional handball games that have been played in Europe since the Early Middle Ages, I am convinced that *pelota mixteca* in its current form was introduced by the Spaniards after the conquest of Mexico and is, thus, formally of European origin[1]. Nonetheless, since the game has been played by Indigenous people in Oaxaca for centuries, I do think that *pelota mixteca* is a genuinely Indigenous sport.

From the beginning of the 20th century onwards, the game has spread from Oaxaca to other parts of Mexico as well as the USA because of the extensive labor migration of Oaxacan *indígenas* and *mestizos*. At the moment, the main hotspots for the game outside of Oaxaca are Mexico City in Mexico and Los Angeles and the San Joaquin valley in the state of California in the United States. In terms of numbers, a 2012 estimate showed there are about 100 active players of *pelota mixteca* in Los Angeles alone (Leopoldo Peña, personal communication 2012). In Mexico City the number of players is somewhat larger. In Oaxaca it is hard to determine the actual number of players because of the large geographical spread and the different varieties that are played, but the number of players is definitely larger than in California.

The game has three variants: *pelota mixteca de hule, pelota mixteca de forro* and *pelota mixteca de esponja*. These variants are distinguished on the basis of the equipment that is used in the different games. *Pelota mixteca de hule* is the variant that is played most, both in Oaxaca, Mexico City and the United States. For *hule*, a large leather glove of about 5 kilograms is used to propel a solid rubber ball that weighs about 900 grams. The *forro* variant, which is the most endangered of the three, is played with a type of "gardening glove" wound with cotton bands and a ball made of leather of about 300 grams. The last variant, *pelota mixteca de*

1 See Berger 2010 for a detailed argumentation of these points. See Bernal and Oliveros; Sweezey; Taladoire for the pre-Columbian origins argument, see Berger and Gillmeister for the European origin.

esponja, is the most recent of the three, as it was only invented around 1950 in the southern part of the valley of Oaxaca. *Esponja* is played with a wooden board of about 20 x 20 centimeters and a sponge ball about the size and weight of a tennis ball. This variant is gaining ground on the others, as it is much easier to make a wooden board and buy a sponge ball to play with than to buy an expensive glove (2011 price: around 300 USD) for *hule* or the special ball used for *forro*.

Despite the fact that there are several hundred players of *pelota mixteca* on both sides of the Mexico-U.S. border, the number of players has declined steadily over the past decades and the sport may risk extinction if this pattern is continued for the decades to come. The main problem is that young people turn to other sports than *pelota mixteca*. Basketball, football and baseball are the most popular sports among youngsters in Oaxaca, as they are in the whole of Mexico. In the face of this threat, the Mexican state, as well as the players themselves, have developed different initiatives to ensure the survival of the game. Below, we will first examine the initiatives taken by the state, followed by the reaction of the players to these actions and the way that both might impact the development of the game for the decades to come.

2. Mexican governments' policies on Indigenous sports

Traditionally, *pelota mixteca* has been considered a game of pre-Columbian origins. Under the influence of this conception of *pelota mixteca* as a pre-Columbian game, the traditional representation of *pelota mixteca* by the Mexican administrations was based on three basic assumptions. Firstly, that *pelota mixteca* is a game that has been played for over 3000 years and is a variation of the ancient Mesoamerican ballgame, second, that *pelota mixteca* is a tradition particular to certain Indigenous peoples, mainly Mixtecs and Zapotecs, and lastly, that *pelota mixteca* is an Indigenous cultural tradition rather than a sport – more similar to a type of Indigenous cultural activity or ritual than to a "real" sport like football or basketball.

Accordingly, the way that the game was approached and the actions – if any – that were undertaken by different state institutions did not aim to preserve *pelota mixteca* as a living sport, but rather to promote the game as a tourist attraction and the continuation of the game as a cultural tradition. To substantiate this argument, I will present a very brief historical overview of Mexican policies related to Indigenous sport, followed by a more detailed examination of some examples of government communication and initiatives in relation to *pelota mixteca*.

Early twentieth century Mexican Indigenous sports policy

From the 1920s onward, the Mexican government has tried to encourage physical exercise and sports through educational programs. The sports that were encouraged by the Mexican governmental programs were primarily sports of European and North American origin (Arbena; Brewster; Joseph). Indigenous sports, games and other physical activities were not generally included into nationwide sports programs. One could ask: why did the Mexican government not choose to promote Indigenous pastimes, such as *pelota mixteca*?

Truth is that, at least officially, it did. In 1935 the Secretaría de Educación Pública (SEP) launched a national program that was aimed at reviving Indigenous sports and games. These Indigenous sports would form the basis for "a new form of national physical education" (Brewster 224). The program tried to promote not only Indigenous games but also traditional dances of different Indigenous groups from all around Mexico by teaching them at rural and urban schools. It seems that a *reglamento* of *pelota mixteca* that was published around 1946 by Juan Bolaños Cacho, Oaxacan Secretary of Public Education, was possibly created as part of this particular program. In the introduction, Bolaños Cacho states:

> when the great Mixteca Zapoteca culture blossomed, the sport known by the name of '*pelota mixteca*' appeared, an autochthonous activity that is practiced up to the current day by our indigenous population [...]. One of the greatest errors that we have committed, is based in the fact that we have forgotten ourselves, the sport history of our country is largely unknown, we live accustomed to playing foreign sports[2] (Bolaños Cacho i).

This introduction reflects the concern of the State to promote Indigenous sports, games, and other pastimes, favoring them over imported sports, such as basketball and baseball.

Despite attempts such as Bolaños Cacho's, however, this program never achieved its goal to put Indigenous sports center stage in national physical education programs. On the contrary, over the past century Indigenous sports have suffered and most, if not all, of the Indigenous sports that were presented at the "Juegos Nacionales de la Revolución" – an annual (folkloric) sports festival held

---

2 "al florecer la gran Cultura Mixteca Zapoteca, apareció la actividad deportiva conocida con el nombre de '*pelota mixteca*' actividad autóctona que hasta la actualidad viene siendo practicada por nuestra población indígena [...] Uno de los errores más grandes que hemos cometido, radica en que nos olvidamos de nosotros mismos, en mucho se desconoce el pasado histórico deportivo de México, vivimos familiarizados con deportes extranjeros." (This, and further, translations from Spanish to English by the author.)

in honor of the Mexican Revolution organized in the mid-twentieth century – seem to have disappeared. What is important to note is that "the ideological thrust of projected physical education programs was to direct social change and enhance state consolidation" (Arbena "Sport and Society" 354). Therefore, it can be questioned whether the SEP's program for encouraging Indigenous sports was ever bound to be successful, and whether *pelota mixteca* ever stood a real chance of being incorporated fully into the national Mexican system. Actively stimulating *pelota mixteca* to *indígenas* would only reinforce the sense of "Indigenousness" that the participants in these games would have, preventing their incorporation into *mestizo* society, one of the main goals of the post-revolutionary Mexican government.

In the post-Revolutionary programs aimed at creating a national Mexican cultural identity, the emphasis "was always on belonging or being alike, not on separation or distinctiveness" (Arbena "Sports, Development" 362). Hence, since the Mexican *mestizo* elite and middle class were players of baseball, football, and basketball, it seems that *pelota mixteca* never stood a real chance of being a sport played by non-*indígenas*. These programs led to a situation in which Indigenous sports, and other traditions, "were faced with one of two possible outcomes: either a process of incorporation leading to folklorism, or continued marginalization" (Brewster 215). It seems that *pelota mixteca* took the latter of the two paths, continuing as a sport in the margin over the course of the twentieth century. As we will see in the following, this early twentieth century choice of folklorism versus marginalization is quite similar to the predicament faced by early twenty-first century players of the game, who resist the "museumization" of their game as intangible heritage. Both folklorization and museumization eventually seem to lead to the extinction of these practices, as evidenced by the fact that the overwhelming majority of the (folklorized) games that were showcased at the 1941 Juegos Nacionales de la Revolución are not practiced anymore. On the other hand, the number of players of (marginalized) *pelota mixteca* has also been declining steadily over the course of the past century, so it is clear that some kind of action needs to be taken.

Late twentieth century and twenty-first century developments

In 1994, Indigenous games reappeared in Mexican federal sports' policies with the "Ley de Estímulo y Fomento al Deporte." One of the main priorities of this law were the so-called "Juegos y Deportes Autóctonos." As a result, Indigenous sports were included as a separate program within the "Programa Nacional de Educación

Física y de Deporte 1995–2000"[3] (*pelota mixteca* is noted especially as being "uno de los deportes más notables"). The aim of this program was somewhat different from the programs that we have seen from the 1920s and 30s. Whereas earlier programs were aimed at incorporation and acculturation of Indigenous peoples into Mexican *mestizo* society, the 1995–2000 program explicitly states that the goal of the diffusion of Indigenous sports is to "develop the sense of identity, solidarity and unity of the indigenous peoples through sports"[4].

One of the results of this program was the introduction of a workshop on Indigenous sports into the "Carrera Magisterial" in 1999 by the SEP. Courses were aimed at future teachers of physical education around the country, in the hope that they would incorporate Indigenous sports within their curricula. While these seem promising developments, it should be noted that the program for the development of Indigenous sports is absent from the "Programa Nacional de Educación Física y de Deporte 2008–2012"[5], so it is doubtful how long these changes will last and whether these courses will continue to be taught. These doubts are especially pertinent if we examine recent (2008–2012) government initiatives related to *pelota mixteca*.

3. Politics and *pelota mixteca*: a more detailed look

Sabias que los Mixtecas contaban con un juego parecido al tenis?

In order to sketch the context in which different initiatives were undertaken, we will first examine the pamphlet "Did you know that the Mixtecs played a game similar to tennis?", which was published by the Oaxacan State Secretary of Tourism. Several aspects of this pamphlet clearly illustrate the traditional view mentioned before of *pelota mixteca* by the state.

The first point that jumps out in terms of the representation are the images that are used in this pamphlet. While one of the images depicts a ball used for *forro*, the most endangered variety of *pelota mixteca* and also the one that uses a type of ball that looks least modern, the other two images are illustrative of the "casting back" of *pelota mixteca* in the past. One image shows a ring from a

---

3 The program is available at http://info4.juridicas.unam.mx/ijure/nrm/1/333/default.htm?s=iste.

4 Desarrollar el sentido de identidad, solidaridad y unidad de los pueblos indios mediante el deporte.

5 Available at http://www.conade.gob.mx/PNCFD_2008/PNCFD.pdf.

pre-Columbian Mesoamerican ballcourt and the other is a picture of the Classic era (AD 200–900) ball court from the archaeological site of Monte Alban.

Looking past the images at the text of the pamphlet, we see that *pelota mixteca* is described as "a sport that was played for hundreds of years before the Spanish conquest by Mixtecs and Zapotecs [...] one of the places where the game was played, was at Monte Alban and the winner would receive the heart of a young woman." This again evokes a pre-Columbian context for the game, casting the practice of the game back in the past, and emphasizes the (Mixtec and Zapotec) cultural particularity of *pelota mixteca*. Additionally, the mention of the fact that the winner of the game would receive the heart of a young woman – this is meant literally, not figuratively – connects the game with "barbaric" practices of the pre-Columbian past and stresses the ancient game's ritual aspects. Lastly, the fact that this pamphlet was published by the Secretary of Tourism rather than by the Secretary of Sport and Physical Education clearly has many repercussions for the treatment of the game by Oaxacan government.

In its presentation of *pelota mixteca* as an historic, Indigenous tradition that is linked to pre-Columbian ballcourts and human sacrifice, this pamphlet is characteristic of a broader pattern of associating Indigenous cultures with the past. Indigenous culture is seen as one of the foundations on which Mexican national identity was built, but, at the same time, is a cultural element that has no place in the present other than as a (touristic) spectacle to be marveled at. This self-image of the Mexican nation-state dates back to the years after the Mexican Revolution, when, under the strong influence of José Vasconcelos' 1925 *Raza Cósmica*, Mexican identity was defined as an amalgam of Mexico's pre-Columbian cultures and Spanish/Western models of governance. The main objective was to "modernize" Mexico, at the expense of traditional culture and Indigenous languages. Hence, the only contribution of Mexico's Indigenous population to the Cosmic Race was that of their prehispanic ancestors, denying the value of contemporary Indigenous traditions (del Val; Friedlander).

Nonetheless, while stressing all these historical aspects of the game, its link to particular ethnic groups and its touristic potential, the pamphlet ends with: "Commentary: It is important that our young people practice this type of sports that [...] form part of our culture, which we cannot permit to disappear." This commentary is virtually the only part of the pamphlet that recognizes *pelota mixteca* as a living tradition that can be practiced by others than the "ancient" Mixtecs and Zapotecs. However, it is not entirely evident whom this commentary is addressing, since the pamphlet is a publication of the Secretary of Tourism, which normally publishes material for domestic and foreign tourists. Still, if the Oaxacan government really aimed at promoting *pelota mixteca* as a sport that should be played by more people, what actions did it actually undertake to promote it?

4. State government promotion of pelota mixteca

In the period up to 2010, the Oaxacan city and state government generally promoted *pelota mixteca* in two ways. One was to (partly) sponsor the annual *pelota mixteca* tournament that is held during the festivities of the Guelaguetza festival in July/August. In this tournament teams from all over Oaxaca, and also from Mexico City, participate in three divisions for the title of *pelota mixteca* champion of the state of Oaxaca.

Another way of promoting the game was the plan to build three *pelota mixteca* courts at so-called *paradores turísticos*. These tourist centers were placed along the newly-formed *Ruta Domínica* that led tourists around the three famous sixteenth century monasteries of Teposcolula, Coixtlahuaca and Yanhuitlán. Ironically, *pelota mixteca* is actually not played in two of these communities, so teams would have had to be brought in from other places to give exhibitions. As such, priority was given to constructing courts for tourists over spending funds on the construction of courts in places where the game was actually still played actively. Another example that illustrates the "tourist focus" of the Oaxacan government is the proposal of *diputada* Margarita García in the state parliament in December 2011. The proposal read: "I encourage the Secretary of Tourism and the State Commission of Sports, to work together in the spread and promotion of the game of *pelota mixteca*, and to institute a state championship." In conclusion, it seems that up to 2012, initiatives in Oaxaca in regard to *pelota mixteca* were in large part aimed at promoting the sport as a tourist attraction to outsiders rather than as a sport to Oaxaca's own population.

5. Mexico City

In Mexico City, *pelota mixteca* has been played since the 1930s or 40s, when the first sizeable groups of Oaxacan immigrants established themselves in the city. The *pasajuego de Balbuena*, a court that was constructed through the communal labor of the players, functioned as an important meeting place for Oaxacan immigrants in an era when modern means of communication were not available. *Pelota mixteca* has a long history not only in the Oaxacan "homeland" but also outside of Oaxaca in Mexico's capital.

It seems that the authorities in Mexico City first started to take an interest in *pelota mixteca* when plans were formed to construct a new edifice for the city's security forces at the location of the *pasajuego de Balbuena*. Since these courts lie close to the *cámara de diputados*, they are strategically located for the construction of this type of building. Around 2006 the Mexican city authorities started to threaten to expropriate the land that was granted to the players of *pelota mixteca* in 1950. In reaction the players of *pelota mixteca* and *pelota tarasca*, a similar sport played by Tarascans from western Mexico, united in the "Asociación Mexicana de Jugadores de Juegos de Origen Prehispánico A.C." (AMJJOP). This association of players put "traditional sports" on the political agenda. As a result, several members of the Mexico City senate proposed initiatives that were aimed at promoting *pelota mixteca* and other traditional sports. Here we will examine the two most prominent bills of which one succeeded and the other failed.

6. The proposal that failed

First, we will examine the proposal that was unsuccessful. This proposal of Francisco Sánchez Ramos (PRD) was heard in senate on the 27th of February 2007. The point of agreement reads: "The Secretary of Public Education is requested to intensify the practice of autochthonous and traditional sports at the level of primary education. The National Committee of Physical Culture and Sport is requested to increase the support for the Federación Mexicana de Juegos y Deportes Autóctonos y Tradicionales, with the aim of promoting and preserving traditional sports."[6] This proposal addresses the Secretary of Public Education and stresses the importance of teaching traditional sports to children in primary school, an excellent way of making sure that the sport is preserved for and by future generations. It also requests an increase of the support for the Federation of Traditional Games. In short, this proposal is explicitly aimed at the needs of the *pelota mixteca* players themselves as well as at the preservation of the sport as a sport rather than a cultural phenomenon or a tourist attraction. However, this proposal was not successful, most probably because, as it focused on sport and education rather than on cultural heritage and tourism, it did not adhere to the generally accepted ideas on the significance of *pelota mixteca*.

---

6 "Se solicita a la Secretaría de Educación Pública incentive la práctica del deporte autóctono y tradicional en los niveles de educación básica, y al titular de la Comisión Nacional de Cultura Física y Deporte (Conade) incremente el apoyo económico destinado a las tareas de la Federación Mexicana de Juegos y Deportes Autóctonos y Tradicionales, AC, con el fin de difundir y preservar los juegos y deportes autóctonos tradicionales."

7. Declaration as intangible cultural heritage

The proposal that *was* successful was signed by Marcelo Ebrard, the president of Mexico's federal district, on July 14, 2008. This declaration proclaimed *pelota mixteca* and *pelota tarasca* intangible cultural heritage of the city of Mexico. This decision was the outcome of a long process of negotiation and research by the Mexican district government, started in 2005. The "Consejo de Fomento y Desarollo Cultural de la Ciudad de Mexico" asked the National Institute of Anthropology and History (INAH) for advice on the matter. The INAH advised that, because of their history, the games were worthy of protection and revalorization in order to guaranty the continuity of the sport.

The declaration consists of five points, two of which are of particular interest here.

Firstly, the third point of the declaration, following the normal trajectory of decisions concerning Cultural Heritage, makes the Secretary of Culture (not the Secretary of Education or the Committee for Physical Education and Sports) responsible for following up on the actions derived from the declaration. The second point of the declaration explicates what the Secretary of Culture is expected to do: "To contribute to the preservation and promotion of the ballgames of prehispanic origin [...], the Secretary of Culture will, in agreement with the organizations of players of prehispanic ballgames and the relevant authorities, create a cultural program of stimulation and spread of said games, also aiming to promote them as a cultural tourist attraction."[7] Clearly, this declaration places the importance of culture above that of physical education.

8. Comparison

When comparing the failed proposal and the successful declaration, it is clear that the proposal that failed was explicitly aimed at the necessities of players. It aimed to promote the sport among children in order to increase the number of players. The state entities that were expected to take on the challenge of promoting the sport were the Secretary of Education and the Committee for Physical Education and Sports. This proposal recognized *pelota mixteca* as a sport that can be played

7 "Para contribuir a la preservación y promoción de los juegos de pelota prehispánica [...], la Secretaría de Cultura acordará con las organizaciones de jugadores de pelota prehispánica y con las autoridades competentes, un programa cultural de fomento y expansión de dichos juegos, tratando de promoverlos también como atractivo turístico cultural."

not only by Oaxacan immigrants, but also by schoolchildren from Mexico City and other non-Oaxacans. In contrast, the declaration that resulted from the second proposal departs from a view of *pelota mixteca* as a cultural tradition rather than a sport. In the proposal and declaration, the Secretary of Culture is requested to undertake action to stimulate the survival of the sport, but also to promote it as a cultural tourist attraction.

An illustration of what the declaration of *pelota mixteca* as cultural patrimony leads to can be seen in a demonstration of Indigenous games that was held during the celebrations of the Days of the Dead at the Zócalo, Mexico City's central square. This demonstration was held in November 2008, one month after the declaration of the games as Intangible Cultural Heritage. During these demonstrations several Indigenous ballgames were played inside a replica of a pre-Columbian Mesoamerican ballcourt. This replica of a ballcourt included the rings that are traditionally found in many pre-Columbian courts as well as Aztec calendar signs and plastic skulls on the walls. At the line-up before the match, the captains were asked to wear a shield that was adorned with a painted illustration of an Aztec-type representation of a skull and a serpent, clearly situating these games in the past.

9. Players' reaction

The view of the Mexican state of *pelota mixteca* as an ancestral tradition particular to certain ethnic groups from Oaxaca led to initiatives that promoted the game as intangible cultural heritage and an attraction for tourists. It was thought that these actions, including the organization of a "Day of the *pelota mixteca*", the institution of a cultural program to promote the sport and using the sport as a means to attract tourists would ensure the survival of the sport.

However, many players of *pelota mixteca* themselves thought differently. Their idea of how to save the game from extinction was predicated on the belief that the only way forward was to have it played, not to confine it to the (open-air) museum. According to them, the promotion of *pelota mixteca* by the state as a tourist attraction and the representation of the game as a culturally particular tradition of the past do not contribute to the survival of the game. On the contrary, these initiatives cast back the game in time and represent it as a cultural tradition that is not open for others. People who have not grown up with *pelota mixteca* will hardly ever start playing, not only because the majority of them will not know of its existence but, more importantly, because *pelota mixteca* has the image of something of the past, played only by *indígenas* as part of a family tradition. In the words of Eduardo Arellanes, a member of one of the best *pelota mixteca* teams for Mexico City: "When we give exhibitions of the game, people don't know if the game is being promoted so that it will be played, or whether we are being brought in as a circus phenomenon, that people see us as something strange, they don't see it as something they can also practice."[8]

Therefore, many players, acutely aware of the urgency to take action, argued for a different route to ensure the survival of *pelota mixteca*. Naturally, they also see the problems that the game faces and understand what is needed to make the game a more widely played sport: that young people start playing the game. In order to achieve this goal, several individual players and teams as well as self-organizations of pelota mixteca players have started initiatives to grow the number of young *peloteros*. These initiatives can be divided into two categories: 1. Plans to incorporate pelota mixteca into the curricula of primary and secondary schools, and; 2. Spectator-oriented activities that aim to stimulate more people to take an interest in the game, either as a player or as a spectator. All these initiatives form a stark contrast to previous government interventions; they argue for a detraditionalization of the game, so that the game could be taught at schools, played in sports clubs and become more spectator-friendly rather than enshrining pelota mixteca as a cultural tradition in the canon of Mexican national heritage.

The spectator-oriented initiatives focus on making the game easier to follow for outsiders. Through these modifications in the way games are being played and tournaments are organized, it is hoped that more outsiders will see the beauty and spectacle that *pelota mixteca* has to offer. One of the teams that has been most active in trying to "professionalize" the marketing and "spectator-friendliness" of the sport is the *quinta Los Gemelos* from Mexico City. By using social media and creating merchandise, they attempt to encourage new players to practice *pelota mixteca*. Like other teams in Oaxaca had done before them, the Arellanes brothers have been creating their own team jerseys,which they customize especially for every event that they compete in. They also created a team logo which they also use for general marketing of *pelota mixteca* and have created stickers that showcase this logo. They also set up a Facebook page called "pelota mixteca" which uses the logo and aims to promote the game through social media. There is also a separate "pelota mixteca Arellanes"-team Facebook page (which has over 500 likes) on which team members post pictures of the games they attended as well as announcements of where they will be playing next. Some other teams have

8 "cuando damos exhibiciones la gente no sabe bien si se esta fomentando para que se practique, o si nos llevan [...] como un fénomeno de feria, donde la gente parece que alli nos ve como algo extraño, no lo toma como algo propio que pueda practicar."

also created Facebook accounts through which they communicate with their fans and invite spectators to visit upcoming matches. Naturally, using the Internet and social media is a novel and bottom-up approach that provides players and teams with their own media outlets, which can be a powerful tool to encourage more young people to learn about the game.

When demonstrations of *pelota mixteca* were organized by the Secretary of Tourism or by the INAH, many players were often hesitant to participate because they feared that they and their sport would be exoticized. In contrast, many *peloteros* actively try to be part of exhibitions that are currently organized by the Comisión Nacional del Deporte (CONADE). During exhibitions of the CONADE, players bring their gloves and balls for playing the game and give spectators the opportunity to practice with the ballgame equipment, so that they can appreciate the incredible weight of ball and glove and the power and skill involved in playing. They hope that outsiders are encouraged to start playing *pelota mixteca* themselves. At demonstrations, players often bring along gloves that were made especially for children, so that they too can develop an interest in the game from an early age. Considering the short time that has passed since the players started organizing and lobbying for their needs, it remains to be seen whether this reaction from the players will have the desired outcome. However, some steps in this direction have been taken both in Oaxaca and in Mexico City. In Oaxaca, the Colegio de Bachilleres del Estado de Oaxaca (COBAO), which organizes secondary education throughout the state, has adopted *pelota mixteca* as its official sport. In addition, the Committee of Sports of the state of Oaxaca has announced that it will make funds available to buy equipments for the game. Considering the high cost of these objects, free equipment could be an impulse for young people to start playing. In Mexico City, the players have been lobbying for the same kind of actions and time will tell if their efforts are successful. Clearly, now that *pelota mixteca* is being introduced into the physical education classes of Oaxaca's largest institute for secondary education (the COBAO), the game will be taken out of its traditional sphere of village fiestas and Indigenous culture. In short, the game will become a true sport, if it was not already, that is played by Mixtecs, Zapotecs, *mestizos*, and other Mexicans alike.

10. Discussion

In the foregoing, I have argued that the view of Mexican and Oaxacan state government of *pelota mixteca* was based on three main assumptions that, in combination, resulted in an appraisal of the game as an activity with cultural, historical and touristic value rather than a regular physical activity or a means of creating social cohesion through sport. As a result, the state's initiatives in relation to the game were aimed towards the cultural sphere as well as its touristic value. In contrast, players of the game themselves argued for a detraditionalization of the game. As such we see here an apparent paradox: the state argues for the continuation of tradition inside the traditional sphere (a form of "museumization"), whereas the players of the tradition themselves argue for detraditionalization of their game.

"Tradition" seems to be the one thing that has ensured the survival of *pelota mixteca* from the days of the Spanish Conquest in the sixteenth century up to the present day. The game continued to be played during *fiestas patronales* in communities across the Mixtec and Zapotec areas, and migrants took the game with them to their new homeland because it was tradition. The "traditional" game was passed on from father to son for many generations as a form of (Indigenous) cultural reproduction that preserved cultural knowledge and traditions and prepared youngsters for life in Oaxacan communities. In the words of Chivis, a *pelota mixteca* player in his twenties from Fresno (California) "todo este deporte consiste en una cadena", this whole sport consists of a chain. This chain links young players today to their past and their ancestors.

However, tradition also seems to be the one thing that keeps young people today from starting to play *pelota mixteca*. Since the sport is not as popular among young people as modern sports and there are no role models outside the family sphere that play the game, the number of players is greatly decreasing. The "Indigenousness" of *pelota mixteca* – that is to say, the representation of the game as something purely Mixtec or Zapotec and its associations with traditional village life and culture and the pre-Columbian past – is one of the important factors that make young people decide not to start to play the game. Due to 500 years of discrimination against and oppression of Indigenous language and culture, the adjective "Indigenous" is seen by many Mexicans as a pejorative. For years, Indigenous culture has implied backwardness, lack of civilization and degeneracy to large sectors of mestizo Mexican mainstream society. As a result, the irony of the situation is that, in order for more people to play *pelota mixteca* – and *pelota mixteca* to survive – it seems that the sport will have to be, at least partly, "detraditionalized". *Pelota mixteca* has to become a sport, preferably a professionalized sport, in which teams compete in different leagues and not only men, but also women can participate.

How can we understand this paradox, this disjuncture between the aims of the government and those of the players? I think that globalization and modernization offer a framework through which we can come to a better understanding of the historical processes at work. First of all, the decline in the number of players of *pelota mixteca* over the course of the twentieth century is clearly related to globalization and modernization. Not only did the advent of new sporting possibilities draw potential *pelota mixteca* players away from it simply because it created new options, these new introductions also occasioned a change in perspective in which pelota mixteca became "the old and traditional option" whereas other sports represented "the modern alternative". Another factor that played a role in the decline was the fact that *pelota mixteca* lacked an "aura of globalization" (van Bottenburg). Whereas the Western sports that were introduced were all played abroad and had their associated World Cups and Leagues, the highest award that one could win with *pelota mixteca* was becoming state champion of Oaxaca, and even this trophy was introduced relatively recently. This problem was exacerbated during the second half of the twentieth century, when mass media started broadcasting and publishing on the World Series and the NBA. This shift from *pelota mixteca* to "modern" Western sports was endorsed by the Mexican state which aspired to make Mexico a "modern" Western-oriented country. This state-led attempt at "modernizing" Mexico in the early twentieth century, however, did not mean that "pre-modern" traditions, such as *pelota mixteca*, were prohibited, as they had been as a result of sixteenth-century globalization. Rather, they were kept at hand as spectacles to be marveled at and as proof of Mexico's pre-Columbian heritage.

In contrast, what mattered most to the players of the game was the survival of their sport. Of course, they feel attached to the traditions surrounding the game, but they are also acutely aware of the decline in the number of players. They understood that only through including *pelota mixteca* in the education system would the game be passed on to future generations. But why did their efforts to have *pelota mixteca* included in the education system succeed? Again, I think that globalization offers a way of understanding the increased political presence and power of Mexico's Indigenous peoples. A major turning point in the approach of the Mexican state and its most important indigenist institute, the INI (Instituto Nacional Indigenista), came in the 1970s, when the country abandoned its economic isolationist policies and opened up for participation in the global economy (Friedlander; Jung). With the abandonment of these policies came the dismantling of the revolutionary project, which included the idea of the *Raza Cósmica* and the racially and culturally unified Mestizo nation. This opened up the possibility of seeing Mexico as a multicultural rather than a culturally homogenous country, creating more space for the recognition of Indigenous cultures. At the same time, the number of Indigenous transnational migrants from Mexico to the US skyrocketed. As a result, Indigenous transnational self-organizations arose. These associations had a form of "privileged agency" as they were able to break out of Mexico's traditional ethnic-political constraints. This privileged agency and these self-organizations, such as the many *pelota mixeca* associations that have since seen the light, were able to set their own agendas for the survival of *pelota mixteca*. As such, (economic) globalization played a clear and distinctive part in the altering of traditional ethnic relationships in Mexico from the 1970s onwards and, consequently, also had a significant impact on the survival of *pelota mixteca* as a living sport.

In the twenty-first century, with the adoption by the COBAO of *pelota mixteca* as its official sport, we see, for the first time in a century, that the number of *pelota mixteca* players is starting to grow. Unique about this adoption of *pelota mixteca* in the COBAO curriculum is that the Mexican state not only "stimulates indigenous activities", but actually incorporates cultural elements that are considered Indigenous into mainstream cultural practice and daily life. Naturally, this is the diametric opposite of the traditional, assimilationist practices of the INI that were prevalent for many years. It is also markedly different from those 1970s policies that aimed to encourage the practice of Indigenous traditions inside Indigenous communities, confining these practices to their traditional cultural spaces and setting them apart from the mainstream. Quite possibly this willingness to adopt *pelota mixteca* into the mainstream flows from the fact that under the influence of twenty-first globalization many countries around the world feel an increased need to express their own identities, "returning to their roots", legitimizing their national identities through an appeal to the historical depth of their traditions (Hall; Robertson). In looking for these roots, Mexico will always find Indigenous cultures and traditions underlying the foundations of the nation-state. As a result, it seems that there might be a positive transformative potential in twenty-first century globalization for the position of the Indigenous peoples of Mexico within mainstream society, which might eventually help *pelota mixteca* to survive and thrive as a truly Mexican national sport inside a globalized world.

Works cited

Arbena, Joseph. *Sport and Society in Latin America: Diffusion, Dependency, and the Rise of Mass Culture*. Westport: Greenwood Press, 1988. Print.

–. "Sport, Development, and Mexican Nationalism, 1920–1970." *Journal of Sport History* 18.3 (1991): 350–364. Print.

Berger, Martin E. "El Juego de Pelota Mixteca: Tradición, Cambio y Continuidad Cultural." *Itinerarios* 12 (2010): 157–177. Print.

–. "The Ballplayers of Dainzú? An alternative interpretation of the Dainzú iconography." *Mexicon* 33.1 (2011): 46–51. Print.

Bernal, Ignacio, and Arturo Oliveros. *Exploraciones arqueologicas en Dainzú, Oaxaca*. México: INAH, Colección Científica, 1988. Print.

Bolaños Cacho, Raúl. *Reglamento de Pelota Mixteca*. Oaxaca: Dirección de Educación Física. 1946. Print.

Bottenburg, Maarten van. *Verborgen competitie, over de uiteenlopende populariteit van sporten*. Uitgeverij Bert Bakker, Amsterdam. 1994. Print.

Brewster, Keith. "Redeeming the Indian: sport and ethnicity in post-revolutionary Mexico." *Patterns of Prejudice* 38.3 (2004): 213–231.

Friedlander, Judith. *Being Indian in Hueyapan: A Revised and Updated Edition*. London: Palgrave Macmillan. 2006. Print.

Gillmeister, Heiner. *Tennis: A Cultural History*. London: Leicester University Press, 1997.

Joseph, Gilbert. "Forging the Regional Pastime: Baseball and Class in Yucatán." *Sport and Society in Latin America: Diffusion, Dependency, and the Rise of Mass Culture*. Ed. Joseph Arbena. Westport: Greenwood Press, 1988. 28–61. Print.

Jung, Courtney. *The Moral Force of Indigenous Politics: Critical Liberalism and the Zapatistas*. Cambridge University Press. 2008. Print.

Robertson, Roland. *Globalization: Social Theory and Global Culture*. Sage Publications.1992. Print.

Hall, Stuart (ed.). *Representation: Cultural Representations and Signifying Practices*. Sage Publications & Open University. 1997. Print.

Sweezey, William R. "La Pelota Mixteca." *Religión en Mesoamerica, XII Mesa Redonda de la Sociedad Mexicana de Antropología*. Eds. Noemi Castillo Tejero and Jaime Litvak. Mexico, 1972. 471–477. Print.

Taladoire, Eric. "Could we speak of the Super Bowl at Flushing Meadows? *La pelota Mixteca*, a third pre-Hispanic ballgame, and its possible architectural context." *Ancient Mesoamerica* 14 (2003): 319–342. Print.

List of Contributors

Grit Alter is a Postdoc at the Department of Subject Didactics, Section for Language Education at the School of Education at the University of Innsbruck. She finished her PhD project on inter- and transcultural learning in the context of Canadian young adult fiction at Münster University in 2014. She has been a board member of the DGFF (German Association of Foreign Language Research) since 2013. Her research interests include inter- and transcultural learning, teaching literature (children's literature and young adult fiction), textbook research and new media and TEFL methodology as well as North American studies, esp. Canadian literature. In March 2011, Grit Alter was awarded the Graduate Student Scholarship by the International Council for Canadian Studies.

Hans Bak is professor of American Literature and American Studies at Radboud University, Nijmegen, The Netherlands. He served as President of the Netherlands American Studies Association (1990–2000), President of the Association for Canadian Studies in the Netherlands (2000–2003), and Treasurer of the European Association for American Studies (2000–2004). He is the author of *Malcolm Cowley: The Formative Years* (University of Georgia Press, 1993), the editor of *The Long Voyage: Selected Letters of Malcolm Cowley, 1915–1987* (Harvard University Press, 2014), and is currently at work on a full-fledged biography of Cowley. He has published many articles mostly on 20th-century American and Canadian fiction, drama, biography, and the discipline of American Studies; among the volumes he has edited are *Multiculturalism and the Canon of American Culture* (1993); *Writing Lives: American Biography and Autobiography* (with Hans Krabbendam, 1998); *'Nature's Nation' Revisited: American Concepts of Nature from Wonder to Ecological Crisis* (with Walter Hoelbling; 2003); and *First Nations of North America: Politics and Representation* (2005). Research interests: American and Canadian fiction (Native American/First Nations literatures); instruments of culture (publishers, periodicals, "middlemen" of letters); transatlantic cultural mobility.

Martin Berger is Assistant Curator for Middle and South America at the National Museum of World Cultures, Leiden, The Netherlands, and is pursuing a PhD degree within the program of Religion and Society in Native American Cultures, Faculty of Archaeology, Leiden University. He received his BA and MPhil from the same institution. His research focuses on the archaeology and ethnography of Mesoamerican ballgames, and on the impact of present-day globalization and migration on Indigenous Mexican culture and traditions. Other research interests include the cultural history and significance of turquoise in Mesoamerica, the trade in Mesoamerican antiquities between 1920 and 1970, and conceptions of authenticity and forgery in ethnographic museums. His work has been published in such journals as *Itinerarios*, *Mexicon* and *Streetnotes*.

Merel de Buck is a PhD student at the Department of Cultural Anthropology at Utrecht University where she is studying socio-political processes of Afro-Mexican and Indigenous communities in Guerrero, Mexico. This investigation involves two interrelated projects, an intercultural university and community police forces, set up by social movements in the area. Specialized in political anthropology, her interests are focused on politics of difference, citizenship, sovereignty, the state, and autonomy. Furthermore, she applies collaborative and activist approaches in her engagement with marginalized communities.

Daniel Chartier is Professor at the Université du Québec à Montréal, Research Chair on Images of the North, Winter and the Arctic, and director of the International Laboratory for the Comparative Multidisciplinary Study of Representations of the North. He is the founder of the *Revue internationale d'études québécoises, Globe*, which he directed from 1998 to 2003. He published 20 books and many articles on Images of the North, Winter and the Arctic, and on Québec studies, including a special edition on « Les modernités amérindiennes et inuites » (*Globe*, 2005), *L'idée du lieu* (2012), *Le lieu du Nord* (2015) and *La nordicité du Québec* (2014) with Jean Désy and Louis-Edmond Hamelin. In 2010, he published an essay on the foreign image of Iceland during the crisis (in French: *La spectaculaire déroute de l'Islande* (2010); translated in English: *The End of Iceland's Innocence* (Reykjavik, 2010; University of Ottawa Press, 2011).

Kim van Dam is Associated Researcher at the Arctic Centre of the University of Groningen. Research interests include Indigenous people, place attachment, and identities, particularly in remote and rural areas. In 2008, Van Dam published her PhD thesis on place and regional identities of Nunavut, *A Place called Nunavut. Multiple Identities for a New Region* (Groningen: Barkhuis Press). In addition, Van Dam is Coordinator for Energy Education at the Energy Academy Europe in Groningen. The Energy Academy Europe is a partnership between the University of Groningen and the Hanze University of Applied Sciences on issues relating to energy.

Caroline Desbiens is a Professor in the Department of Geography at Laval University where she holds the Canada Research Chair in Historical Geography of the North. Based on an intercultural approach, the main objective of her research is to foster greater harmonization of the territorial perspectives of aboriginal and non-aboriginal peoples in managing the North and its resources, and in working toward social and economic development. The territorial knowledge and experiences of aboriginal women are also a key axis of Professor Desbiens' research. In addition to her individual research projects, Dr. Desbiens is part of three major collaborative research teams with Inuit, Innu and urban aboriginal communities. She is also a Commissioner for the Quebec place names commission (Commission de toponymie du Québec). She has published numerous articles in French and English and her book *Power from the North: Territory, Identity and the Culture of Hydroelectricity in Quebec* was published with UBC Press in 2013.

Andreas Huck holds a Bachelor's degree in Spatial Planning from Technical University Kaiserslautern (Germany) and a Master's Degree in Regional Studies from University of Groningen (Netherlands) where he focused on political and social geography. For his research in British Columbia (presented in this book) and beyond, he was besides others awarded with the Canadian Studies Student Research Award of the Association for Canadian Studies in the Netherlands (ACSN), with the GUF-100 Award of the Groningen University Fund, with a student scholarship of the RUG center for Canadian Studies, and with the ICURD-NEURUS Scholarship of the Network for European and U.S. Regional and Urban Studies. Currently, Andreas works as Project Manager and Content Developer for various education related projects in the European Knowledge and Innovation Community "Climate-KIC".

Wil Pansters is head of the Department of Social Sciences at University College Utrecht and professor of Social Sciences at Utrecht University. He is also Professor of Latin American Studies at the University of Groningen and director of the *Centro de Estudios Mexicanos* in Groningen. Over the years, he has done ethnographic and historical field research in Mexico. He has published on political culture, regional history, democratisation and social change. Currently he focuses on the meanings of (drug-related) violence in politics and society, and on the search of people for justice in environments of insecurity. His most recent book is *Violence, Coercion and State-Making in Twentieth-Century Mexico. The Other Half of the Centaur* (Stanford: Stanford University Press, 2012). In 2011 he received the Orden del Águila Azteca from the Mexican government.

Laurence Simard-Gagnon is a PhD student in the Department of Geography at Queen's University in Kingston, Canada. Her work is centered on daily practices of care of women in a situation of cultural minority, and on the meanings and significance of these practices in terms of gender and cultural identity. She is particularly interested in ways in which different acts of care are constructed or mobilized by women as resistance to multidimensional cultural and gender marginalizations. Laurence completed her Master's thesis "Eating and Living the Territory: Inuit women's contemporary management of berry picking and use" under the supervision of Dr. Caroline Desbiens at Laval University. Her master's work explored the contemporary unfolding of Inuit women's practices of berry picking and use in the community of Inukjuak, Nunavik, Canada. This research highlighted the meanings of berries and their social trajectories for women's gender identity and family belonging, as well as for cultural continuity within the community. Laurence's work is funded by the Fond de Recherche du Québec sur la Société et la Culture (FRQSC).

Fjære van der Stok holds a bachelor's degree in Romance Languages and Cultures and a master's degree in North American Studies from the University of Groningen. Her current research interests include Indigenous film and digital art, and the role of street art in contemporary social movements.

Jeanette den Toonder is Assistant Professor of French and francophone literatures at the University of Groningen and Director of the Centre for Canadian Studies at this university. Her research interests include questions of identity, autobiography, journey and space in the contemporary francophone novel in Canada. She is particularly interested in migrant writing and has published in *Voix et Images*, *Francophonies d'Amériques*, *Revue d'études canadiennes*, *Canadian literature* and *Dalhousie French Studies*. She has co-edited *Romans de la route et voyages identitaires* with Jean Morency and Jaap Lintvelt (Québec: Éditions Nota Bene, 2006), *Écritures de l'intime dans la littérature francophone du Canada (1980–2005)* with Madeleine Fréderic and Jean-Pierre Bertrand (Québec: Éditions Nota Bene, 2011) and *Re-exploring Canadian space / Redécouvrir l'espace canadien* with Bettina van Hoven (Groningen: Barkhuis Press, 2012).

Index

D

INTERAMERICANA

Inter-American Literary History and Culture
Historia literaria interamericana y sus contextos culturales
Histoire littéraire et culture interaméricaines

The new series continues, in substance, series C, "Inter-American Literary Studies" published by Wallstein-Verlag for the Göttingen Center for Advanced Studies in the Internationality of National Literatures (1997-2001).

Publications in the former series:

Frank, Armin Paul, & Helga Eßmann, eds. *The Internationality of National Literatures in Either America: Transfer and Transformation 1. Cases and Problems* (1999 – vol. 1:1).
Frank, Armin Paul, & Kurt Mueller-Vollmer. *The Internationality of National Literatures in Either America: Transfer and Transformation 2. British America and the United States, 1770s–1850s* (2000 – vol. 1:2).
Glasenapp, Jörn. '*Prodigies, anomalies, monsters*': *Charles Brockden Brown und die Grenzen der Erkenntnis* (2000 – vol. 2).

Publications at Peter Lang GmbH:

Vol. 1 *Do the Americas Have a Common Literary History?* Edited by Barbara Buchenau and Annette Paatz, in cooperation with Rolf Lohse and Marietta Messmer. With an Introduction by Armin Paul Frank. 2002.

Vol. 2 Barbara Buchenau: *Der frühe amerikanische historische Roman im transatlantischen Vergleich.* 2002.

Vol. 3 *Internationality in American Fiction. Henry James. William Dean Howells. William Faulkner. Toni Morrison.* Edited by Armin Paul Frank and Rolf Lohse. 2005.

Vol. 4 Rolf Lohse: *Postkoloniale Traditionsbildung. Der frankokanadische Roman zwischen Autonomie und Bezugnahme auf die Literatur Frankreichs und der USA.* 2005.

Vol. 5 Armin Paul Frank / Christel-Maria Maas: *Transnational Longfellow. A Project of American National Poetry.* 2005

Vol. 6 Kurt Mueller-Vollmer: *Transatlantic Crossings and Transformations. German-American Cultural Transfer from the 18th to the End of the 19th Century.* 2015.

Vol. 7 Marietta Messmer / Armin Paul Frank (eds.): *The International Turn in American Studies.* 2015.

Vol. 8 Gabriele Pisarz-Ramirez / Markus Heide (eds.): *Hemispheric Encounters. The Early United States in a Transnational Perspective.* 2016.

Vol. 9 Jeanette den Toonder / Kim van Dam / Fjære van der Stok (eds.): Native America. Indigenous Self-Representation in Canada, the U.S. and Mexico. 2016.

www.peterlang.de

www.ingramcontent.com/pod-product-compliance
Ingram Content Group UK Ltd.
Pitfield, Milton Keynes, MK11 3LW, UK
UKHW041828100926
8556IPUK00002B/78

9 783631 640821